VOLUME 490

MARCH 1987

THE ANNALS

of The American Academy *of* Political
and Social Science

RICHARD D. LAMBERT, *Editor*
ALAN W. HESTON, *Associate Editor*

FOREIGN LANGUAGE INSTRUCTION: A NATIONAL AGENDA

Special Editor of this Volume

RICHARD D. LAMBERT

University of Pennsylvania
Philadelphia

Ⓢ SAGE PUBLICATIONS *NEWBURY PARK BEVERLY HILLS LONDON NEW DELHI*

THE ANNALS

© 1987 *by* The American Academy *of* Political *and* Social Science

ERICA GINSBURG, *Assistant Editor*

Editorial Office: 3937 Chestnut Street, Philadelphia, Pennsylvania 19104.

For information about membership* (individuals only) and subscriptions (institutions), address:

SAGE PUBLICATIONS, INC.

2111 West Hillcrest Drive   275 South Beverly Drive
Newbury Park, CA 91320   Beverly Hills, CA 90212

From India and South Asia,   *From the UK, Europe, the Middle*
write to: *East and Africa, write to:*
SAGE PUBLICATIONS INDIA Pvt. Ltd.   SAGE PUBLICATIONS LTD
P.O. Box 4215   28 Banner Street
New Delhi 110 048   London EC1Y 8QE
INDIA   ENGLAND

SAGE Production Editor: JACQUELINE SYROP

*Please note that members of The Academy receive THE ANNALS with their membership.

Library of Congress Catalog Card Number 86-061219
International Standard Serial Number ISSN 0002-7162
International Standard Book Number ISBN 0-8039-2932-3 (Vol. 490, 1987 paper)
International Standard Book Number ISBN 0-8039-2931-5 (Vol. 490, 1987 cloth)
Manufactured in the United States of America. First printing, March 1987.

The articles appearing in THE ANNALS are indexed in *Book Review Index; Public Affairs Information Service Bulletin; Social Sciences Index; Monthly Periodical Index; Current Contents; Behavioral, Social Management Sciences;* and *Combined Retrospective Index Sets.* They are also abstracted and indexed in *ABC Pol Sci, Historical Abstracts, Human Resources Abstracts, Social Sciences Citation Index, United States Political Science Documents, Social Work Research & Abstracts, Peace Research Reviews, Sage Urban Studies Abstracts, International Political Science Abstracts, America: History and Life,* and/or *Family Resources Database.*

Information about membership rates, institutional subscriptions, and back issue prices may be found on the facing page.

Advertising. Current rates and specifications may be obtained by writing to THE ANNALS Advertising and Promotion Manager at the Beverly Hills office (address above).

Claims. Claims for undelivered copies must be made no later than three months following month of publication. The publisher will supply missing copies when losses have been sustained in transit and when the reserve stock will permit.

Change of Address. Six weeks' advance notice must be given when notifying of change of address to insure proper identification. Please specify name of journal. Send change of address to: THE ANNALS, c/o Sage Publications, Inc., 2111 West Hillcrest Drive, Newbury Park, CA 91320.

Origin and Purpose. The Academy was organized December 14, 1889, to promote the progress of political and social science, especially through publications and meetings. The Academy does not take sides in controverted questions, but seeks to gather and present reliable information to assist the public in forming an intelligent and accurate judgment.

Meetings. The Academy holds an annual meeting in the spring extending over two days.

Publications. THE ANNALS is the bimonthly publication of The Academy. Each issue contains articles on some prominent social or political problem, written at the invitation of the editors. Also, monographs are published from time to time, numbers of which are distributed to pertinent professional organizations. These volumes constitute important reference works on the topics with which they deal, and they are extensively cited by authorities throughout the United States and abroad. The papers presented at the meetings of The Academy are included in THE ANNALS.

Membership. Each member of The Academy receives THE ANNALS and may attend the meetings of The Academy. Membership is open only to individuals. Annual dues: $26.00 for the regular paperbound edition (clothbound, $40.00). Add $9.00 per year for membership outside the U.S.A. Members may also purchase single issues of THE ANNALS for $6.95 each (clothbound, $10.00).

Subscriptions. THE ANNALS (ISSN 0002-7162) is published six times annually—in January, March, May, July, September, and November. Institutions may subscribe to THE ANNALS at the annual rate: $52.00 (clothbound, $68.00). Add $9.00 per year for subscriptions outside the U.S.A. Institutional rates for single issues: $10.00 each (clothbound, $15.00).

Second class postage paid at Philadelphia, Pennsylvania, and at additional mailing offices.

Single issues of THE ANNALS may be obtained by individuals who are not members of The Academy for $7.95 each (clothbound, $15.00). Single issues of THE ANNALS have proven to be excellent supplementary texts for classroom use. Direct inquiries regarding adoptions to THE ANNALS c/o Sage Publications (address below).

All correspondence concerning membership in The Academy, dues renewals, inquiries about membership status, and/or purchase of single issues of THE ANNALS should be sent to THE ANNALS c/o Sage Publications, Inc., 2111 West Hillcrest Drive, Newbury Park, CA 91320. *Please note that orders under $20 must be prepaid.* Sage affiliates in London and India will assist institutional subscribers abroad with regard to orders, claims, and inquiries for both subscriptions and single issues.

THE ANNALS

of The American Academy of Political
and Social Science

RICHARD D. LAMBERT, *Editor*
ALAN W. HESTON, *Associate Editor*

———————————— **FORTHCOMING** ————————————

See page 3 for information on Academy membership and
purchase of single volumes of **The Annals.**

CONTENTS

BOOK DEPARTMENT CONTENTS

ECONOMICS

PREFACE

The articles in this volume comprise the working papers for a week-long meeting held at the Aspen Institute for Humanistic Studies in June 1986. That meeting, supported by the Exxon Education Foundation and the Ford Foundation, was in preparation for the establishment of the National Foreign Language Center.

Those in attendance at that meeting were Lyle Bachman, University of Illinois; Richard Brod, Modern Language Association; Russell N. Campbell, University of California at Los Angeles; John L. D. Clark, Defense Language Institute; Ray T. Clifford, Defense Language Institute; Helen Cunningham, Pew Memorial Trust; John Fought, University of Pennsylvania; Phyllis Franklin, Modern Language Association; Claire L. Gaudiani, University of Pennsylvania; Ralph Ginsberg, University of Pennsylvania; Frank Heny, State University of New York at Albany; Ralph Hester, Stanford University; Randall Jones, Brigham Young University; Eleanor Jorden, Cornell University; Cornelius Kubler, American Institute in Taiwan; Richard D. Lambert, University of Pennsylvania; Dale Lange, University of Minnesota; Diane Larsen-Freeman, Experiment in International Living; Steven Lavine, Rockefeller Foundation; Michael Long, University of Hawaii at Manoa; Nancy McCarthy, Ford Foundation; Sarah Jane Moore, American Academy of Political and Social Science; Alice Omaggio, University of Illinois; C. Edward Scebold, American Council on the Teaching of Foreign Languages; Arne Shore, Exxon Education Foundation; Peter Stanley, Ford Foundation; G. Richard Tucker, Center for Applied Linguistics; and A. Ronald Walton, University of Maryland.

The articles in this volume are an attempt to capture the essence of a great deal of planning and advocacy currently taking place around the country in the field of foreign language pedagogy. The authors of the articles were asked to summarize the current state of knowledge and to make recommendations for future action on particular aspects of foreign language instruction. Together, these articles constitute a fresh statement of what the nation must do to improve the foreign language competencies of our citizens.

By the time this volume is published, the National Foreign Language Center will have been established. It will be the primary purpose of that center to provide national leadership in the fulfillment of this agenda. It is hoped that other organizations and individuals will find this compilation of analyses and recommendations useful for their own efforts as well.

RICHARD D. LAMBERT

ANNALS, *AAPSS*, **490**, March 1987

The Improvement of Foreign Language Competency in the United States

By RICHARD D. LAMBERT

ABSTRACT: A great deal of discussion and planning is under way the purpose of which is to upgrade our national system of foreign language instruction. Out of that discussion has emerged a consensus on a few key points of leverage to supplement and improve the system. These include focusing on adult language needs; the development of consistent measures of individual and program performance; the elaboration of the technology of teaching upper-level language skills; and the establishment of empirically oriented experimental classrooms. To carry out this agenda, the creation of a national foreign language center is proposed.

Richard D. Lambert is editor of The Annals, *professor of sociology at the University of Pennsylvania, and the first director of the National Foreign Language Center at Johns Hopkins University. He was formerly president of the Association for Asian Studies and of the American Academy of Political and Social Science. His most recent books are* Beyond Growth: The Next Stage in Language and Area Studies; A National Agenda for International Studies; *and* The Transformation of an Indian Labor Market.

NOTE: Parts of this article are drawn from an agenda statement for a proposed National Foundation for International Studies. The writing of that agenda was supported by the Carnegie Corporation, the Exxon Education Foundation, the Ford Foundation, the Andrew W. Mellon Foundation, and the Rockefeller Foundation.

THERE is nothing more damaging to the American capacity to cope in a global society than the abysmally low level of foreign language competency of most Americans. Most of us are devoutly monolingual. This is not for want of investing money and time in trying to get American school children to learn a foreign language. Our annual investment in teaching foreign language in our schools is more than $2 billion. Millions of students study French, Spanish, or German for at least two years, and often four or six years, of their high school and college education. And the number of students enrolled in foreign language classes, after a period of decline, has begun to rise again. Many colleges and universities are reinstituting a foreign language requirement for admission or graduation, and several of our largest states are proposing to require foreign language instruction for all high school students.

The trouble is that while in our educational system we invest an immense amount of student and teacher time and huge amounts of money in foreign language teaching, survey after survey documents how inadequate our current foreign language capacity is: the skills it imparts are too low and too scholastic; the languages taught were appropriate for the nineteenth century but not for the twenty-first; the ways of measuring skill acquisition are outmoded; the levels of instruction are totally unarticulated so that the cumulative aspect of skill acquisition by a student is unattended and accidental; and no one knows or seems concerned about how much of early foreign language training survives to be available for adult use.

I mean this as no criticism of the many hardworking teachers and students now involved in foreign language

education. It is various aspects of the system as a whole that present the problem: too limited time given to language acquisition; too many students dragging their feet in learning a skill whose utility to them is, at best, unclear; the low average level of foreign language competency of too many teachers; the compartmentalization of instruction by semesters and between primary, secondary, and tertiary schools; the lack of a way to measure well just how much competency a student really has acquired. Thus, while we welcome the growing foreign language course enrollments and requirements as a recognition of the importance of foreign language competency, putting more and more students through, and pouring more and more resources into, the current foreign language teaching system will not solve the national problem.

Hence, before we plunge ahead into an expansion of the current system, which gives millions of students a little foreign language training and relatively few a genuinely usable competency, a major shift in emphasis, organization, and teaching technology in our foreign language educational system is needed. Otherwise, we will look back after another decade of spending increasing amounts of student time and scarce national resources on teaching foreign languages, and we will find ourselves just where we are now: all but a few of us able to communicate only in English in a polyglot world. We need a freshly thought-through national foreign language policy and a redirection of national will and resources to improve the system.

The federal government can only play a marginal role in that process. The administration of foreign language teaching policy is the responsibility of the state or of the local school district, and almost all of the billions of dollars spent in the United States on foreign language instruction appears on state budgets. There is, nevertheless, an important collective responsibility at the national level that can assist in making the marginal investment and providing the necessary intellectual catalyst that a major shift in national policy demands. The high degree of dispersion of foreign language instruction throughout our thousands of school districts makes it unlikely that such a transformation will well up spontaneously from the thousands of classrooms. There are some things, such as setting national standards, that must be done centrally or they will not be done at all. Thus there must be a national as well as a state effort to strengthen our foreign language teaching and learning system.

An attempt to create a coordinated national policy comes at a propitious time; there are many, many separate initiatives afoot to work at pieces of that agenda. For instance, 32 of the major national language education associations have grouped together into a Joint National Committee for Languages to develop and work for a national agenda. The major private foundations have begun to invest in a transformation of the language teaching system. With the support of a number of private and public funders, plus moneys contributed by school systems throughout the country, a system of Academic Alliances has been created to bring together language teachers and administrators from high schools and colleges and universities throughout the country to help improve foreign language instruction. The Rockefeller Foundation has provided $1.5 million in fellowship support to send teachers of foreign languages in high

schools abroad to upgrade their own language competencies. The federal government has been funding work on the improvement of language teaching capacity in the less commonly taught languages through Title VI of the Higher Education Act, and in the reauthorized, 1986 version of that act Congress has authorized the creation of two to five centers to improve language pedagogy. The National Institute of Education included improvement of foreign language instruction in its recent grants to establish major centers for research on bilingual education. The National Security Agency has funded development efforts in foreign language pedagogy, particularly in the use of high technology in language teaching. The Department of Defense is considering how it may help in the development of our national capacity for instruction in the languages spoken in the Pacific Rim countries. The Education for Economic Security Act (Public Law 98-377) provides $5 million for the improvement of instruction in the critical languages. A number of bills aimed at this same general purpose have been or are about to be introduced in Congress; examples are Senator Simon's Foreign Language for National Security Act of 1984 and Congressman Panetta's Foreign Language and National Security Act of 1985.

These many initiatives in the improvement of the national capacity to teach foreign languages are most encouraging. Right at the beginning of this upsurge of interest and investment in the improvement of foreign language instruction, however, it is extremely important that a central planning, initiating, coordinating, and implementing organization be put into place to assure that the scattered efforts in the area of foreign language education are cumulative, that they address the central agenda issues, and, above all, that they are effective and comprise the best use of our national resources. This is particularly true of the many federal funding programs, but is equally true of those in the private sector. Language instruction has become an area where the American penchant for pluralism has become a vice. What follows is both a preliminary attempt to set a portion of the new national agenda and a recommendation for the creation of a mechanism to carry it out.

THE AGENDA

Where are the points of leverage for change in our foreign language instructional system? How can an immense, highly dispersed foreign language education system begin to transform itself? What can a centralized effort accomplish? How can the various initiatives now under way be coordinated to make a major difference? How can the collective national interest be expressed as a determinant of priority areas of development? How can we measure the effectiveness of efforts to introduce change? In short, what should the agenda for a national foundation be in the strengthening of our national capacity to teach foreign languages?

Adult use of
foreign language

The first agenda item is an action plan that starts with a point of view. Stated simply, the national interest is not in the language instruction system per se, but in the production and maintenance of usable foreign language competencies among adults, particularly those occupational groups who need, or should need, them in their work. I add the phrase "should need" because it can be reasonably argued that, from the perspective of the national interest, some groups, such as internationally oriented business leaders, foreign service officers, staff members of key congressional foreign affairs committees, military attachés, or technical assistance workers, may need more foreign language competency than we currently demand of them.

By focusing on adult needs and use for foreign language skill we mean to dramatize the point that the national payoff for the large investment of time and money that we currently invest in foreign language instruction must be measured against adult use. If, for instance, very few people acquire enough skill to use it in real-life situations, or if whatever skill they learn in school has totally evaporated by the time they are fully functioning adults, then the system must be changed. The trouble is that we know almost nothing about the current or the most desirable adult use of foreign language skills in the United States. Establishing what adult foreign language skills are, perhaps at the outset only for key occupational groups, and how those skills are used is a necessary first step in the reorientation of our foreign language instructional system. The technology for such adult needs and use surveys is well established in Europe and elsewhere and needs only to be adapted for use in the United States.

Focusing on foreign language skills held by adults dramatizes another difference between our own society and that of others. We concentrate virtually all of our foreign language instruction on young people enrolled in our formal education system. In other societies, there are facilities for adults to learn other languages as the need for them becomes apparent. Here, adults' only recourse is to a few proprietary language schools, and they tend to concentrate on a single teaching method, teach only the first levels of language competency, and cover only the most commonly taught languages. Our formal educational institutions, even in their continuing education divisions, provide very little foreign language instruction for adults. When they do give instruction, they tend to force it into the same time frame, teaching style, and pacing of regular school classes, while the needs and timing of adults are often quite different. Moreover, we have virtually no facilities for maintaining or refreshing language skills once they are acquired.

While the success of fresh educational ventures must depend upon their long-term economic viability, the current organization of our language teaching system and the fiscal constraints that colleges and universities now face make it difficult for them to take the risks involved in experimenting with the creation of new teaching facilities aimed specifically at adult audiences. What may fill a national need in the long term is not tried by individual institutions for want of venture capital. Since the collective, national need for language teaching facilities aimed particularly at adults is so clear, however, a few individual institutions should be given the entrepreneurial support to develop model programs for this purpose.

A common metric

An equally important agenda item for the foundation is the creation and diffusion of a common metric measuring in an objective, consistent fashion the degree of proficiency a person—student or adult—has in a foreign language. This metric should be equivalent across all languages and be used to certify general competency in all jobs for which a knowledge of a foreign language is relevant: business, government, education, journalism, and so forth. In addition, the foundation should assist in the diffusion of the metric throughout the society so that its use becomes truly universal and so that a measurement of proficiency in one language or occupation is equivalent to another. Our current metric for the measurement of language competency—the length of time a language has been studied when it was first acquired—is not sufficient. A new metric must be established that expresses an individual's competency in a language in terms of his or her ability to use the language in increasingly demanding real-life situations with increasing effectiveness. The metric must measure genuine proficiency in the language, not just time spent in learning it.

The importance of establishing a common metric cannot be exaggerated. For one thing, only with the widespread application of a common metric will we have any reliable way of expressing the real demands on foreign language skill of particular jobs. Once developed, the common metric can be adopted as a criterion of employment in language-relevant government occupations. This in turn would dramatize to students the utility of foreign language competency for future employment, providing the motivation for foreign language learning so sorely needed in our educational system.

The development and adoption of a common metric will have other beneficial effects as well. Only with the adoption of a common metric will we begin to be able to measure the effectiveness of all or parts of our foreign language teaching system. Only with the adoption of a common metric will individual students or adults have any idea of how much language competency they do or do not possess compared both to others like themselves and to the goal of attaining full proficiency. Only with the adoption of a common metric will we begin to know how the various language teaching methods work best and for what kinds of students in what kind of learning situation.

Fortunately, over the past decade a fair amount of work toward establishing this common metric has been done. A measurement scale ranging from zero for no competency to 5 for educated-native-speaker competency, with half-point increments in between, was developed in the federal government's language teaching programs—first the Foreign Service Institute, then the Department of Defense and other agencies. Steps are currently being taken to make such a scale applicable for employment, job qualification, and promotion in as many federal agencies as possible. Further, a joint government-academic effort has been launched under the aegis of the American Council on the Teaching of Foreign Languages to adapt the metric to the academic learning situation.

As this worthwhile effort toward the establishment of a universally used metric has progressed, a number of crucial issues have arisen that must be faced. For one thing, the scale has to be expanded at its lower end to provide rating gradations fine enough at the beginning stages of learning to measure the small incremental increases in language proficiency that are characteristic of academic classroom situations.

Second, the scale works best for speaking and for listening comprehen-

sion, skills that are best measured in face-to-face interviews. Making the metric equally effective for reading and writing skills remains a challenge.

Third, as the metric expands into the difficult languages, particularly those with especially complex orthographies such as Japanese, Chinese, and Arabic, some of the criteria used for dealing with the European languages that are most like our own have to be specially adapted to their needs.

Fourth, the development of proficiency-testing strategies that are consistent and valid in a large number and variety of testing situations is a major challenge just beginning to be faced. What works well in a few, tightly controlled testing situations with an experienced staff is easily corrupted when large numbers of people are to be tested and when the staff administering and judging the tests have widely varying amounts of experience. Transforming pilot programs in applying the common metric into institutionalized, large-scale programs inevitably runs into a series of major problems: inventing new ways of testing a person's language competency that measure genuine proficiency but are relatively immune to variations in the ability and perspectives of those doing the rating, developing tests that can be administered to large numbers of people at the same time, providing training for substantial numbers of professionals to administer and interpret accurately the test results, and constructing a national network of testing sites to make proficiency certification universally available are major challenges yet to be faced.

When these challenges have been met, getting the use of the metric to be near universal in as many sections of the population as possible, particularly among major employers such as international business and government, will be a difficult marketing task that will take years to accomplish.

With all of its difficulties, retaining momentum in the movement toward a common metric is essential for the development of a meaningful national policy in foreign language learning and use. Without such a metric we will continue to have no way of measuring performance against objectives, no way of distinguishing excellence in teaching from pro forma, low-quality pedagogy, no way of setting up occupational qualifications that can recognize and utilize foreign language skills, and no way of moving foreign-language-competent individuals from one job to another with a meaningful certification of their skill level in that language. It is, indeed, an indication of the non-goal-oriented nature of our language teaching system, and the low value that we place on foreign language competency, that we have not created such a metric before.

Research

Many of the necessary prerequisites to an improvement in our foreign language teaching system are not ready on the shelf, just waiting to be applied. A number of them require prior research, but that research must be highly focused, highly applied in its orientation. It should lead directly to the preparation of new teaching materials or pedagogical practices. As I will note, such applied research in the field of language pedagogy is precisely the kind of inquiry that the existing national programs in support of research, both public and private, tend not to reach. First, however, what are some of the items on the research

agenda that are important to the development of our national foreign language policy?

1. We need to develop criteria for evaluation of the many competing innovations in language instructional pedagogy. Another revolutionary teaching method—the monitor method, suggestopedia, total physical response, to name just a few of the more recent ones— seems to come along every year or so. We have no systematic way of determining what work best with what kind of students, at what level of instruction, and in what kind of learning situation. It would seem that such information would be essential for teachers or school administrators who are trying to decide what works for them. But such a methodology for evaluating the effectiveness of language instructional programs is not now available in even the most rudimentary form. At present, the foreign language field is decidedly nonempirical in its decisions about the use of pedagogical techniques; this situation must be changed.

2. If we are to focus on adult language competencies, then knowing something about the loss, retention, and rejuvenation of school-learned language skills would seem to be a crucial ingredient to the formation of sensible policy. While in the past two or three years, two major research projects have developed, one in the private sector and one in the Department of Defense, to discover something about the rate and pattern of skill loss, we have a long way to go before sensible skill maintenance and rejuvenation programs can be developed.

3. Most of the existing technology for foreign language instruction is appropriate for the beginning and intermediate

competency levels. We must develop the capacity to train people to a near-native level of competency in a foreign language or even the best-trained Americans will continue to be language cripples, using their foreign language skills haltingly and inaccurately. There are no materials available or even any general pedagogical guidelines for upper-skill-level instruction.

4. Much of the demand among adults for foreign language competency—for instance, among international business managers assigned abroad—is idiosyncratic, comes in fits and starts, and may be highly specialized in purpose. This situation clearly calls for the development of individualized and, to the extent possible, self-instructional materials. Our foreign language teaching system, however, tends to be classroom oriented, with sets of students sitting together in a class and marching in step through a common set of materials. Except for some commercially available materials that are of uncertain quality, tend to be limited to the early stages of language learning, and are concentrated in the most commonly taught languages, self-instructional materials are not generally available. Recently, a number of substantial efforts have been made to remedy this situation by the National Association for Self-Instructional Language Programs, by Ohio State University, and by the Foreign Service Institute. Research leading to the development of materials and teaching strategies for individualized or self-instructional materials is an important area for national investment.

5. Language instruction lends itself well to automation of some of the teaching and testing process. A major national investment in the development of effective automated teaching technology may help alleviate some of the problems of the uneven quality of instruction in our highly dispersed language teaching system. It can assist in the development of a common metric and a viable testing network. It can help us to create a more individualized teaching system and make language instruction more available to learners outside the classroom. Within the last ten years there has been a major flowering of research and experimentation in the applicability of the newer high-technology teaching devices to foreign language instruction, much of it funded by the National Security Agency. What has been accomplished so far, however, is just a beginning. With a few exceptions, application of the newer technology tends to be limited to the most commonly taught languages, and to the early learning stages of those. Some of the most promising developments are in the use of live video programs picked up via satellite from broadcasts in the Soviet Union and other countries. Research and materials development in this area should be encouraged and made more widely available.

It is one of the peculiarities of the way in which support is distributed throughout the government agencies—and until very recently, private support in this area has been conspicuously lacking—that there is no program under which the funding of the kind of research previously listed fits comfortably. Or rather, it is more accurate to say that while the government has invested substantial sums of money in research on foreign language instruction, the money has almost all been spent on the improvement of teaching within its own language teaching programs. It has invested very little in the diffusion of the knowledge gained within that system to the nongovernment world, nor has it been engaged in supporting research to improve the national language teaching system as a whole, and no one else has moved in to fill the vacuum. In this regard, it is useful to quote the findings in a recent report, *Beyond Growth: The Next Stage in Language and Area Studies.*

The private foundations have, by and large, not been interested in investing in the research and development necessary for the improvement of language instruction. Until recently, there has been almost no place to go for such support. The International Education Program of the Department of Education has some research funds under Title VI, but they have generally amounted to less than $1 million annually and must also be used to support all other evaluative and prescriptive research on area studies. Moreover, in part because of the limitation of funds, the International Education Program's tendency has been to fund small, isolated projects; larger, longer-term ventures that might have greater impact cannot be supported.

Research on language pedagogy has not been part of the mission of any of the other granting agencies of the federal government. The Education Division of the National Endowment for the Humanities (NEH) has supported the development of teaching materials—even this seems to be coming to an end—and the training of language teachers on a pilot program basis, but neither the Education nor the Research Divisions of the NEH can support basic pedagogical research for the transformation of the field. The Research Division of NEH does include research related to language learning, but to qualify for funding under NEH's research program, work must be on literature or linguistic features of the language, not language learning itself, and, in particular, not on anything measuring language proficiency

or evaluating the effectiveness of alternative methods of language teaching. Even though almost half of the humanists on our campuses are engaged in language instruction, as a research topic, language instruction is not a humanity! Even when the staff of the NEH chooses to encourage the submission of such projects, the screening committees tend to weed them out. . . .

The National Science Foundation's (NSF) linguistics section might have been expected to be interested in language pedagogy, but it is not. As in the NEH, the moment a research topic becomes applied and particularly when it touches upon language testing or pedagogical research, it falls outside of the self-defined mission of the NSF. . . .

For most of its history, the Fund for Improvement of Post-Secondary Education was not interested in language instruction. Although it is now interested—it has recently awarded a grant for the creation of a major proficiency testing center for the commonly taught languages—its funds are extremely limited. Moreover, it has the same bias as the NEH; it will fund experimental action programs, but not the basic research to inform those programs before they are created.

The National Institute of Education, which does fund pedagogical research and institution formation, has traditionally limited itself to secondary and primary education, to the commonly taught languages, and to bilingual education. Moreover, that agency has had drastically reduced funding over the past several years so that a new definition of scope is unlikely.

Recently, the National Security Agency has been awarding funds for research on foreign language pedagogy. It has been particularly active in promoting the use of high-technology instrumentation in language instruction and in the establishment of criteria for proficiency testing.[1]

1. Richard D. Lambert with Elinor G. Barber, Margaret Merrill, Eleanor Jorden, and Leon I.

There have been some changes in this situation during the past year. For instance, the National Institute of Education has appended funding for research on second-language learning to a recent grant for bilingual education research. But basically, the situation just described still obtains. Support for research in foreign language pedagogy falls through the crevices of federal programs in support of research.

A NATIONAL CENTER

The transformation of such a large and diffuse enterprise as our national language teaching system is not likely to occur without the assistance of one or more organizations whose principal task is the carrying out of that transformation. Just casting government and private funds widely on such an extensive sea will not accomplish the purpose. Nor will the traditional, relatively passive role of government funding suffice. If major changes in the national language teaching system are to occur, more proactive programs, ones specifically created to effect change, not just support existing activities, must be developed. What is needed is the development of a national foreign language resource center to serve as a catalyst in that transformation. Its tasks would be to create, evaluate, and work for the adoption of satisfactory techniques of language instruction capable of carrying a wide variety of learners to a high enough level of competency to permit genuine use. The functions of the center would be (1) to carry out or commission the research

and materials development required for that transformation; (2) to implement the change strategies developed in that research and development; (3) diffusion and articulation; and (4) evaluation. The center, in terms of audience, would serve the needs of:

—primary and secondary school teachers and administrators;

—college and university teachers providing language instruction as part of the general education requirement;

—language teachers training area specialists;

—language teachers for government employment;

—language teachers in proprietary institutions; and

—teachers of foreign business language.

The research agenda of the center would parallel the items listed earlier in the overall national agenda. I include under the rubric of research the conduct of experimental classrooms to ensure that theoretical findings are translated into actual pedagogical practice. Since not all of the requisite skills would be gathered into the center, some of the necessary research would be conducted in a more dispersed fashion in all the major language teaching institutions throughout the country, including those in the federal government. With respect to research, in addition to conducting some crucial work in-house, the center's added functions would be to set a collective agenda for research relating to effective language pedagogy, to coordinate it, to make it cumulative, and to make sure that research advances actual classroom teaching and student learning.

Twarog, *Beyond Growth: The Next Stage in Language and Area Studies* (Washington, DC: Association for American Universities, 1984), pp. 89-90.

In terms of materials, if a major advance in language pedagogy is to take place, the center must be able not only to create new materials, but to gather and collect feedback from the many dispersed innovators now producing language teaching materials all over the country. The need is particularly great where the preparation of language teaching is a cottage industry.

Training, the first aspect of implementation, includes all of the following priorities:

1. The center will develop a capacity to train teachers whose education has been in linguistics and/or literature of the language. The pedagogical training envisioned will have to be language specific and geared as much to the linguistic needs of American speakers as to the structure of the language itself.

2. The center will create and administer intensive instruction programs for students enrolled in secondary schools and colleges, as well as those in business and government. That is, the center will offer intensive study abroad, as it were, as an alternative to extensive language programs. Another major audience will be the lay public who want to study a foreign language intensively and exclusively.

3. The center will act as an institution of last resort for instruction in the truly scarce languages as universities curtail their language and area studies programs, tending to drop the same peripheral languages.

Diffusion and articulation can be considered together, for we need to think of ways to involve teachers at all levels in the education system in ongoing study of foreign language pedagogy and refinement of teaching techniques. The center will put in place collaboratives that will not only enable professionals to stay in touch with primary research, but also to make contributions to the research agenda. A renewed sense of professional rigor will likely accompany the growth of greater understanding of the teaching of foreign languages.

In terms of evaluation, the center would serve as an impartial evaluator of the effectiveness of teaching programs and teaching methods for different types of students, learning time required, and cost. It would also serve as a major administration and validation center for the common metric.

The creation of such a center should follow the model of the National Institutes of Health centers, or the regional centers established by the National Institute of Education, or the collaborative science centers established by the National Science Foundation. One difference would be that the foreign language center would be expected to gain nonfederal support as well. Several of the private foundations—the Exxon Education Foundation, the Ford Foundation, the Pew Memorial Trust—have already provided funds for the creation and maintenance of such a center.

Whether through a center or through the existing organizations in the field of foreign language instruction, we must improve our foreign language teaching system in the United States. The agenda is immense; the resources are beginning to be assembled; it is time we got on with the task.

ANNALS, *AAPSS*, **490**, March 1987

The Measurement of Foreign/Second Language Proficiency

By LYLE F. BACHMAN and JOHN L. D. CLARK

ABSTRACT: Based on and synthesizing recent advances in both psychometric procedures and communicatively oriented linguistic analysis, a theoretical framework for describing factors affecting performance on foreign/second language tests is presented. Included within this framework are both test method factors—such as the testing environment, the nature of the instructions to the examinee, and the stimulus and response modalities represented in the test—and linguistic factors, including the examinee's organizational and pragmatic competence, strategic competence, and psychophysiological skills involved in the proper reception or production of the test language. Implications of the framework for the development and validation of communicative language proficiency tests are discussed and an action plan is suggested, including further refinement of the theoretical framework; development of large-scale, highly authentic criterion measures operationalizing each of the framework factors; and subsequent validation of both existing and to-be-developed practically oriented communicative proficiency tests against the criterion measures. Establishment of a working group of interested individuals from several institutions and disciplinary areas is proposed as an appropriate administrative vehicle for these activities.

Lyle F. Bachman is associate professor of English as an international language and associate director of International Programs and Studies, University of Illinois at Urbana-Champaign. He has published widely in the areas of language testing, language program design, and evaluation.

John L. D. Clark, dean of evaluation and standardization, Defense Language Institute, Monterey, California, has worked and published widely on foreign language testing and test-related research. His major current interests include language proficiency assessment and technology applications in foreign language instruction.

IN the past five years, language testing research has seen dramatic developments on two fronts: applications of current psychometric theory to language testing problems, and the incorporation of current theories of the nature of language proficiency into test design. Each of these two areas is complex in its own right, and inasmuch as they intersect, language testing researchers have been faced with increasingly complex problems and have sought solutions to these problems in diverse ways. As a result, language testing researchers are not working within a single paradigm, with respect to either a theory of language proficiency or a measurement theory.

On the practical side, there is an increasing need for measures of language proficiency for use in language acquisition and attrition research, in language program evaluation, and for making decisions regarding whether individuals have attained levels of language proficiency required for various educational and employment goals. Most currently available measures are inadequate for these purposes in two respects: they are based on a model of language proficiency that does not include the full range of abilities required for communicative language use, and they are based on norm-referenced principles of test development that only permit interpretation of ability levels relative to the performance of specific groups of language users.

To address both the theoretical and practical problems in language testing, there is a pressing need for the development of a theoretical framework, or domain specification, of factors that affect performance on language tests, and for empirical research into both the measurement characteristics of language

tests based on such a theoretical framework and the validity of the framework itself and of tests based on it.

This article will consider issues related to the domain specification of language proficiency and the measurement characteristics of tests developed from this domain specification. It will also suggest a program of research that needs to be undertaken in the service of developing and determining the validity, reliability, authenticity, and practicality of language tests, focusing on their use in program evaluation and in making decisions about individuals.

CURRENT RESEARCH AND DEVELOPMENT IN LANGUAGE TESTING

Current research and development in language testing can be characterized both in terms of the applications of psychometric theory to language testing problems and in terms of the language abilities and the characteristics of language use that are being incorporated into language tests.[1] The major applications of psychometric theory to language testing research in the past five years have been in the areas of construct validation, item-response theory, generalizability theory, and criterion-referenced (CR) measurement. Simultaneously, much effort has been directed toward developing tests that not only measure a broad range of language abilities, including grammatical, discourse, sociolinguistic, and strategic competencies, but that are also authentic, in that they require test takers to interact

---

1. We will use the term "ability" to refer both to the knowledge, or competence, involved in language use and to the skill in implementing that knowledge, and the term "language use" to refer to both productive and receptive performance.

with and process both the explicit linguistic information and the illocutionary force of the test material.[2]

Applications of measurement theory

Although research into the construct validity of language tests can be traced at least to the 1940s, with Carroll's factorial study of verbal abilities,[3] interest in this area was rekindled in the seventies by Oller's research aimed at verifying the notion that language proficiency was a single unitary ability.[4] Oller's research also brought renewed interest in factor analysis as an analytic procedure. Subsequent studies disconfirmed the hypothesis that language proficiency is a single unitary ability;[5] several also applied the multitrait-multimethod design, which had been used extensively in construct validation studies in other fields, along with causal modeling and confirmatory factor analysis, to language tests for the first time.[6]

More recently, item-response theory, which has the potential for providing estimates both of the characteristics of test items—difficulty, discrimination—and of individuals' ability levels that are stable across different samples of individuals and across different testing occasions, has been introduced into language testing research and is being used in-

2. The terms "functional," "communicative," and "authentic" have been used by language testing researchers to refer to the extent to which the tasks required on a given test are similar to some standard of real-life language use. See, for example, Keith Morrow, "Communicative Language Testing: Revolution or Evolution?" in *The Communicative Approach to Language Teaching,* ed. Christopher J. Brumfit and Keith Johnson (Oxford: Oxford University Press, 1979), pp. 143-57; Marjorie B. Wesche, "Communicative Testing in a Second Language," *Canadian Modern Language Review,* 37(3):551-71 (1981); Lyle F. Bachman and Adrian S. Palmer, "The Construct Validation of Some Components of Communicative Proficiency," *TESOL Quarterly,* 16(4):449-65 (Dec. 1982); Michael Canale, "On Some Dimensions of Language Proficiency," in *Issues in Language Testing Research,* ed. J. W. Oller (Rowley, MA: Newbury House, 1983), pp. 333-42; Andrew Harrison, "Communicative Testing: Jam Tomorrow?" in *Current Developments in Language Testing,* ed. A. Hughes and D. Porter (London: Academic Press, 1983), pp. 77-86; John C. Alderson, "Who Needs Jam?" in ibid., pp. 87-92; Dan Douglas and Larry Selinker, "Principles for Language Tests within the 'Discourse Domains' Theory of Interlanguage: Research, Test Construction and Interpretation," *Language Testing,* 2(2):205-26 (Dec. 1985); Charles W. Stansfield, ed., *Technology and Language Testing* (Washington, DC: Teachers of English to Speakers of Other Languages, 1986); *Language Testing,* 2(1) (June 1985); Lyle F. Bachman, *Fundamental Considerations in Language Testing* (Reading, MA: Addison-Wesley, forthcoming). Given the problems of clearly delineating real-life from non-real-life language use, however, we prefer Widdowson's notion of authenticity, which he defines essentially as the interaction between the language user and the discourse, in which the language user responds to and interprets both the propositional and illocutionary meaning. Henry G. Widdowson, *Teaching Language as Communication* (Oxford: Oxford University Press, 1978).

3. John B. Carroll, "A Factor Analysis of Verbal Abilities," *Psychometrika,* 6:279-307 (1941).

4. John W. Oller, "Evidence of a General Language Proficiency Factor: An Expectancy Grammar," *Die Neuren Sprachen,* 76:165-74 (1976); idem, *Language Tests at School: A Pragmatic Approach* (London: Longman, 1979).

5. John B. Carroll, "Psychometric Theory and Language Testing," in *Issues in Language Testing Research,* ed. Oller, pp. 80-105; H. J. Vollmer and F. Sang, "Competing Hypotheses about Second Language Ability: A Plea for Caution," in ibid., pp. 29-74.

6. Lyle F. Bachman and Adrian S. Palmer, "The Construct Validation of the FSI Oral Interview," *Language Learning,* 31(1):67-86 (Mar. 1981); idem, "The Construct Validation of Some Components of Communicative Proficiency"; John A. Upshur and Taco J. Homburg, "Some Relations among Language Tests at Successive Ability Levels," in *Issues in Language Testing Research,* ed. Oller, pp. 188-201.

creasingly in the analysis of language test scores.[7]

Generalizability theory, a powerful extension of classical measurement theory that permits researchers to examine several different sources of measurement error simultaneously, has recently been used to analyze different sources of measurement error in ratings of oral interviews.[8]

Finally, the principles of CR measurement have been applied to the development of language achievement tests.[9]

As a result of these studies, research and development in language testing is now making use of the most current models and techniques in psychometrics.[10]

Applications of linguistic theory

Although much foreign/second language test development continues to be based on a skills and components frame-

work such as those proposed by Lado and by Carroll,[11] language testing researchers are now for the most part working within an expanded framework of communicative language proficiency of which the major distinguishing characteristic is its recognition of the importance of context beyond the sentence level to the appropriate use of language.[12] This context includes both the discourse of which individual sentences are part and the sociolinguistic situation that governs, to a large extent, the nature of that discourse, in both form and function.

Along with this recognition of the context in which language use takes place has come a recognition of the dynamic interaction between that context and discourse, and an expanded view of communication as something more than the simple transfer of information. This dynamic view of communication is reflected in the literature on interlanguage communication strategies and has been included in frameworks of communicative competence as strategic competence.[13]

7. See, for example, Grant Henning, "Advantages of Latent Trait Measurement in Language Testing," *Language Testing*, 1(2):123-33 (June 1984); Grant Henning, Thom Hudson, and Jean Turner, "Item Response Theory and the Assumption of Unidimensionality," ibid., 2(2):141-54 (Dec. 1985); Fred Davidson and Grant Henning, "A Self-rating Scale of English Difficulty: Rasch Scalar Analysis of Items and Rating Categories," ibid., pp. 164-79; Patrick E. Griffin, "The Use of Latent Trait Models in the Calibration of Tests of Spoken Language in Large-scale Selection-placement Programs," in *New Directions in Language Testing*, ed. Y. P. Lee et al. (Oxford: Pergamon Press, 1985), pp. 163-70.

8. For example, Robert E. Bolus, Frances B. Hinofotis, and Kathleen M. Bailey, "An Introduction to Generalizability Theory in Second Language Research," *Language Learning*, 32(2):245-58 (June 1982).

9. For example, Thom Hudson and Brian Lynch, "A Criterion-referenced Measurement Approach to ESL," *Language Testing*, 1(2):171-201 (June 1984).

10. Many of these developments are represented in the papers included in Stansfield, ed., *Technology and Language Testing*.

11. Robert Lado, *Language Testing* (New York: McGraw-Hill, 1961); John B. Carroll, "Fundamental Considerations in Testing English Proficiency of Foreign Students," in *Testing the English Proficiency of Foreign Students* (Washington, DC: Center for Applied Linguistics, 1961), pp. 31-40.

12. Carroll discusses "linguistic performance abilities," such as speed and diversity of response, complexity of information processing, and awareness of linguistic competence, but considers these as essentially outside the construct of language proficiency. See John B. Carroll, "The Psychology of Language Testing," in *Language Testing Symposium: A Psycholinguistic Approach*, ed. Alan Davies (Oxford: Oxford University Press, 1968), pp. 46-69.

13. Michael Canale and Merrill Swain, "Theoretical Bases of Communicative Approaches to

Frameworks of communicative competence thus provide a much more inclusive description of the abilities required to use language effectively than do earlier models, in that they include, in addition to the knowledge of grammatical rules, the knowledge of language functions, or illocutionary acts, and of sociolinguistic conventions, and the recognition of language use as a dynamic process. These new frameworks have influenced research and development in language testing in two ways. First, language test developers are now concerned with the extent to which language tests are capable of measuring the various abilities associated with communicative language use. The second, related, concern has been with developing tests that are more highly authentic.

Thus there are two main problems facing current language testing research. First is the problem of specifying communicative language proficiency and other factors that affect performance on language tests precisely enough to provide a basis for test development and for characterizing the notion of test authenticity. The second problem is determining the scaling and measurement properties of tests of language proficiency. This determination is made difficult by the fact that such tests may measure several distinct abilities and by the need for scores from such tests to be interpreted with reference to externally defined ability domains rather than to comparative performance of individuals.

FACTORS THAT AFFECT PERFORMANCE ON LANGUAGE TESTS

A theoretical framework for describing factors that affect performance on language tests should specify both the domain of language proficiency and the test method characteristics that may systematically affect performance on language tests.

Communicative language proficiency

Bachman defines communicative language proficiency as consisting of both knowledge, or competence, and skill in implementing, or executing, that competence, and he describes a framework of communicative language proficiency that includes three components: language competence, strategic competence, and the psychophysiological skills required to implement these abilities in language use.[14]

Language competence. Language competence can be classified into two types: organizational competence and pragmatic competence. Organizational competence comprises those abilities involved in controlling the formal organization of language for creating or recognizing grammatically correct sentences, comprehending their propositional content, and ordering them to form texts. These abilities are of two types: grammatical and textual. Grammatical competence includes rules of lexis, morphology, and syntax, which govern the choice of words to express specific significations, their forms, and their arrangement in sentences to express propositions. Textual competence includes the knowledge of the conventions of cohesion and rhetorical organi-

Second Language Teaching and Testing," *Applied Linguistics,* 1(1):1-47 (Spring 1980); Canale, "On Some Dimensions of Language Proficiency"; Sandra J. Savignon, *Communicative Competence: Theory and Classroom Practice* (Reading, MA: Addison-Wesley, 1983).

14. Bachman, *Fundamental Considerations in Language Testing.*

zation for joining utterances together to form a text.

Pragmatic competence includes those abilities that, in addition to organizational competence, are employed in the contextualized performance and interpretation of socially appropriate illocutionary acts in discourse. Pragmatic competence thus includes illocutionary competence, or the knowledge of how to perform illocutionary acts, or language functions, and sociolinguistic competence, or the knowledge of the sociolinguistic conventions that govern appropriate language use in a particular culture and in varying situations in that culture.

Strategic competence. As has been indicated, communication involves a dynamic interchange between context and discourse, so that communicative language use resides not in the production or interpretation of texts, but in the relationship that obtains between a text and the context of the situation in which it occurs. The interpretation of discourse, in other words, requires the ability to assess the context for relevant information and then to match this information to information in the discourse. This matching of the new information to be processed with relevant information that is available—including presupposition and real-world knowledge—and mapping this onto the maximally efficient use of existing language abilities is a function of strategic competence.

Strategic competence may affect test scores in several ways. Correctly answering inference questions, for example, requires strategic competence, in that the test taker must recognize what information outside the discourse itself is relevant to answering the question, and he or she must then search for that infor-

mation in his or her memory. Another example would be certain performance tests in which test takers can successfully complete the required tasks by utilizing their strategic competence to compensate for deficiencies in other competencies.

Psychophysiological skills. The abilities described thus far may be implemented or executed in listening, speaking, reading, and writing. In order to distinguish these skills, it is necessary to consider the modes and channels that are involved in language use. Thus in the receptive mode—listening, reading—auditory and visual skills are employed, while in the productive mode—speaking, writing—the neuromuscular skills—articulatory or digital skills—are employed. Likewise, the auditory channel—listening, speaking—can be distinguished from the visual channel—reading, writing.

Test method factors

Numerous research studies attest to the fact that the test method influences performance on language tests.[15] A

15. Ray T. Clifford, "Reliability and Validity of Language Aspects Contributing to Oral Proficiency of Prospective Teachers of German," in *Direct Testing of Speaking Proficiency: Theory and Application,* ed. J.L.D. Clark (Princeton, NJ: Educational Testing Service, 1978), pp. 191-209; idem, "Convergent and Discriminant Validation of Integrated and Unitary Language Skills: The Need for a Research Model," in *The Construct Validation of Tests of Communicative Competence,* ed. A. S. Palmer, P.J.M. Groot, and G. A. Trosper (Washington, DC: Teachers of English to Speakers of Other Languages, 1981), pp. 62-70; Susanna M. Brütsch, "Convergent-discriminant Validation of Prospective Teacher Proficiency in Oral and Written French by Means of the MLA Cooperative Language Proficiency Test, French Direct Proficiency Tests for Teachers (TOP and TWP), and Self-ratings" (Ph.D. diss., University

framework for characterizing method factors has been described by Bachman.[16] This framework includes the following categories: (1) the testing environment; (2) the nature of the test directions; (3) the nature of the stimulus the test taker receives; and (4) the nature of the response to that stimulus.

The testing environment includes factors such as familiarity of place, time of day, familiarity of equipment, familiarity and status of personnel administering the test, and noise. Test directions include the following factors: language, channel, explicitness of criteria for correctness, and specification of task. The stimulus includes the following factors: channel, whether auditory or visual; format, including type of presentation, type of language sample, specification of problem, and speededness; and nature of discourse, including propositional content, textual characteristics, and illocutionary characteristics. The response includes the following factors: channel; type of response—identification, selection of correct alternative, production; form of response—language or nonlanguage; nature of discourse—propositional content, textual characteristics, and illocutionary characteristics; and restrictions on response, such as requiring specific grammatical forms or organizational patterns in a test of writing.

CHARACTERISTICS OF LANGUAGE TESTS

In some tests the channel of either the stimulus or the response or both matches

that of the language ability being tested, in which case the test method and language proficiency factors overlap. This matching between test stimulus and/or response channels and language ability channels is one characteristic of performance tests, such as an oral interview being used as a measure of speaking ability or a reading passage used as a measure of reading ability. Such tests are sometimes referred to as direct or semi-direct, depending upon the extent to which both stimulus and response channels match the language ability channel. Tests in which the test method and ability channels do not match might be called nonperformance tests, sometimes called indirect tests. An example of such a test would be one that requires test takers to identify written words that rhyme as an indication of their speaking ability.

Authenticity

The stimulus and response can also be characterized in terms of their illocutionary force, or the language functions performed. The overall function performed by any language test is to elicit a response that can be evaluated, so that a stimulus consisting of a language sample thus performs the obvious function of eliciting a response and could, in this somewhat trivial sense, be regarded as functional. More important, however, is the extent to which the stimulus embodies communicative functions in addition to this. At one extreme are nonfunctional tests in which neither the stimulus nor the response performs any communicative function, such as a multiple-choice test of grammar in which the stimulus material in the stem and choices serves solely as a medium for focusing the test taker's attention on the

of Minnesota, 1979); Bachman and Palmer, "Construct Validation of the FSI Oral Interview"; idem, "Construct Validation of Some Components of Communicative Proficiency."

16. Bachman, *Fundamental Considerations in Language Testing.*

grammatical form of the language and in which the response in simply a mark on a piece of paper.

At the other end of the spectrum are tests in which both the stimulus and the response involve the performance of a variety of language functions. An example of this is a well-conducted oral interview in which both the examiner and the examinee are involved in the conversation to the extent that they virtually forget the formal organizational characteristics of the discourse and the test situation.

Since authenticity depends on the interaction between the test taker and the test material, a given test may be authentic for some test takers and not for others. This is because the extent to which test takers are aware of and respond to the illocutionary force of the test stimulus is likely to vary from individual to individual. Determining the authenticity of a given test or test item, therefore, is difficult and cannot be done on the basis of content or appearance alone.[17]

Artificiality

Language tests are sometimes characterized as nonnatural or nonnormal, or relatively artificial. One way to characterize artificiality of language use is in terms of the extent to which variation is inappropriately restricted. In virtually all language use, even in situations that

17. The extent to which a given test or test item needs to be authentic will depend, to a large degree, upon its purpose. Thus, if the purpose of the test is to measure grammatical competence, the need for authenticity may be less than if sociolinguistic or illocutionary competence is to be measured. The effect of authenticity or lack of authenticity on test performance is, of course, an empirical question and is the proper object of construct validation research.

might be characterized as authentic or natural, variation is restricted to a large extent by the context of the situation. Upon meeting a colleague on the way to class, for example, we are usually not free to utter whatever may come into our head, but are restricted both in the illocutionary act we perform—greeting—and in the register we use—informal. Language use can be restricted in terms of channel and mode as well as its propositional, organizational, illocutionary, and interactional characteristics. Whenever artificial restrictions are imposed by the format or manner of operation of the test, some of the variability encountered in normal language performance is likely to be lost, and some of the authenticity as well.

CRITERION-REFERENCED
SCALES OF COMMUNICATIVE
LANGUAGE PROFICIENCY

Two areas of great current interest and need for language test development are those of language method evaluation studies and the evaluation of individuals' levels of language proficiency. Most currently available language proficiency tests are norm referenced, which means that their scores can be interpreted only with reference to the performance of other individuals. The norm-referenced interpretation of test scores is not suitable for use in either formative program evaluation or in comparative program evaluation, since it fails to reflect the degree of mastery of specific objectives and since both the score norms and the content may be inappropriate to either or both groups that are being compared.[18]

18. We would note that it is possible for a given test to be both criterion and norm referenced,

Common metric scales

The need for a common metric scale for measuring language proficiency in a wide variety of contexts, at all levels, and in many different languages has been recognized and discussed by testing researchers for some time.[19] The obvious advantage of such a scale and tests developed from it is that they would provide a standard for defining and measuring language proficiency that would be independent of specific languages, contexts, and domains of discourse. Scores from such a test would thus be comparable across different languages and contexts.

Such a scale would necessarily be CR, since norm-referenced test scores must be referenced to specific groups and specific contexts. Unlike norm-referenced test scores, the interpretation of CR test scores is independent of the performance of other individuals on the test. A CR test score is one that can be

interpreted as an indication of an individual's attainment with respect to a given domain of proficiency. Thus the primary concern in developing a CR test is that it be sensitive to different levels of proficiency in the domain.

Criterion-referenced scales

There are two necessary conditions for the CR interpretation of test scores: the test content must be sampled from a well-defined domain of abilities, and the scores must be defined in terms of an absolute scale of proficiency.

In order to interpret test scores as indicators of language proficiency, we must define the domain of language proficiency in a way that clearly distinguishes it from test-method factors. That is, in order for test scores to be comparable across content domains and contexts, the abilities that are reflected in these scores must be defined independently of these factors.

The specification of the domain of language proficiency in terms of specific content areas and contexts is illustrated in the following example:

Able to satisfy the requirements of everyday situations and routine school and work requirements. Can handle with confidence but not with facility complicated tasks and social situations, such as elaborating, complaining, and apologizing. Can narrate and describe with some details, linking sentences together smoothly. Can communicate facts and talk casually about topics of current public and personal interest, using general vocabulary.[20]

One problem this type of domain specification creates is lack of comparability of

---

since a test developed by CR procedures could be normed to various groups of test takers. Criterion referencing a norm-referenced test is much more difficult, since it depends on the availability of a well-defined domain of abilities and involves statistical assumptions in score equating. An example of this latter procedure is provided in John B. Carroll, *The Foreign Language Attainments of Language Majors in Their Senior Year: A Survey Conducted on U.S. Colleges and Universities. Final Report*, ERIC document ED 013-343 (Cambridge, MA: Harvard University Graduate School of Education, 1967).

19. Protase Woodford, "Let's Speak the Same Language" (Paper delivered at the National Conference on New Directions in Foreign Language Studies and Language Policy, Wayne, NJ, 17 Nov. 1978); Brendon J. Carroll, *Testing Communicative Performance* (London: Pergamon Institute of English, 1978); John L. D. Clark, "Toward a Common Measure of Speaking Proficiency," in *Measuring Spoken Language Proficiency*, ed. J. R. Firth (Washington, DC: Georgetown University Press, 1980).

20. American Council on the Teaching of Foreign Languages, *ACTFL Proficiency Guidelines* (New York: American Council on the Teaching of Foreign Languages, 1986), p. 2.

ratings. This is because it is not likely that these specific functions—elaborating, complaining, apologizing, narrating, and describing—will be of equal relevance to different language use contexts. Another problem is that test scores are highly dependent upon context factors and thus susceptible to the effect of test method. Because of this, both the use of context-dependent domain specifications in developing tests and the interpretation of scores on such tests are limited to the specific situations for which they are designed, and are of little use for comparative purposes.

Therefore, although it is essential for our tests to be appropriate for and sensitive to specific language learning and language use contexts, there is a dilemma involved in increasing the specificity of scale definitions: the most appropriate domain specification would be for a single individual in a specific context. Thus the more narrowly we define the domain of language proficiency in terms of specific forms, functions, contexts, and content areas, the less generalizable our tests become.

The second requirement for the CR interpretation of test scores is that they constitute an absolute scale of measurement, that is, one that has true zero and perfect points.[21] Achieving an absolute scale of foreign language proficiency with true zero and perfect levels is virtually impossible if one attempts to define this scale in terms of actual language use or actual language users. If we consider language proficiency to be similar to other cognitive abilities, such as intelligence, that may not have true zero points, as well as the likely existence of elements of the native language that are either universal to all languages or shared with the foreign language, then true zero second language proficiency does not exist in actual individuals.

At the other end of the spectrum, the individual with absolutely complete language proficiency also does not exist. Not only does language proficiency develop diachronically as a function of language change, it also develops in the way that all cognitive abilities constantly develop. Although the language use of native speakers is frequently advocated as a criterion for absolute language proficiency, such a criterion is clearly inadequate for several reasons.[22] First, native speakers show considerable variation in proficiency, particularly with regard to abilities such as cohesion, discourse organization, and sociolinguistic appropriateness. Second, there is the problem of identifying which variety or dialect to adopt as the native-speaker criterion. This question, which is often political or social rather than linguistic, is further complicated by the fact that boundaries between language varieties are not necessarily clear-cut. Finally, we must also consider differences in usage even within varieties or dialects, as well as differences between prescriptive norms and the norms of actual usage.[23]

---

21. Glaser states that "the notion of a continuum of knowledge acquisition ranging from no proficiency at all to perfect performance" underlies CR measures. Robert Glaser, "Instructional Technology and the Measurement of Learning Outcomes," *American Psychologist,* 18(8):519 (Aug. 1963).

22. Discussions of the problems involved in attempting to define native-speaker norms are included in Florian Coulmas, ed., *A Festschrift for Native Speaker* (The Hague: Mouton, 1981); James Lantolf and William Frawley, "Oral Proficiency Testing: A Critical Analysis," *Modern Language Journal,* 69:337-45 (1985).

23. Variation in native norms is discussed in Braj B. Kachru, "Standards, Codification and Sociolinguistic Realism: The English Language in

Because of these problems, it is virtually impossible to define criterion levels of language proficiency in terms of actual individuals or actual performance. Rather, such levels must be defined abstractly, in terms of the relative presence or absence of the abilities that constitute the domain.

In summary, to develop tests that are adequate for the uses of language program evaluation, that will yield scores that are comparable across a wide range of language learning and language use contexts, and that require authentic language use, we must begin by (1) specifying a domain of foreign language proficiency that is consistent with current frameworks, and specifying the characteristics of test methods that affect test performance; and (2) defining levels or scales of proficiency abstractly, in terms of relative degrees of ability, and independently of contextual features of language use.

RESEARCH AND DEVELOPMENT CONSIDERATIONS

As may be readily inferred from the preceding discussion of an expanded conceptual model for foreign/second language proficiency assessment, further development and validation of both the model and the testing instruments derived from it will require a substantial and highly focused effort that may well extend over a number of years before achieving a good level of both theoretical and practical success. With regard to the implementation of such a development effort, a very useful strategy would seem to be to work more or less simultaneously on four separate but interrelated fronts, specifically, to:

—continue to refine the theoretical model of communicative language proficiency as briefly described earlier in this article, with particular attention to defining the specific ability domains in operational terms;

—develop, based on the operational definitions of the individual domains of the model, highly authentic measures of performance within these domains, for use as criteria in proficiency testing or proficiency development studies;

—survey currently available proficiency testing instruments with respect to their degree of congruence with the requirements of a more fully elaborated proficiency model, selecting the most promising instruments and validating them against the criterion measures at issue in the development of the authentic performance measures; and

—develop and validate, through a joint effort of language testing practitioners, applied linguists, evaluators, and psychometricians, batteries of new instruments of optimum reliability, validity, and practicality for use in a variety of real-world testing contexts.

Refinement of the theoretical model would involve the fleshing out of each of the major components of the model in operationally verifiable terms; such fleshing out would include useful input from several linguistic areas, especially discourse analysis and pragmatics. For example, the nature of textual compe-

the Outer Circle," in *English in the World: Teaching and Learning the Language and Literature,* ed. R. Quirk and H. G. Widdowson (Cambridge: Cambridge University Press, 1985), pp. 11-30.

tence could be elaborated with reference to its typical—and differing—manifestations in both receptive and productive modes. Well-constructed and adequately detailed characterizations of each of the components of the model would, in and of themselves, point rather directly to the particular types of testing contingencies that would need to be set up to assess performance on these components in a highly criterial manner.

Development of the necessarily lengthy, research-oriented, and—for practical purposes—unwieldy criterial measures would be a painstaking job the nature and scope of which have been described in some detail by Clark.[24] Notwithstanding the difficulty of the task, it would appear that the development of such measures, to serve as conceptual and statistical criteria against which the performance of less highly authentic instruments would be gauged, would be a sine qua non for the entire undertaking, since in the absence of such instruments and the correlational data that they would provide, validity assertions concerning the less authentic instruments would have little or no extrinsic grounding. In addition to serving as criterion measures against which other instruments would be validated, these tests would provide highly useful feedback on the accuracy and adequacy of the communicative proficiency model itself and would almost certainly lead to the properly informed fine-tuning of the model in several respects.

While developing the research-oriented criterial tests, as well as the more practically oriented operational tests, it would not be appropriate, or cost- or labor-effective, to reject out of hand the quite large number of proficiency tests and testing formats that have been developed over the past five to ten years or, in some instances, even earlier. Detailed reviews of these tests should be conducted and reported, consisting of an informed analysis of (1) the extent to which the test addresses each of the performance domains at issue in the expanded proficiency model; (2) the authenticity of the test, as reflected in the realism and naturalness of both the test stimuli and the examinee responses as exemplary of real-life language use situations; (3) the absence of test method factors that would negatively influence the degree of authenticity, even though the instruments may have the appearance of validity; (4) the amount and nature of developed field experience with the test, including correlations with other instruments, predictive studies, and other validation or interpretation activities; and (5) the overall practicality of the test for administration, scoring, and score reporting in a variety of operational situations.

At present, there is a reasonably large inventory of instruments that could and would undergo a detailed review of this type. For example, the Foreign Service Institute oral interview and scoring scale,[25] as well as recent modifications of the traditional procedure by the Interagency Language Roundtable[26] and by the Educational Testing Service and the American Council on the Teaching of

24. Clark, "Toward a Common Measure of Speaking Proficiency."

25. Claudia P. Wilds, "The Oral Interview Test," in *Testing Language Proficiency,* ed. R. Jones and B. Spolsky (Arlington, VA: Center for Applied Linguistics, 1975), pp. 29-38; Howard E. Sollenberger, "Development and Current Use of the FSI Oral Interview Test," in *Direct Testing of Speaking Proficiency,* ed. Clark, pp. 1-12.

26. P. Lowe, *ILR Handbook on Oral Interview Testing* (Washington, DC: DLI/LS Oral Interview Project, 1985).

Foreign Languages,[27] might be expected to receive mixed reviews emphasizing, as positive points, both the high degree of authenticity of the approach for one particular type of communication situation—polite conversation between relative strangers on a variety of general topics—and the vast amount of accumulated experience with test administration and interpretation of testing results. On the negative side, the lack of realism of the pure interview as reflective of communicative performance in other than conversational situations would need to be emphasized, as well as the relatively cumbersome and labor-intensive administration and scoring procedures.

The so-called semi-direct speaking tests, typified by the Recorded Oral Proficiency Examination[28] and the Chinese Speaking Test,[29] are intended to provide a reasonable surrogate for face-to-face proficiency tests through a tape- and booklet-mediated testing procedure that is considerably more practical, but also appreciably less authentic, than the direct interview.

For the receptive skills, a variety of potentially useful instruments already exist or are under development, including, for example, listening comprehension and reading tests in Japanese,[30] Chinese,[31] and Russian.[32] In all cases, the aural and visual stimuli are typical of those encountered in real-life contexts and are representative of a wide number of topics and content areas within the listening comprehension and reading domains. These and numerous other tests demonstrate combinations of qualities that make them appropriate for consideration for use as proficiency testing instruments during a period in which even more highly valid instruments and procedures would be under active development.

Proper use and interpretation of such existing instruments would be guided both by an informed, thoroughgoing review of their merits and shortcomings vis-à-vis an expanded conceptual framework for communicative proficiency testing and by the accumulation of empirical validation data as these tests are increasingly used in a variety of contexts. For example, a study of the intercorrelations of the Chinese Speaking Test with an interview of the Interagency Language Roundtable type is nearing completion, with very encouraging results from a statistical perspective.[33]

27. American Council on the Teaching of Foreign Languages, "The ACTFL Provisional Proficiency Guidelines," in *Teaching for Proficiency: The Organizing Principle,* ed. T. Higgs (Lincolnwood, IL: National Textbook, 1984), app. A; idem, *ACTFL Proficiency Guidelines;* Judith Liskin-Gasparro, "The ACTFL Proficiency Guidelines: A Historical Perspective," in ibid., pp. 11-42; Pardee Lowe, "The ILR Proficiency Scale as a Synthesizing Research Principle: The View from the Mountain," in *Foreign Language Proficiency in the Classroom and Beyond,* ed. Charles J. James (Lincolnwood, IL: National Textbook, 1985).

28. Pardee Lowe and Ray T. Clifford, "Developing an Indirect Measure of Overall Oral Proficiency," in *Measuring Spoken Language Proficiency,* ed. Firth, pp. 31-39.

29. John L. D. Clark, "Development of a Tape-mediated, ACTFL/ILR Scale-based Test of Chinese Speaking Proficiency," in *Technology and Language Testing,* ed. Stansfield, pp. 129-46.

30. Educational Testing Service, *Japanese Proficiency Test* (Princeton, NJ: Educational Testing Service, 1981).

31. Center for Applied Linguistics, *Chinese Proficiency Test* (Washington, DC: Center for Applied Linguistics, 1983).

32. Educational Testing Service, *Russian Proficiency Test* (Princeton, NJ: Educational Testing Service, in preparation).

33. John L. D. Clark, *Final Report: The Development, Validation and Dissemination of a Proficiency-based Test of Speaking Ability in Chinese and Associated Assessment Model for*

Of the four suggested activity paths to be followed more or less simultaneously, the last—development of operational instruments exemplifying a fully elaborated communicative language proficiency model to the maximum extent possible within real-life administrative and scoring constraints—will at the same time pose the greatest challenge and offer the greatest practical rewards.

In order to accomplish such a task, the continued input and close collaboration of individuals working in each of the other three areas will be required. The first area will provide conceptual and theoretical guidance for test content and for elicitation and scoring procedures. The second area will provide the necessary research-oriented criterion instruments against which the new tests would need, in part, to be validated. The third area will provide detailed information about current proficiency-oriented testing instruments and techniques, which will furnish a good point of departure for the new test development effort.

Other Less-commonly Taught Languages (Washington, DC: Center for Applied Linguistics, forthcoming).

From a structural point of view, it may be useful to think of establishing an at least semiformal working group of interested individuals, each of whom would concentrate his or her efforts in one of the four major areas, but who would also have access and input into the activities of those in the other three areas. A variety of networking procedures might be considered, including an informal newsletter, use of electronic mail, and at least annual reports to the profession, possibly through the vehicle of the annual Language Testing Research Colloquium.

By way of brief conclusion, it is fair to say that the language proficiency testing field has reached an important watershed, at which recent statistical advances, increased attention to the development of detailed theoretical models of communicative language proficiency, the existence of a number of useful prototype instruments, and growing practical interest in proficiency-based language teaching and assessment on the part of both language teachers and researchers all combine to produce a very opportune moment for the field to make rapid, synergistic advances in both the theory and the practice of language proficiency assessment.

ANNALS, *AAPSS*, **490**, March 1987

Advanced Technology in Foreign Language Instruction and Translation

By JOHN FOUGHT

ABSTRACT: The hardware available for computer-assisted language learning is rapidly improving. Software development continues to lag, and the empirical foundation for second language acquisition research is inadequate. A strategy for remedying these deficiencies is outlined. Networked microcomputers whose software for computer-assisted language learning generates logs of user activity for analysis of second language acquisition offer interesting possibilities both for practical applications and in research. With access to a national network of data, testing, and teaching materials, such local networks will support advanced workstations and software allowing more complex interactions with the learning environment.

John Fought received his doctorate in linguistics from Yale University in 1967. Except for one year as a Fulbright lecturer at the University of Innsbruck, he has taught linguistics since then at the University of Pennsylvania. Field linguistics and linguistic anthropology, especially the study of the Mayan languages of Mesoamerica, as well as the hieroglyphic writing system of the ancient Mayas, and instruction in the basic technical skills required for fieldwork have been his main focus. Since 1983, he has directed the Language Analysis Project at Penn, an effort to apply modern technology to general linguistics.

M ANY commissions and individuals concerned with foreign language study and policies have pointed out that in the United States, foreign language skills are most often thought to have instrumental rather than intrinsic value. Within the federal government, as within the business and academic communities, language skills are valued principally for their contribution to job performance. Foreign language proficiency is associated with the specialist, not the generalist; with low-level rather than high-level responsibilities. For all but the language teacher, time and resources needed just to maintain language skills, let alone to enhance them, are sharply restricted. Hard-pressed administrators may see them as a distraction from one's real job or as just a waste of time. The commitment of private and public resources to developing and maintaining these skills has accordingly been relatively limited, and there is good reason for language professionals—all of them volunteers in the best sense—to feel overworked and at times undervalued. These institutional realities are always in the background of discussions of foreign language needs, resources, and policies.

In such circumstances, both managers and teachers have and exercise the right to seek methods that are not only effective but actually cost effective. Now, for teachers and administrators alike, there is urgent concern as a powerful, rapidly changing technology spreads everywhere, even at last into the language classroom. What might it do for the learners? What will it do to the teachers? Computer-assisted language learning (CALL) is no exception to the rule: to prosper, it must not only work, but be efficient. There is a clear danger, often noted, of overselling it to the language profession,

and a serious, still-unsolved problem of mutual adjustment between computer and language specialists involved in the development of CALL systems at what is, after all, a relatively high cost when compared with traditional tools.

It is gratifying to see how consistently the participants in the Aspen conference have pointed out the need for sound empirical foundations, for careful planning and evaluation, and for systems that will free rather than replace the teacher. No computer system now available can interact conversationally or translate automatically with even remotely human skill, nor is any such system visible on the horizon. But while indeed there are roles, human roles, vital to the success of language learning, it is perhaps not too subversive to suggest that some roles commonly played by human teachers are not vital. It should be seen as a hope, rather than a threat, that the computer can, with proper handling, replace the human teacher as drillmaster, as word-by-word translation coach, as spelling corrector, as roll taker, as drudge. The increasing use of the new technology will bring changes in institutional functioning and will shift the demands made on language teachers into a new, but possibly more satisfying, pattern.

Computers—more specifically, microcomputers—are at the focus of educational technology now and are likely to remain there for the foreseeable future. Micros earned their prefix by being much smaller—and many times cheaper—than their predecessors. They do not require a prepared site, but just plug into an ordinary outlet. They are meant to serve one user. Peripheral devices augment their capabilities; networks connect them to each other and to larger computers to create very powerful retrieval and information-processing resources; pure and applied thinkers with every imaginable kind of credentials ponder their uses and implications. But the main reason they are gaining in the marketplace much faster than larger systems is their low cost per user and per unit of computing power.

Microcomputers are different in some significant ways besides size and cost from the larger mini and mainframe computers that became familiar to most academics in the twenty or so years ending around 1975, when these large systems were installed, almost emplaced, in specially designed and chilled quarters with raised floors and dropped ceilings to conceal the maze of cables connecting their many large components. Micros are much easier to use, and to learn to use, yet they now have enough power and capacity to serve most individual users very well, and when linked into networks, they jointly wield enough power for almost any task. With the admittedly even greater computing power and capacity of mainframes and minis comes a very much higher cost of purchase and operation; consequently these are used as time-sharing systems supporting many terminals in imperceptibly fast succession, so that each does indeed experience the computer for fleeting instants in all its manifold and feudally arbitrary complexity. This is just the trouble: not only is all its power yours to command, but all its commands are yours to figure out. Elsewhere I likened the process of opening and using an account on a mainframe system to that of obtaining and using influence at the court of the Sun King.[1] The vassals

1. John Fought, *Interactions with Computers* (Paper delivered at the Temple University Conference on Culture and Communication, Philadelphia, PA, 1983).

of the Sun King are still to be found working in every mainframe computer center, jealously guarding and aggrandizing their master, regulating access to it, charging fees whose tiny components somehow amount to startling monthly totals. The cost of use, whether measured in dollars or in humiliation, but even more, the bewildering complexity of the operating systems and embedded environments found on any mini or mainframe are the main reasons time-sharing systems have had so little appeal to humanists in general. With the appearance of cheap, adequately powerful, and now networked microcomputers, the mainframe systems have become largely irrelevant to the humanities, including, most particularly, the foreign language professions, whose special needs are no doubt farthest of all from the center of the world of time-sharing systems.

To be sure, there are foreign language instructional systems of relatively long standing and some merit on two mainframe systems. I will have very little to say about them here, however, since the realities of the market have forced the release of scaled-down versions of both in microcomputer formats. These are the Plato system, developed at the University of Illinois and promoted by Control Data, and the TICCIT system, developed by Brigham Young University and MITRE and now owned by Hazeltine. The difficulty with these systems in their original form is their high cost per user, especially high in the case of Plato, with its requirement of specific hardware, including very expensive terminals. Plato has its strong partisans, and there are surely worthwhile elements to be salvaged from it. It is available for remote access, and interesting user data have surely been accumulated. Nevertheless, I am convinced that systems requiring large investments in specific hardware, particularly time-sharing systems, should be regarded by now as victims of the institutional realities of both the computer industry and the system of priorities within which the foreign language professions operate.

LESSONS FROM YESTERDAY'S ADVANCED TECHNOLOGIES

Microcomputers are not the first wave of technological aids to be put into wide use in foreign language instruction, however. There have been a number of these over the past half century, and each has left behind valuable lessons deserving of our attention.

Audiovisual aids

Perhaps the earliest of these we need to consider was the introduction of audiovisual equipment: record players, film, filmstrip, and transparency projectors. The costs of production of quality disks and film were high enough so that audiovisual materials were largely outside the control of their users, who could not modify them or, indeed, even obtain them in sufficient quantity for use as primary learning materials. As they were from the beginning, they are still confined to a supplementary role in the classroom or auditorium in all but the rarest cases. Thus their use depends on the proportion of classroom time set aside for them by teachers or administrators, and this in turn is presumably regulated by their perceived effectiveness in relation to a given curriculum or lesson plan.

Language laboratories

Beginning in the 1950s, partly with a view to implementing a fashionable system of language instruction, schools across the nation installed language laboratories. At first these consisted of little more than assemblages of disk and then tape recorders crowded together into hastily converted classrooms.[2] Soon, however, manufacturers adapted or designed equipment especially for language laboratories. Even so, labs were and are a fairly cheap way to provide authentic spoken material under controlled conditions, an advantage whose novelty and appeal it is easy to forget now, in the age of the ubiquitous cassette. Another application they are well known and disliked for is the delivery of pattern drills, typically the substitution of one focal element for another in a framing environment, while the student follows along in a workbook. Audiolingualism, supported by stimulus-response psychology, led to their use in simulated interactions.[3] These interac-

2. Standard methodological publications on language laboratories date from the 1960s. See Elton Hocking, *Language Laboratory and Language Learning* (Washington, DC: National Educational Association, 1964). Wilga M. Rivers, *Speaking in Many Tongues: Essays in Foreign-language Teaching,* 3rd ed., (New York: Cambridge University Press, 1983), pp. 131-40, surveys the topic from the current perspective. Labs are used more for listening nowadays and less for exercises.

3. Audiolingualism arose from instructional methods developed by the Army Specialized Training Program during World War II. Small classes, a live informant, and a supervising linguist were featured. Although there were theoretical points at stake for the linguists who developed the methods, the linguists were also all experienced language teachers under severe time pressure and in many cases lacking access to teaching materials apart from what could be hastily created. The success of the wartime program should be judged against several factors: the relatively poor quality of the competing approaches, the high motivation of students and teachers, and the intensive exposure. Transferred to an environment where skills,

tions, dialogues with a voice on tape, inevitably lack the key elements that make human interaction so helpful: immediate feedback, both audible and visible, and the capacity for cooperative repair of damaged communication. Most of the time, of course, they lack much more than that, being generally unconnected with any useful situational context the user might actually encounter and, often enough, not even embodying a very useful linguistic structural pattern. They soon produce in all but the most fervent student a profound anomie.

There are instructive parallels between these two waves of technology-driven innovation. Most obviously, in both, the hardware manufacturers played a major role, and questionable theorists were easily found to sanctify the enterprise, just as publishers were found to put out first the disks and films and then the collections of magnetic media and textbooks to use with them. Like computer labs, audio labs were grossly oversold at the beginning, and both have suffered from backlash due in part to an astonishing disregard of their inherent strengths and an insistence on using them in ways dictated by pedagogical theories or classroom practices established independently of the technology and not well adapted to technological support or mimicry. In this regard the history of audiolingualism as a theory and practice of second language teaching is especially noteworthy: stimulus-response theories of human learning and the associated narrow variant of the then-dominant structuralist approach to linguistics provide a sobering precedent from which to view the current partnership of broadly transformational linguistic theories, cognitive psychology, and computer science known as cognitive science. Only an unflinching commitment to empirical validation will protect us against buying more nostrums.[4]

Teaching machines

An interesting episode in the story of educational technology is the teaching machine, worth remembering here as the immediate ancestor of computer-assisted instruction and for its software, which bears an uncomfortable resemblance to much of what can be found right now on computer diskettes in its generally linear progression with little use of branching and looping.[5] Although they were mechanical or electromechanical appliances, sometimes actual books, teaching machines were the first serious attempts at programmed learning and should be understood as an effort to apply the methods of problem solving appropriate for low-level programming

---

4. The research model of hypothesis confirmation used so frequently both in psychology and in education should be regarded with special suspicion. Unless accompanied by independent and convincing evidence that alternative hypotheses must be excluded, this model is an instance of the classical fallacy of affirming the consequent: if x then y; y; therefore x.

5. See H. Kay, B. Dodd, and M. Sime, *Teaching Machines and Programmed Learning* (New York: Penguin Books, 1968), and its bibliography. As with computer-assisted instruction, much of the motivation for development seems to have come from industry and government, with their needs for unconventional patterns of instruction and cost savings. A substantial body of development and evaluation research with direct application to CALL awaits exploitation.

motivation, and exposure were generally lower, and where an undeniably pretentious theorizing was included in the package, the method came to be seen as a failure by many, though not always for the best reasons.

languages to the needs of human learning without the then-prohibitive cost of computer access. More even than language labs, teaching machines apparently produced often violent aversion in teachers and learners alike. If language labs often made students feel like inept parrots, teaching machines made them feel even worse—like incompetent learning machines.

Computers and translation

Research on computerized translation began in the late 1940s. These efforts received considerable support until the publication report of the Automatic Language Processing Advisory Committee (ALPAC) in 1966.[6] That report reviewed the disappointing lack of progress made up to that time toward the goal of automated translation and compared the cost and quality of human translations with the computer-aided and human-edited translation systems then available, leading to a conclusion that (1) there was no prospect of satisfactory fully automatic translation in the then-foreseeable future; and (2) machine-aided translation was nearly as costly as and significantly less effective than human translation.

Support was sharply restricted after the ALPAC report, but it did not end. A number of findings and possibilities mentioned in the report have served since then as the basis for successful systems of machine-aided translation systems: improved dictionary lookup, convenient word-processing systems, and the development of suitably power-

ful microcomputers with sufficient mass storage have brought the cost effectiveness of machine-assisted translation systems into a very appealing range.[7]

CALL TODAY

Although substantial resources have been committed by government and private sources to the development of computer-assisted foreign language learning software, there are a number of areas of conspicuous underdevelopment in CALL: solid data on the effectiveness of various approaches to CALL across a full range of individual learners, skills, and languages; and support for individual users of CALL, both teachers and learners, comparable to that supplied by the textbook publishing industry to users of conventional classroom instruction in languages.[8] Both these lacks are especially serious for the less commonly taught critical languages; both are indirect consequences of a generally low level of sophistication and power in available CALL software, it being far less developed than the hardware it was made to run on.

6. *Language and Machines: Computers in Translation and Linguistics* (Washington, DC: National Academy of Sciences, National Research Council, Automatic Language Processing Advisory Committee, 1966).

7. The European Economic Community, the North Atlantic Treaty Organization, the Canadian government, and various branches of the U.S. government use machine-assisted translation systems routinely. As in much current practically oriented computer software development, the emphasis has shifted from automatic to interactive operation. Research and development are proceeding vigorously in the United States, in Europe, and in Japan, driven by the prospect of a very large market.

8. This familiar mode of development is due in part to the lack of centralization characteristic of our educational system overall. Although CALL installations are not yet as common as language labs, they are in place in many language departments across the country. They usually work independently, however, and there is little sharing of resources and research results.

An overview of current hardware

The largest populations of computers in educational institutions are Apple II, Commodore 64, and Radio Shack TRS 80 machines. These are incompatible with each other, but have some similarities: they have from 48 to 64 kilobytes of random access memory (RAM), an eight-bit processor, and, at least in the first two cases, quite easily used screen graphics. Typically, a school will place its computers together in a room under the supervision of a teacher who is either a volunteer or a draftee in the role of computer expert; donated and purchased educational software and a few simple peripherals—a shared floppy disk drive, a printer—will be found with them, sometimes in working order. The very limited memory capacity of these computers is more of a handicap than their relatively weak processing power, which is, after all, still great enough to be of considerable use to language learners and teachers blessed with a supply of useful software.

The IBM PC is not nearly as common in the schools as it is in colleges and universities. There, as in the business world, it is the most influential microcomputer on the market. The PC and its many imitators have a 16-bit processor chip, either an Intel 8088 or the more powerful 8086; a much larger RAM, usually from 256 to 640 kilobytes; and an ever growing selection of peripherals and aftermarket enhancements. Because of the prestige of the manufacturer, the IBM PC has come to dominate the business and government microcomputer markets. As a tool for foreign language work, however, the PC leaves much to be desired: the screen graphics until recently have not been good, making it somewhat difficult to provide multiple character sets without sacrificing other conveniences of operation, for example. What is perhaps more serious in the long run is the limitation of the operating system—whether PC DOS or MS DOS—to 640 kilobytes of directly addressable memory. This limit is proving troublesome for some computer users and surprisingly difficult for software developers to remedy. It limits the speed of execution of some kinds of programs, provides cramped quarters for so-called memory-resident convenience software, and calls for more expensive measures than would otherwise be needed to upgrade the performance of the basic unit.

The Macintosh is just beginning to emerge as a serious foreign language workstation, having been delayed by its original hardware design limitations and the company's policy of making expansion difficult: a single drive, and 128 kilobytes of RAM, with some of this taken up by its graphics-dominated user interface, with the now very familiar and rather tiresomely cute little icons. With more RAM—now as much as 4 megabytes—and a fast hard disk interface making 20 megabytes of mass storage available, the only serious limitation remaining is its small screen and relatively high cost in its fuller configurations. The radically different operating system design and graphics management makes it very inviting to develop and use multiple fonts and character sets, though the number of individual symbols per set is not especially large. When coupled with an inexpensive laser printer, the Mac makes an attractive small-scale office publishing system. Moreover, since it provides a scaled-down version of the performance features found on the high end of the microcomputer market, the professional workstations, the Mac permits its users to add multilingual capabilities to a workstation network.

A very recent rule of thumb for defining a workstation refers to a minimum configuration of one megabyte of RAM, 1 million separately managed pixels—picture elements—forming a graphics image on screen, and 1 million instructions per second of central processing unit operation, a level of performance calling for a fast 32-bit processor or its equivalent. Typical business applications of such equipment are in computer-aided design and engineering, fields that have been drawn far into a revolution by the widespread use of workstations in this class. In the last couple of years, predictably, the RAM standard has doubled or tripled, and the speeds of the central processing unit have nearly doubled as well; mass storage capacities have increased comparably. These devices, as currently manufactured by Apollo, DEC, in the form of the Microvax series, Sun, and a number of smaller companies, represent the high end of the professional workstation market right now, giving an individual user computing and storage resources costing as little as $10,000 to $15,000 per user but equivalent to those found a couple of years ago only on minicomputers costing ten or twenty times as much. Competitive pressures will drive the price and performance of these workstations into very advantageous ranges for academic users in a matter of a few months.

Current CALL software

We recently completed a survey of software suitable for use in skill maintenance for intermediate and advanced users of seldom taught languages. Like many other surveys with more broadly defined criteria, we found that:

—most of the software available is designed for elementary language training or testing, not for skill maintenance;

—most CALL software is of the drill-and-practice type; and

—most CALL software does not allow modification of content or structure.[9]

These are serious shortcomings, even allowing that the first is merely a consequence of an overall preoccupation with elementary levels in language teaching generally. The very notion of courseware represents a rather unimaginative adaptation of the textbook to the computer environment. Withholding from either the learner or the instructor the capability of modifying the content or structure of the learning materials goes far toward canceling any advantages of using the computer as an instructional tool. Drill and practice exercises have their merits, to be sure, but their dominance in CALL software gives some point to the criticism that much of it is little better than a workbook transferred to the computer screen. The greatest potential strength of the computer as an educational tool, its ability to adapt to the needs of the individual user, is exploited least of all.

9. John Fought, C. Doughty, and D. Boatman, *A Survey of Foreign Language Software for the Microcomputer*, Automated Methods in Foreign Language Training and Instruction, 3rd technical report (Washington, DC: Defense Intelligence College, 1986). See also R. Baker, "Foreign Language Software: The State of the Art, or Pick a Card, Any (Flash) Card," *CALICO Journal*, 2(part 1): 6-10 (1984).

In the genealogy of computing, hardware and software belong to distinct lineages. It is customary to reckon a hardware generation as the time required to double the power available to the user at a given price—or to halve the cost of the same computing power. Recently this period has been estimated at 18 to 24 months. As a corollary development to reduced cost per unit of power, generally the bulk and manufacturing complexity of the system is sharply reduced also. This is easy to see in the world of IBM PC aftermarket products. The IBM PC at the time of its introduction was often purchased as a monochrome system with two floppy drives and 128 kilobytes of memory to use with its processor chip, the 16-bit internal and 8-bit external Intel 8088. Now most are configured as maximum units, with an internal hard disk of 10 or 20 megabytes of capacity, 640 or more kilobytes of RAM, and a high-resolution color display. The aftermarket provides a selection of coprocessor cards, however, which use the IBM chassis and power supply, but leave the original computer and RAM as an input-output server for the more powerful coprocessor card, which may contain a full 32-bit processor and two or more megabytes of RAM, supporting UNIX or some other more advanced operating system. The cost of such a card is usually less than the original cost of the complete system it takes over. Thus the useful life of PC hardware already purchased can be stretched out for at least a few more years.

At the same time, more powerful multi-user or multitasking UNIX-based computer systems are becoming available at costs per user not far above the cost of an IBM PC two years ago. With these systems, mass storage devices such as compact disk systems—compact disk read-only memory—continue to improve in speed and capacity, and other peripherals, including especially printers, optical scanners, and voice input/output devices, grow more flexible and less expensive at the same pace as the computers themselves.

Finally, it must be repeated that networking, especially the linking of less powerful PC-class equipment to more powerful network servers, promises to increase the effective power of the entire networked system far beyond the gains realized through file transfer alone. Both resources and tasks can be shared in ways limited only by the imagination and the programming sophistication of the system users and administrators.

In the software marketplace there is nothing like the degree of organization and capitalization found in the implacably competitive world of computer hardware. The established software development companies seem to concentrate on the business market with its growing needs for both separate and integrated word, graphics, and number processing packages. The educational market is left to the relatively small software branches of educational publishing houses and to a few small start-up companies. For the present, then, the educational software market is caught in a bind: without the hardware base, software developers are reluctant to invest time in it; without the software, the educators are reluctant to commit themselves to large-scale hardware investments.

The most pressing need in CALL is for an empirical foundation for software validation. Without it, as is the case now, there is nothing but intuition and expediency to guide the creation of software, and no reason to expect marked improvement in the current situation, whose shortcomings have been pointed out with remarkable unanimity in a number of recent surveys.[10]

THE PROMISE OF THE FIFTH GENERATION

Hardware development has far outpaced software development. The now-frequent references to fifth-generation computer technology refer to generations of programming languages, the first being hard-wired programs, the second being machine language, specific to each central processor, and the third being procedural languages like Fortran or Cobol, much more compact than machine language and portable from machine to machine thanks to compilers that automatically translate expressions in the third-level language into expressions in machine language. Fourth-generation languages are the so-called high-level languages now in use: Pascal, Ada, Prolog, and others. Commercial packages are now available to generate the relatively prolix Cobol code equivalent to much more compact expressions coded in the C language. Thus the vast and ancient government and business

inventory and accounting software systems written in Cobol can be maintained and modified without the agony of Cobol programming. In effect, the software compiles C into Cobol, and then into machine language. The distinction between the third- and fourth-generation languages is sometimes imperfect, however, for both conceptual and chronological reasons. Some languages, like LISP, have been around as long as Fortran and Cobol, but, because of some of their special traits, are used as high-level languages. Others, like C, the language of the UNIX operating system, have both high-level and low-level traits and are used across a wide range of machines and problems.

Cheap memory, dataflow processing, knowledge engineering

Fifth-generation languages, when they come, will presumably be as much more compact and powerful than fourth-generation languages as these are in relation to third-generation languages. The much publicized Japanese fifth-generation project will develop software that will be compiled into Prolog code, for example; much comparable work in the United States is based on the LISP language. Moreover, these more powerful and flexible programming instruments will be accompanied by still further enhanced hardware capabilities, designed in conjunction with the software.

In one or two years, computers with very large RAM and mass storage capacity, fast execution of parallel and other types of responsive or interactive processing capabilities, and the skeleton of knowledge-based software development systems will become available and affordable. If the formidable programming

10. The Computer Assisted Language Instruction Consortium at Brigham Young University maintains a data base of CALL software; see also H. Weller, *Computer Assisted Instructional Programs in Foreign Languages* (Holland, MI: Hope College, 1984).

problems can be resolved even in part, we can expect parallel processing, fast RAM in the 4-16 megabyte range, and comparably large mass storage capacity of hundreds or thousands of megabytes. The operating systems and compilers of such computers will dissect programs and data, apportioning work and data among any or all of the processors, which may be nets of identical units or heterogeneous teams of specialized chips, passing intermediate results around for use in both simultaneous and subsequent steps, and coming up with solutions at speeds now available only on very large computers.

On this hardware foundation, extremely powerful expert associates can be created. Such systems do much more than solve problems once these have been exactly posed and programmed. They actively assist the user in finding and defining the problem to be solved, bringing to bear not only immense raw calculating power, but large stocks of organized expert knowledge as well. They remember and make use of past interactions with their users; they are capable of explaining the steps they have taken in reaching a given result; and they are able to reconcile conflicting needs according to metarules built into the system. What could such software and hardware do for the foreign language community?

Interactive text, interactive media, and other possibilities

Interactive text, sometimes called hypertext, is a way of integrating information in and about a document so that the reader has access to it from any point in the document by any number of relational pathways. For example, a reader might ask for information about a word in the document by placing the cursor on it with a mouse or other pointing device and then clicking the appropriate button. A window would then pop up near the word, showing a dictionary entry or other form of explanation. If something in the explanation is queried in turn, any or all of several possibilities might be exploited: (1) references to other parts of the original document might be given, moving the user across to an earlier or later mention of the relevant word or fact; or (2) a more detailed explanation might be offered by moving down to another window with information about the form, content, or vocabulary of the explanation, as if it were part of the original document. It is obvious that eventually, a persistent questioner would need access to the greater part of human knowledge, not just to a document and a dictionary.

Consider now the further possibility of finding interactive visual data integrated with the interactive text, so that an image—a drawing, map, photograph, or chart—could be examined or interrogated in addition to or instead of verbal information. Diagrams could be animated; maps could display the type of information desired; photographs could be linked to captions or to other photographs.

Moving to another plateau of computing power and memory requirements, it is possible to provide audio and video integrated with other types of data in a learner's information resource of this kind. A stock of cultural information in video form would be an obvious asset to the language learner, especially if it could be reached by various pathways of inquiry starting from any number of documents. All that is lacking is sophisticated, rapid speech recognition. Since this problem is under intensive attack in a number of labs, and since it is in part amenable to brute force, it can be predicted with some confidence that highly accurate systems of this kind will become available in the next few years.

SUPPOSE WE COULD START OVER ...

In view of these technological developments, current and imminent, it is time to consider not only likely changes in the study and teaching of foreign languages brought about by the continuing evolution of technology, but also desirable changes. Discouragement is one reaction experienced by many when first confronting possibilities so radically different from our accustomed working environment. It must be remembered that these tasks, however monumental they may seem at the beginning, can rather easily be divided among a number of centers, and fall into a natural sequence.

Finding out more about how people learn

One neglected aspect of the computer as a learning tool is its capacity for retaining information about what has been done with it. It can thus be used to log information about the performance of a learner as a by-product of the learning process. This information has two obvious and important potential uses:

—to investigate individual differences in learning strategies; and

—to refine learning materials.

By "learning strategies" in this context, I mean the strategies implied by the learners' actual moves in dialogue with the sources of instruction or information, whether a human or a computer. This level of strategy is more fundamental than the sense given to learning strategies in much current pedagogical writing, where they are presented almost as maxims or presumably good study habits. A greater understanding of the ways different individuals go about the humble tasks of learning would obviously be of great help in designing materials adaptable to the wide range of needs presumably represented in the community of learners.

Creating an integrated learner/user system

As a learner in today's schools moves upward through the system toward professional practice, the books and personal notes used for instruction and reference by the learner grow more and more advanced and comprehensive in their coverage of the chosen topic. In an educational system making intensive use of the computer, it is easy to imagine learning tools organized in a modular fashion and provided with entry points, or hooks, enabling the learner to modify and extend them. In this way, reference materials and notes can be integrated into a personal tool kit and knowledge base that will graduate along with their user from learner to practitioner status and will continue to evolve, reflecting the experience, taste, and needs of the individual user. Mastery of these tools will imply control of their form and function as well as their content, in the same way that mastery of an art or craft once implied full control of the entire process of creation.

TOWARD A CRITICAL LANGUAGES
KNOWLEDGE BASE
AND SUPPORT NETWORK

Although substantial resources have been committed by government and private sources to the development of computer-assisted foreign language learning, there are still two areas of conspicuous underdevelopment in CALL:

—solid data on the effectiveness of various approaches to CALL across a full range of individual learners, skills, and languages; and

—support for individual and institutional users of CALL, both teachers and learners, comparable to that supplied by the textbook publishing industry to users of conventional classroom instruction in languages.

In the space remaining, I wish to outline a way of meeting these needs through the establishment of a knowledge base and an electronic distribution network for the critical language expertise organized and stored within it. Selected sites would contribute instructional, test, and evaluation materials in the form of text, audio, and video documents in critical languages; users, whether individuals alone or in instructional programs led by teachers, would download needed materials. Logs of the performances of learners could be transmitted back through the network to researchers for analysis and refinement of the learning materials; templates and authoring systems—and guidance in their uses—would also be available for teachers preferring to customize their materials using the text files, audio and video resources, and background information available through the system. It is important to realize that these two resources—the knowledge base and the national network—depend upon and enhance each other.

THE NEED FOR GENERAL-PURPOSE ANALYTICAL TOOLS

At most a handful of the languages of the world have been analyzed and described adequately. Most published linguistic reference and instructional materials reflect incomplete or outdated source materials, antiquated or substandard descriptive practice, or other serious shortcomings. Notations and technical criteria differ so much that comparisons and upgrading of these substandard works is difficult or uncertain. Balance among the needed types of reference tools is generally poor: grammars are not matched with dictionaries; reading selections are unavailable or are concentrated in a few topic areas. Projects go through a predictable life cycle, leaving behind a few rapidly aging publications after the development team has dispersed.

The microcomputer in its most recent and powerful forms, supported by optical scanning, can do much to improve this situation. In place of the one-by-one, bottom-up creation of computerized materials, the University of Pennsylvania is developing general-purpose analytical tools adaptable to any language and to a wide range of linguistic approaches and goals. These tools, and the text data bases accompanying them, have been planned as a foundation stone for continuing analysis and description of critical languages in support of both linguistics and language teaching. In its final form, the tool kit will enable linguists singly or in groups to analyze a language and to produce the core reference tools required for further work on the language by specialists: morphological and grammatical analyses, concordance and lexical files, and specialized glossaries and indexes of various kinds, as well as rich text-based statistical profiles. The Linguists' Toolbox is expected to reach its currently planned final form in late 1987 or early

1988, at which time it will be available in several hardware environments.

The need for a critical languages knowledge base

In order to take the fullest advantage of the wide availability of optical scanning and well-developed analytical software, it is essential to organize and give open access to a critical languages knowledge base. Without such a resource, the currently prevailing lack of coordinated efforts whose results are shared will continue indefinitely. The computer will indeed provide faster results than older methods of work, but its greatest benefits are only available within networks where tasks and findings can be shared.

The critical languages knowledge base could contain information giving a user access to a full range of knowledge about each language, including crucial cultural information, and will also contain in its lower layers abundant text and reference material, including translations, and learning materials needed to begin—and eventually to continue—the study of the language. Continued additions to the knowledge base will keep it up-to-date. Analytical and query tools will facilitate many kinds of exploitation for pure and applied linguistics, content analysis, dictionary building, and other uses as well as the creation of learning materials. In its mature stages of development, the knowledge base would contain a hierarchy of information about and in each of the critical languages covered. As more material is added, it will evolve under administrative control into an integrated store of information capable of supporting specific or limited inquiries, more sustained study, or prolonged instruction at inter-

mediate- or high-skill levels as well as introductory course support.

Foundations for the knowledge base and the network

I will not survey here the language and area studies experts and programs inside and outside the government that could both contribute to and profit from the availability of the system under discussion. That has been done very capably elsewhere. These essential participants must be brought into the planning process as well as into the operation of any nationally organized system in the future, as they are now. In addition, however, certain specific administrative, software, and hardware elements must be developed and tested.

Pilot-scale testing of the Teacher/ User Support Net idea is now beginning at the University of Pennsylvania as part of the Language Analysis Project. Thus the project, with its powerful network of Apollo computers, Kurzweil optical scanner, and expert staff of software developers and linguists, will have the same role of direct support for the learners and teachers in the pilot network at Penn that the input-producing support sites would have in the larger network. These network pilot program efforts, which I am directing with the assistance of Dr. Ralph Ginsberg, will devise and test appropriate centralized—networked—support systems for students engaged in computer-assisted foreign language study as a means of expanding and consolidating our already ongoing research, which aims at tracing and evaluating individual learning strategies used in CALL. We will apply both existing and new resources at the University of Pennsylvania to developing learning resources suitable for use in two local area networks of IBM PCs dedicated to language instruction, and we will test the effectiveness of the network both as a primary learning resource for individualized language instruction and as an adjunct to regular instruction in which it will take over some functions commonly assigned to the classroom teacher.

The need for evaluative measures of structural salience and difference

A recent survey of instructional theory and practice has shown that current approaches to second language acquisition concentrate on theories of the learning process. Genuinely empirical confirmation of one or another of these theories receives far less attention. The notions of difficulty, degree of difference, or salience are left at the intuitive level by almost everyone. Some early and admittedly inadequate work discussed the notion of functional load; somewhat more recent approaches to structural comparison known as contrastive analysis and error analysis sought to predict or assess sources of difficulty for learners by comparing inventories of elements in the learner's language and the target language. Still more recently, attention has centered on interlanguage theory, an approach based on the notion that the learner uses an interlanguage, a system different from both the first language and the target language. Many researchers have attempted to measure the convergence of interlanguage and target language by looking for the target-like use of particular elements; much of this work has been criticized for omitting consideration of key contextual and stylistic variables, while concentrating on rather tightly circumscribed linguistic environments. Critics of this approach have emphasized that the interlanguage must be approached as a linguistic system in its own right. These efforts amount to viewing the process of second language acquisition as being more comparable to that of first language acquisition than past research has done. Notice, however, that to emphasize the importance of understanding the immediate communicative functions of interlanguage forms and patterns on their own terms does nothing to solve the problems of how to assess progress toward other communicative norms—those of the target language—nor the attainment of communicative efficiency when engaged in written or spoken dialogue with a native user of the target language. It remains true that there has been little or no concerted effort to develop measures of salience, that is, of the communicative importance, of a particular structural feature or subsystem in a language, or to go beyond this to consider how structural differences might be evaluated for their significance in the learning process.

We believe that worthwhile progress toward these goals will be made by using the local network as a tool for exploring individual learning strategies against the background of the learner and target language systems; that to develop such measures of saliency will require the structural and statistical analysis of variation in linguistic performance by learners; and that the evaluation of salience and difference can only be approached usefully in a relativistic way, through attention to all of these variables. We anticipate that very interesting results will quickly emerge from this research program and that future support will be amply justified.

Prospects for enhancement of classroom instruction

In the commonly taught languages, there is usually a sufficient concentration of both students and teachers to make conventional classroom instruction economical. For teachers hoping to use computers as teaching and learning aids, however, as many are now expected to do, there is, once again, no counterpart of the conventional textbook publishing industry to provide support to individual teachers or learners. Consequently, the teacher, often a novice computer user, must find or even create material afresh in addition to meeting the ordinary and very heavy responsibilities of classroom teaching. Here, too, an electronic network is an attractive solution, making possible the immediate distribution of fresh, expertly prepared materials backed up by reference and pedagogical utilities to all users. Standardized testing, particularly through computerized adaptive tests, which automatically adjust their difficulty to the skills of the test taker, are an especially advantageous application of the support network concept. Moreover, the same harvesting of research data about the use of the resources is possible when the network is in place.

Establishing and using the support network

The suggested network should piggyback on one or more already existing systems linking the selected locations. These locations would be chosen from among academic and government installations, eventually representing the fullest possible range of critical language resources and needs. Each location would consist of a gateway to the network, either one way or two way, and one or more local computers or networks. That is, each site on the network would operate in either of two ways: as a support site or as a user site. Support sites would furnish fresh material to the network and download research or test results for evaluation as well as downloading learning materials as desired. User sites would only have access to the materials on the network, but would not contribute to them. Selected foreign language, linguistics, or foreign area programs in major universities and the principal federal language schools would form the nucleus of the support component of the network and would also figure prominently among the users; eventually, the number of users—and possibly of support sites also—should grow as the advantages of membership become evident. There is some possibility of cost sharing from a broad membership base, but, especially in its early stages, the network should be operated as a utility. By rigorously distinguishing active and passive relationships to the network, it is hoped that even secure sites, understandably reluctant to risk membership in electronic networks generally, might be willing to participate if sufficient guarantees can be given of one-way—downloading—access.

In broader terms, a facility like the one described here would support those aspects of language use—and thus of language learning—where microcomputers, especially microcomputers forming a network with support from a centralized source for the teacher and the learners, are able now to substitute effectively for at least some aspects of teacher-supervised classroom instruction. These areas are, as we see it, those involving the learners' receptive skills and the judging of written responses, via the keyboard or other graphic input devices. So far, speech recognition software and hardware for microcomputers have been unsatisfactory, largely because of the vastly greater complexity of speech signals compared with writing. It has not been possible to provide quick and accurate vocal answer judging, either in drills or in attempted conversations with computers. This picture may have begun to clear in the last few months, however. Current efforts to simulate human interactions using computers and videodisks have suffered from the same drawbacks, made even more noticeable by the users' need to interact via the keyboard.

In any case, some division of labor between classroom teacher and computer learning station should prove to be more productive than either can be alone. We expect to find through our study how to determine roughly what this division should be and to what extent it should vary according to circumstance.

Recent Innovations in
Language Teaching Methodology

By DIANE LARSEN-FREEMAN

ABSTRACT: Five innovative methodologies currently practiced in the teaching of foreign languages are discussed: the Silent Way, Suggestopedia, Community Language Learning, the Comprehension Approach, and the Communicative Approach. In order to understand how these methodologies are innovative, a discussion of teaching practices during the first half of the twentieth century is offered. Following the historical perspective, the five innovative methodologies are analyzed in terms of their goals, features of the teaching and learning process, characteristics of teachers and learners, and their views of language and culture. Then a summary of what they have in common is provided. The article concludes with the identification of questions concerning methodologies that need to be addressed in the field and with some specific recommendations for a national agenda for foreign language instruction.

Diane Larsen-Freeman (Ph.D. in linguistics, University of Michigan, 1975) is a professor at the School for International Training in Brattleboro, Vermont. From 1980 to 1985 she was the editor of the journal Language Learning. *In addition to numerous journal articles and book chapters, she is editor of* Discourse Analysis in Second Language Research *(1980), coauthor, with Marianne Celce-Murcia, of* The Grammar Book *(1983) and, with Michael Long,* An Introduction to Second Language Acquisition Research *(forthcoming), and author of* Techniques and Principles in Language Teaching *(1986).*

NOTE: I gratefully acknowledge the contributions of my colleagues at the School for International Training. The following people in particular contributed to the second part of the article, in which issues for a national agenda were identified: Pat Moran, Lise Sparrow, Donald Freeman, and Michael Jerald.

IN order to understand in what ways recent language teaching methodologies are innovative, it would be helpful first to adopt a historical perspective. To limit our examination we will only review those methodologies that have achieved prominence in the twentieth century.

HISTORICAL PERSPECTIVE

At the turn of the century, the method most widely practiced in the United States was the Grammar-Translation Method.[1] Some version of this method had been applied by language teachers for centuries; indeed, the method had its antecedents in the teaching of the classical languages. A shared objective of practitioners of this method was to have students achieve enough competence in the foreign language to be able to read and to appreciate foreign language literature. A second objective was to have the students' ability to read and write their native language enhanced by their study of foreign language grammar. Finally, studying a foreign language was thought to be a mentally stimulating, and thus an intellectually enriching, enterprise.

In order to realize these objectives, students spent a good deal of class time translating passages from the foreign language into their native language and vice versa. Discussion of the passages, many of which dealt with some aspect of the foreign culture, was almost always conducted in the students' native language. Grammar teaching was deductive: students were given explicit grammar rules and were expected to memorize

them and to apply them to example sentences. Students were also expected to commit to memory grammatical paradigms such as verb conjugations and foreign language vocabulary lists with their native language equivalents.

Some of the criticisms that were ultimately leveled against the Grammar-Translation Method had to do with its tedium and the inefficiency of its instructional procedures. Moreover, not unexpectedly, students were able to attain only limited oral proficiency.[2] Despite these criticisms, and primarily for a reason to be discussed, Grammar-Translation remained a dominant method on the American foreign language scene up to World War II.

Because of some disenchantment with the Grammar-Translation Method, however, the Direct Method, already established in certain European countries, was attracting increased attention in the United States. As with its predecessor, the Direct Method had its antecedents in antiquity. In modern times, it was resurrected when the goal of instruction became having students learn how to use a foreign language in order to communicate.

Practitioners who adhere most stringently to its principles forbid use of the native language in the classroom. In fact, the Direct Method receives its name from the fact that meaning is to be directly associated with the foreign language, not conveyed by means of translation from the students' native language. In order to associate meaning directly, whenever the teacher introduces a new word or phrase, he or she makes its meaning clear through the use of

1. The description of this method and the others discussed in this article have been drawn from Diane Larsen-Freeman, *Techniques and Principles in Language Teaching* (New York: Oxford University Press, 1986).

2. J. Donald Bowen, Harold Madsen, and Ann Hilferty, *TESOL Techniques and Procedures* (Rowley, MA: Newbury House, 1985), p. 20.

realia, pictures, or pantomime. Another principle implied by this procedure is that the spoken language is accorded primary status. Students learn to read and write only what they have first heard and spoken.

Students often communicate in the foreign language in situations they would encounter in real life. Certain lessons would thus focus on shopping in a market; others, on visiting a bank. Grammar is taught inductively: students are given examples from which they derive the rule. Students practice new vocabulary by using it in contextualized utterances of their own creation.

Although the Direct Method was adopted in this country for use in certain commercial language schools, such as Berlitz, it never achieved widespread acceptance in public education. This was in part due to the difficulty practitioners had in implementing it. Teachers needed to have a very high degree of proficiency in the language and to be highly skilled pedagogues as well, since much of the language instruction was not supplemented by the use of textbooks. Then, too, its efficiency was seriously hampered when teachers had to go to great lengths to convey meaning when a brief translation may have served students better.[3]

A second reason the Direct Method never achieved the same degree of popularity in this country as it had in Europe was due to the widely publicized recommendations of a study, the Coleman report.[4] Given the limited time allocated to foreign language study in this country, the skills of teachers, and the perceived irrelevance of communicative ability in a foreign language for most American students, the study advocated reading a foreign language as a more reasonable goal.[5]

This recommendation contributed to the longevity of the Grammar-Translation Method and set aside the need for students to develop oral proficiency. Then America entered World War II. Involved in a worldwide conflict that would make evident the need for speaking proficiency, the military turned to linguists for assistance in describing exotic languages for which descriptions did not exist and in developing materials that would prepare speakers to be able to communicate. This undertaking resulted in the Army Specialized Training Program, a program that concentrated on oral work and drill.[6]

This program only lasted about two years, but it received a great deal of attention in the press and among academicians.

It was a program innovative mainly in terms of the procedures used and the intensity of teaching rather than in terms of its underlying theory. However, it did convince a number of prominent linguists of the value of an intensive, oral-based approach to the learning of a foreign language.[7]

If the oral-based approach lacked theoretical underpinnings, this condition did not persist. Structural linguists, intent on describing the patterning of language and conducting contrastive

3. Jack C. Richards and Theodore S. Rogers, *Approaches and Methods in Language Teaching* (Cambridge: Cambridge University Press, 1986), p. 10.

4. Algernon Coleman, *The Teaching of Modern Foreign Languages in the United States* (New York: Macmillan, 1929).

5. Richards and Rogers, *Approaches and Methods*, p. 11.

6. Bowen, Madsen, and Hilferty, *TESOL Techniques and Procedures*, p. 33.

7. Richards and Rogers, *Approaches and Methods*, p. 45.

analyses, comparing and contrasting two languages, joined forces with psychologists who saw human behavior explicable in terms of stimulus-response conditioning. What resulted was the view that language acquisition was a process of habit formation in which learners had to inculcate the patterns of the foreign language through overcoming the habits of the native language and overlearning those of the foreign language.

From the confluence of these two views, the Audio-Lingual Method emerged. Typically, new vocabulary and structures are presented through dialogues. The dialogues are then memorized through imitation of the teacher's models and through repetition. The teacher then conducts various drills to reinforce the sentence patterns that are present in the dialogue. Teachers provide positive reinforcement to students' responses. Grammar rules are induced by students and rarely made explicit. Students' reading or writing is based upon initial oral work. Teachers attempt to control the language that students produce as much as possible to avoid students' committing errors. The concern is that if errors are committed, bad habits will be fostered.

Ironically, as the Audio-Lingual Method had looked to linguistics for its theoretical base, it was linguists who presented its greatest challenge.

The publication in 1957 of Noam Chomsky's work on transformational-generative grammar electrified the linguistic community with its dramatic and powerful challenge to structural linguistics. Two years later Chomsky attacked the language acquisition theory of behavioral psychology. This twin assault challenged existing descriptions of language as well as the most basic notions of how language is acquired . . . the new view saw it as rule-governed, with language acquisition a creative process requiring considerable learner initiative rather than learner manipulation through mimicry, memorization and overlearning.[8]

The Audio-Lingual Method had been monolithic on the American foreign language teaching scene. Due to the challenges it had received, teachers searched for an alternative. Since the demise of the Audio-Lingual Method in the early 1970s, no single method has assumed its stature. Perhaps because practitioners in the field realized they could no longer rely on linguists for theoretical support, perhaps because of the shift of focus to the learner, recognizing the indispensable contribution a learner brings to the learning situation, perhaps for some entirely different reason, the language teaching field of modern times has become multidisciplinarian in perspective, drawing insights not only from linguistics but also from psychology, sociology, anthropology, and education. In any event, the lack of a universally attractive alternative to the Audio-Lingual Method has led in the latter 1970s and 1980s to a period of "adaptation, innovation, experimentation and some confusion."[9]

There are at least five methodologies that might be termed innovative in the language teaching field these days: the Silent Way, Suggestopedia, Community Language Learning, the Comprehension Approach, and the Communicative Approach. In order to arrive at an overall understanding of them, it would behoove us first to view each independently. In order to aim for coherence,

8. Bowen, Madsen, and Hilferty, *TESOL Techniques and Procedures*, p. 37.

9. Richards and Rogers, *Approaches and Methods*, p. 60.

however, we will analyze each of the five using a framework that will allow us later to extract the similarities and differences among them.

Ten questions will be addressed to each method.[10] These ten questions will be subsumed into four general categories as follows: goal; teaching and learning process; teacher and learner; and language and culture. With respect to goal, what are the objectives of the practitioner who adopts this method? With respect to the teaching and learning process, what are some general characteristics of the teaching and learning process? How does the teacher respond to student errors? And how is evaluation accomplished? Concerning the teacher and learner, what are the roles of the teacher and of the students? What is the nature of student-teacher interaction and of student-student interaction? And how are the students' affective feelings and cognitions dealt with? Finally, with respect to language and culture, how is language viewed and how is culture viewed? What areas of language are emphasized and what language skills are emphasized? And what is the role of the students' native language?

Silent Way

Goal. The goal of the Silent Way is to prepare students so that they can freely express their own thoughts, perceptions, and feelings. In order to be able to accomplish this, students are encouraged to develop as rapidly as possible an independence from the teacher. Accord-

10. Larsen-Freeman, *Techniques and Principles*, pp. 2-3

ing to its originator, Caleb Gattegno, the Silent Way goes beyond other methods in one important regard: the Silent Way not only teaches students the language, but also furnishes them with a way to learn on their own.

Teaching and learning process. Students begin their study of the language by first learning its sounds. These are introduced through a language-specific sound-color chart. Students learn to associate the sounds with particular colors. Later, using charts called Fidels, the student learns the spelling of different words in the language, aided by the fact that letters or groups of letters are colored to correspond to the sound they represent. Next, students learn to read and pronounce words properly through the use of color-coded word charts.

The structures of the language are often introduced to the students through the use of Cuisenaire rods. The teacher sets up a situation with the rods in which the meaning of a structure is transparent. For example, an initial lesson teaches the use of the imperative and singular versus plural, while introducing the words for the pronouns, colors, and numbers. Students command one another to "give her two yellow rods," "take one blue rod," and so forth.

The teachers use minimal spoken cues while guiding students to produce the structures. They can rely on the fact that students already bring with them some knowledge of how the foreign language operates since they have already mastered their native language. Teachers work with the students, for the most part nonverbally, striving for pronunciation that would be intelligible to a native speaker of the foreign language. They use the students' errors as evidence of where the language is unclear to the students and hence where to work. The teachers try getting students to self-correct first, based on the inner criteria they are developing about the foreign language. If the students are unable to self-correct and their classmates cannot assist, then the teachers supply the correct language, but only as a last resort. They do not praise or criticize the students, not wishing to interfere with the students' development of their own criteria. The teachers expect students to learn at their own rate and never expect perfection at the beginning.

By not repeating a model from a teacher or a classmate, the students receive a great deal of practice in using the language meaningfully. They gain autonomy in the language by exploring it and making choices. After the lesson, the teachers seek feedback from the students as to their reactions to the lesson and what they have learned. Their feedback provides valuable information to the teachers and encourages students to take responsibility for their learning.

Although Silent Way teachers may never administer a formal test, they continually assess their students' learning. Since Gattegno advocates the subordination of teaching to learning, the teachers must be responsive to the immediate learning needs. The teachers put a limited amount of language into circulation among the students and then are silent, free to be aware of what it is students are learning and where they are struggling.

Teacher and learner. Gattegno says that rather than teachers being concerned with modeling language, the teachers should be concerned with what the students are doing.[11] For much of

the student-teacher interaction, therefore, the teachers are silent. They still are very active, however, setting up situations to force awareness, putting a limited amount of language into circulation, listening attentively to students' speech, and silently working with them to shape their production. When the teachers do speak, they offer clues; they do not model the language.

The students are supposed to free themselves from any affective factor—such as a negative attitude—that might impede their learning. They should fully engage their cognitive powers to attend to the language in circulation and to engage actively in exploring the language. Since students can learn from each other, students are encouraged to interact cooperatively. When the teacher is silent, this cooperation is facilitated.

Language and culture. All languages have a great deal in common. This fact can be exploited by the language teacher. Despite this, teachers must recognize that each language has its own unique spirit, which must be conveyed to the student. The culture of the speakers of the language is inextricably interwoven in the language.

Since it is the sounds that are fundamental to any language, it is the sounds that receive initial emphasis. Once the students have been introduced to the melody of the language, they are presented with its structures. No explicit grammar rules are given, but the students receive abundant practice with the basic sentence patterns of the language, using a rather restricted vocabulary.

There is no linear syllabus fixed in advance. Instead, the teacher starts with what the learner knows and builds upon that. One structure evolves into another,

11. Caleb Gattegno, *The Common Sense of*

Teaching Foreign Languages (New York: Educational Solutions, 1976), p. vii.

with the teacher working to expand the learners' repertoire constantly while recycling the structures previously introduced. Although all four language skills are being developed together, the students learn to read and write what they have already learned to listen to and speak about.

The teacher exploits what the students already know, as they have already acquired knowledge and skills in their native language. Certain sounds, for example, will be common to both languages. The students' native language, therefore, is a point of departure, but is not explicitly used in the class. Meaning is, rather, derived through students' perceptions of the situations the teacher has created.

Suggestopedia

Goal. The goal of Georgi Lozanov, the originator of Suggestopedia, is to have students utilize untapped cognitive resources on their way to achieving communicative competence in the foreign language. In order to do this, the teacher must desuggest the psychological barriers to the students' using their full mental potential.

Teaching and learning process. A Suggestopedic classroom is one in which the students are made to be as comfortable as possible. If it can be arranged, easy chairs, soft lighting, and music are employed to contribute to this comfort. Displayed around the classroom are scenic posters of the country where the foreign language is spoken natively, as well as posters exhibiting grammatical information about the foreign language.

At the beginning of a course, each student selects a new name and identity that he or she will use throughout the course. Handouts containing lengthy dialogues in the foreign language are then distributed. On the right side of the page is the dialogue; on the left side of the page is a translation of the dialogue in the students' native language. There are also some notes in the students' native language drawing attention to critical vocabulary and grammar as they are used in the dialogue.

The teacher often begins the lesson with deep-breathing exercises accompanied by music or by speaking in a reassuring manner about what students are about to encounter and expected to learn.

The teacher then presents the dialogue to the class in two phases. In the first, the receptive phase, the teacher reads the dialogue synchronizing the cadence of the language with the rhythm and pitch of the music. The teacher's motivation is to engage the whole brain of his or her students. The students read the dialogue and its translation along with the teacher's rendition. During a second concert, the students close their eyes and relax while the teacher reads the dialogue at a more normal pace, once again accompanied by music.

During the second, activation, phase, the students engage in a number of activities designed to help them gain facility with patterns of the language ensconced in the dialogue. These activities include question-and-answer exercises, games, songs, and dramatizations.

The students leave the classroom with instructions to read the dialogue at night just before they go to sleep and once again in the morning upon rising.

Student errors are not corrected immediately. The teacher's main objective is to get students to communicate. When errors do occur, the teacher attempts to remedy them by using the troublesome forms correctly later on during the class.

Evaluation usually is based upon students' normal in-class performance. Formal tests, which would undermine students' security, are normally not administered.

Teacher and learner. The teacher is responsible for not only presenting the language, but also desuggesting limits that students normally bring with them.[12] In order for the method to be successful, the students must have trust in the authority of the teacher. In turn, they will feel more secure and the defenses they normally bring with them as learners will be dropped. This means students will feel less inhibited and more spontaneous with regard to the learning task.

Although the teacher is usually the initiator of the classroom interaction at first, students are encouraged to interact with the teacher and each other in the beginning. Learning is thought to be facilitated when students are enjoying themselves, so much of the interaction is of a playful nature.

Lozanov believes that everyone can learn and that effective learning can take place when students use their latent cognitive powers. In order for this to happen, the psychological barriers students bring with them need to be desuggested. The teacher makes direct and indirect positive suggestions to enhance students' self-confidence and to convince them that success is attainable. It is thought that if students are relaxed and confident, learning will occur naturally and effortlessly.

Language and culture. There are two planes operating in all languages. The

first contains the linguistic message; the second consists of factors that influence the linguistic message—for example, the nonverbal behavior that accompanies the linguistic forms. Learning a language is learning to control both planes. The culture that students learn concerns the everyday life of people who speak the language; the fine arts—for instance, music and drama—are also incorporated into Suggestopedia classes, however.

The acquisition of vocabulary is considered very important in Suggestopedia. Students are expected to learn large numbers of new words in a short time. Conversely, there is a minimal focus on grammatical structures. It is thought that if students are using the language, the grammar will be learned without it being given conscious attention.

All four skills—reading, writing, listening, speaking—are worked on from the beginning of a course, although speaking communicatively receives primary focus.

The meaning of the dialogues is made clear through translation into the students' native language. The teacher also uses the students' native language when necessary during the class.

Community Language Learning

Goal. Students are to learn to use the foreign language communicatively. They will also learn about their own learning and thus how to take increasing responsibility for it. Learning the language and learning about how they learn will be done most efficaciously if approached in a nondefensive manner.

Teaching and learning process. Charles Curran, the originator of Community Language Learning, claims that learners pass through five stages, from dependence on the teacher to independence

12. Georgi Lozanov, "Suggestology and Suggestopedia," in *Innovative Approaches to Language Teaching,* ed. Robert W. Blair (Rowley, MA: Newbury House, 1982), p. 151.

from the teacher, as they proceed to mastery of the foreign language. In a stage-one class, students typically sit in a circle around a tape recorder. They have a conversation in their native language, which lasts about ten minutes. Right after a student says something in his or her native language, the teacher translates it for him or her in chunks. The students then tape-record the chunks, which when replayed sound like a fairly fluid conversation in the foreign language. A transcript is made of the conversation; this transcript later becomes the text for this class and several successive classes. Various activities revolve around having students work with the text: they work on pronouncing certain words or phrases, they examine a particular grammar point, they create new sentences with the words from the text, and so forth.

At the end of each class, students are invited to make comments about what they learned and how they felt about the class.

The teacher does not overtly correct errors. Instead, he or she works to correct errors in as nonthreatening a way as possible. The teacher might, for instance, repeat correctly what the learner has incorrectly said, without calling further attention to the error.

Although there are no specific prescribed evaluation techniques, the students' performance is presumably continually being assessed as they use the language.

According to Curran, there are six elements necessary for nondefensive learning.[13] The first of these is security. One way students experience this is by

13. Charles A. Curran, "A Linguistic Model for Learning and Living in the New Age of the Person," in *Innovative Approaches to Language Teaching*, ed. Blair, p. 141.

being able to use their native language to converse. The second is aggression, which for Curran means that students should have an opportunity to assert themselves. Having a conversation that they initiate and that later becomes the class text is one way this element is included. The third element is attention; students' attention is directed to one task at a time. Time for reflection, the fourth element, occurs throughout the lesson; students are, for example, allowed time to reflect on the transcript they have created while the teacher reads it aloud several times. Retention is the fifth element, the integration of the new material that takes place within each student. The last element is discrimination, the element that calls for students to sort out the differences between the foreign language forms. This element is present in a stage-one lesson when learners make observations about the grammatical structures present in the text.

Teacher and learner. The teacher acts as a counselor to the student client. This does not mean that the student enters into therapy with the teacher. What it does mean is that the teacher is aware that learning something new can be threatening, especially for adult students. Recognizing this, the teacher helps to support his or her students in their attempts to learn the foreign language. Although initially the student is dependent upon the teacher for support, during stage four the roles switch. It is the teacher who needs the understanding and acceptance in order to continue to impart knowledge of the foreign language. The important point here is to acknowledge that both teacher and students are whole persons—that they have affective reactions to learning and that learning is not merely a cognitive challenge.

As Jennybelle Rardin has observed, Community Language Learning is neither student centered, nor teacher centered, but rather teacher-student centered, with both being responsible for decision making at different times.[14] Students are aggressive in Curran's sense of the word when they are conversing and the teacher actually physically removes himself or herself from the conversation circle. At other times, the teacher provides a good deal of structure and direction in the lesson.

The most important point is that a trusting relationship is built between the teacher and the students and among the students themselves. Trust comes partly from each party's feeling secure. When a sense of community develops, nondefensive learning is promoted.

Language and culture. The language that is used is communicative. Curran also believes that "learning is persons."[15] The focus then shifts from grammar and sentence formation to a sharing and belonging between persons. Culture is integrated with the language.

In the early stages, the syllabus is student generated. At later stages the teacher might work from published textbooks. The most important skills are understanding and speaking; students learn to read and write what they have understood.

Initially, meaning is made clear by using the students' native language. Wherever possible, literal native language equivalents are given for foreign language words. At a later point, conversation in the foreign language can replace native language conversation.

Comprehension Approach and Total Physical Response

Goal. In the Comprehension Approach, the goal is once again to have students learn to communicate in the foreign language. What is seen to obstruct this goal is when the learner is forced to speak before he or she feels comfortable in doing so. With an eye toward how children learn their native language, methodologists who subscribe to the Comprehension Approach advocate a period of delayed speaking until which time students feel they are ready to speak. There are several methodologies that adopt a delayed speaking period as their basic operating principle: James Asher's Total Physical Response,[16] Stephen Krashen and Tracy Terrell's Natural Approach,[17] and Harris Winitz's Learnables.[18] We have chosen to illustrate the Comprehension Approach by analyzing one of these, Total Physical Response.

Teaching and learning process. For an extended period of time at the start of a Total Physical Response course, the students are silent. It is the teachers who do all of the speaking. Their speech is in the form of commands. They tell the students, "Stand up," "Walk forward," "Turn around," "Walk back," "Sit

14. Jennybelle Rardin, personal communication, 1984.

15. Charles A. Curran, *Counseling-Learning in Second Languages* (Apple River, IL: Apple River Press, 1976), p. 41.

16. James J. Asher, *Learning Another Language through Actions: The Complete Teacher's Guidebook*, 2nd ed. (Los Gatos, CA: Sky Oaks Production, 1982).

17. Stephan Krashen and Tracy Terrell, *The Natural Approach: Language Acquisition in the Classroom* (Hayward, CA: Alemany Press, 1983).

18. Harris Winitz, *The Learnables* (Kansas City, MO: International Linguistics, 1978).

down," and so forth. As they issue the commands they act them out. Following the teachers' lead, the students act out the commands, too.

After a certain number of commands have been presented, the teachers no longer act them out. Instead, they observe to see if the students have comprehended and thus can carry out their orders on command. Later the teachers recombine familiar elements in unfamiliar ways to have students develop flexibility in understanding different combinations. These commands, which students perform, are often humorous.

After responding to oral commands, the students learn to read and write them. Later in the course, when they feel ready, students will take more initiative and issue commands to the teachers and their classmates both. Asher claims that a great deal of language can be embedded into the imperative. For example, if the teacher wished to introduce the conditional, he or she might do so through the following sequence: "Joe, go to the blackboard. Amy, if Joe went to the blackboard, please open the door." It is realistic to expect that students will commit a great number of errors when they first begin speaking the foreign language. A teacher is quite tolerant of them and only corrects major errors in an unobtrusive manner. As students progress in the language, a teacher can fine-tune, that is, correct more minor errors.

By observing students' actions, a teacher will know immediately whether he or she has been comprehended or not. Formal evaluation can consist simply of a series of commands to which the student does or does not comply. At more advanced levels, students perform skits that can be evaluated by the teacher.

Teacher and learner. At the beginning of the course, the teacher is the initiator of all the commands and the director of all the activities. As the course proceeds, students take more and more initiative for issuing commands. These initiatives result in a role reversal between teacher and student. Throughout the course, students perform the actions together and thus can learn from one another, as well as the teacher. At some point, however, Asher believes students must actively issue commands or at least demonstrate their understanding of the commands in order to retain them.

Asher feels that a major obstacle to successful acquisition of foreign languages in this country is the motivational factor. Since in Total Physical Response students do not participate until they feel ready to do so, Asher believes that some of the stress of learning a foreign language is alleviated and that therefore students will persist in studying the foreign language beyond beginning levels.

Furthermore, some negative anxiety will be relieved by the fact that students are not expected to perform perfectly. If they feel successful in their communication, that is all that matters initially, as this will encourage students to continue to study.

Finally, it is thought that another way to relieve anxiety is to make language learning as enjoyable as possible. The use of zany commands and humorous skits are two ways of making language learning fun for students.

Language and culture. Oral language is considered primary, with cultural information imparted along with the language.

Acquisition of vocabulary and grammatical structure, particularly the imperative, are given the most attention. One of the reasons for emphasizing the imperative is Asher's observation that input directed to children learning their native language contains a large number of imperatives.

Understanding the spoken word should precede its production. Students learn to read and write the commands they first have carried out.

Although not explicitly forbidden, the students' native language is usually not invoked in class. Meaning is made clear through actions.

Communicative Approach

Goal. The expressed goal of this method is to produce students who are communicatively competent. While this may not seem different from other methods we have considered here, the notion of communicative competence proposed in the Communicative Approach is considerably expanded from previous definitions.

Communicative competence involves being able to use the language appropriate to a given social context. To do this, students need knowledge of the linguistic forms, meanings and functions. They need to know that many different forms can be used to perform a function and also that a single form can also serve a variety of functions. They must be able to choose from among these the most appropriate form, given the social context and the roles of the interlocuters. They must also be able to manage the process of negotiating meaning with their interlocuters.[19]

Teaching and learning process. After an initial presentation by the teacher, students are involved in using the language. They do so through a variety of activities, such as games, role plays, and problem-solving tasks.

Activities that are communicative share these features: an information gap exists; the speakers have a choice as to which linguistic forms to use; and they receive feedback on their attempts to communicate.[20]

An information gap occurs when at least one person in an exchange knows something the others do not. It is the task of the person with the information to convey the missing information.

The speaker has a choice in the way to impart the information. Depending on the social status of the other interlocuters and the speaker's estimation of the usefulness of the information, the speaker must choose from a vast array of linguistic forms that or those which convey the information in an appropriate manner. Following an attempt at communication, the speaker evaluates whether or not his or her communicative intent has been achieved. This evaluation is based on the feedback the speaker receives from his or her listeners.

The communicative activities in this approach often use authentic materials. It is considered desirable to afford students an opportunity to develop strategies for dealing with language as it is actually used by native speakers.

Finally, it is characteristic of the Communicative Approach that much of the class activities are carried out with students working in small groups. Such configurations maximize students' communication and give them ample opportunity to negotiate meaning.

Errors of form are tolerated by the teacher. It is seen to be more important that the students communicate and do so with optimum fluency.

---

19. Larsen-Freeman, *Techniques and Principles,* p. 131.

20. Keith Morrow, "Principles of Communicative Methodology," in *Communication in the Classroom,* ed. Keith Johnson and Keith Morrow (Essex: Longman, 1981), pp. 62-63.

Evaluation would only be performed via communicative activities. Students are evaluated according to their ability to get their message across.

Teacher and learner. The teacher is a facilitator of the students' learning. The teacher manages class activities, acts as an adviser, supplying the language that students need, and at other times is a "co-communicator," engaging in the communicative activities along with the students.[21]

Students are primarily involved in the task of communicating. They learn to communicate by communicating. Since teachers are less dominant in this method, students are seen to be more responsible managers of their own learning.

The teacher establishes activities in which communication naturally follows. What follows is that students interact with each other in various configurations: pairs, triads, and small groups. During these occasions, the teacher circulates from group to group, monitoring students' performance. One of the basic assumptions of the Communicative Approach is that students will feel motivated if they feel they are learning to achieve some purpose with the language they are studying.

Also, teachers give their students an opportunity to express their individuality by having students share their ideas and opinions on a regular basis. Students thus become very interested in the communicative activities in which they are engaged.

Language and culture. Language is for communication. Communicative

competence consists not only of being able to control the forms of the language; speakers must also be able to use the language to accomplish certain functions, such as expressing disagreement, making promises, declining invitations, and the like. Furthermore, they must be able to select from among the various forms of the language the form appropriate to the social situation; that is, they must learn the pragmatics of the language.

Culture is the everyday life-style of the people who speak the foreign language natively. Certain components of culture—for example, nonverbal behavior—are emphasized, as they are indispensable in communicating.

Language functions are emphasized over linguistic forms. Typically a functional syllabus is used in which the units are organized around a function such as seeking information, rather than a form such as the past tense. Students thus work with language units larger than single sentences. We therefore say that they work with language at the suprasentential, or discourse, level.

Students work on all four language skills from the beginning of instruction. Reading and writing are thought to be just as interactive as speaking and listening. For example, the meaning of a written text does not reside in the text itself, but is negotiated through an interaction between the reader and the writer.

The students' native language is rarely used. The foreign language is used during activities as well as in classroom management.

SUMMARY

After this brief review of five current methodologies, three important qualifications need to be made:

---

21. William Littlewood, *Communicative Language Teaching* (Cambridge: Cambridge University Press, 1981), p. 19.

1. Certainly not all practicing language teachers today subscribe to one or the other of these innovative methodologies. There are no doubt many teachers in the United States who practice some form of the Audio-Lingual Method, for example.

2. Even those who do practice more up-to-date methods do not necessarily use one of these methods to the exclusion of the others. It is not uncommon for teachers to practice a principled eclecticism, combining techniques and principles from extant innovative methods.

3. Teachers who use an eclectic approach or even those who apply one method in particular do not necessarily put the principles into practice as the originators of the method intended. A method is, after all, an abstraction. How it is used is left to the interpretation of the practitioner.

As Bowen, Madsen, and Hilferty have expressed it,

We are compelled to recognize those factors that transcend methodology: the teacher's personal mastery of the language principles she is teaching, the students' role in and varied capacities for language acquisition, the varying objectives of instruction from class to class, and finally, the magic of the chemistry in teacher-student interactions, which overrides any method that the teacher might possibly select. But recognizing these factors doesn't negate the importance of utilizing sound methodology.[22]

Having acknowledged these qualifications, it would behoove us to reflect now on the similarities among the innovative methodologies. From our earlier analyses, it might seem that the five methods have little in common. In fact, however, there

22. Bowen, Madsen, and Hilferty, *TESOL Techniques and Procedures*, p. 29.

are a number of principles that the methods share and that do reflect the state of the art of the field. We will summarize these using the same framework we employed for the analyses.

Goal

The goal of most methodologists appears to be to prepare students to be able to communicate in the foreign language. It also seems that methodologists feel that all learners can learn to do this, although certain factors may make some learners less successful than others—for example, excessive reliance on the teacher, as dealt with in the Silent Way; anxiety and defensiveness, as handled by Suggestopedia, Community Language Learning, and the Comprehension Approach; and low motivation, as considered in the Communicative Approach.

A second goal for some methodologists is to teach students how to learn—to help learners develop an approach to learning, and, indeed, a repertoire of learning strategies, that will enable them to maximize the benefits they derive from instruction and even to continue their learning on their own.

Teaching and learning process

Language learning is seen to be a natural process, one that is best accomplished by having the students use the language in a personally meaningful way, rather than repeating a teacher's model or analyzing structures. Thus learners are encouraged to be creative and communicative with the language, often doing so in small-group activities. Thus, also, grammar is taught inductively, often without explicit grammar rules ever being furnished.

With the exception of the speaking skill in the Comprehension Approach, most methodologists call for all four language skills to be worked on from the beginning of instruction. There is an attempt to integrate them, with reading and writing playing a supportive role to speaking and listening.

Learning is a gradual process. Students progress at their own rates. Little by little, errors will be eliminated. Perfection cannot be expected from the start. When the teacher does correct a student's error, he or she should do so as unobtrusively as possible.

Assessment is more informal. To be most effective, the teacher should be conducting continual assessment of what his or her students are learning. When formal assessment is used, tests should focus on how students use the language, not what they know about it.

Teacher and learner

Most innovative methodologies are learner centered. Thus the teacher's role is that of a guide and informant, although the teacher still fulfills the traditional functions of presentation, evaluation, and classroom management. The student is seen as being responsible for the learning and, in some methods, even for its direction. In certain methods, learners' opinions about the instructional processes are sought; adjustments are made based on their views. Learners are encouraged to learn from each other as well as from the teacher.

Importance is given to the affective domain. Learners' feelings and attitudes can act as blocks to the natural process of language acquisition unless they are dealt with appropriately. Learners should thus be engaged cognitively, but they

also should enjoy the process and not feel threatened by it. They should also feel that their needs are being met and therefore see the learning process as a meaningful one.

Teachers need a high degree of proficiency in the foreign language, and some methods require proficiency in the students' native language. Teachers need not only to be teaching the language, but also working with their students to help them overcome any affective blocks that would impede their learning. Although not explicitly dealt with in any method we have examined, it is also commonly expected these days that teachers will address the different learning styles of their students.

Language and culture

Meaning must be present at all times; students should not just be asked to manipulate linguistic forms. The focus is often on getting one's message across fluently, at some cost to accuracy, at least during initial stages of instruction.

The pragmatics of communication, using the language appropriate to the social context, has also received a good deal of attention.

Oral and aural skills are primary, with reading and writing reinforcing what students have already encountered through speaking and listening. Some attention is given to pronunciation, but retention of an accent—at least by older learners—is expected and intelligibility is the goal.

There is not necessarily a syllabus established in advance of a course. In some cases, the syllabus is organic, developed in a student-generated fashion, as in Community Language Learning, or developed by the teacher, according to his or her perceptions of learner needs, as in the Silent Way. Furthermore, although textbooks are often used with some methods, as in the Communicative Approach, other methods rely more on the teacher's creativity and sense of when to introduce what.

What language the teacher does present is authentic, or at least natural and fully contextualized, as opposed to teacher-contrived language.

Culture, for the most part, relates to the everyday life-style of native speakers of the foreign language. It receives little special focus of its own, other than that which arises through fostering a cultural awareness necessary for communication to take place appropriately.

The use of the students' native language varies considerably from method to method. Silent Way teachers do not use it in the classroom, but rely on the knowledge students bring with them of their native language and build from there. Community Language Learning and Suggestopedia make extensive use of the students' native language. A method in the Comprehension Approach, the Natural Approach, allows students to respond initially using their native language; later students respond in the foreign language. Other methods of the Comprehension Approach and the Communicative Approach do not make explicit any role for the students' native language.

AREAS FOR A FUTURE AGENDA

We have summarized the common features stemming from recent innovations in methodologies. No less important are those areas that are not currently addressed by modern methods, but that have considerable import for the effective transmission of language instruction.

The same four-category framework will be adopted for pointing out areas for a future agenda. It is thought that our purposes will be best served by posing a series of questions.

Goal

Most methods strive to have students achieve communicative competence in the foreign language. What is less in accord is exactly what this means. It is acknowledged that there are three dimensions of language—form, meaning, and pragmatics—but what are all the components of these dimensions of communicative competence?[23] Which of these should be introduced and when?

Moreover, what are some appropriate techniques for working on them with students? Of particular need is a repertoire of techniques for addressing the pragmatic dimension of language.

If it is important that learners be educated in how they learn best, what are the strategies that are most useful for them to learn? If we inventory the strategies of successful language learners, does this mean that all learners can learn to use them, and if they do, will the strategies be effective for all language learners?

Teaching and learning process

Does focus on fluency mean that student accuracy has to suffer? It appears that many practitioners present some aspect of the language and then ask students to use it communicatively. Thus students are not really prepared to use the forms accurately. What are some

23. Diane Larsen-Freeman and Marianne Celce-Murcia, "Defining the Challenge: An Additional Choice in Course Design" (Paper delivered at the TESOL Convention, New York City, NY, 1985).

ways to provide structured practice that is meaningful, not tedious, and yet results in students' being able to express themselves both fluently and accurately?

Independent of the innovative methods, applied linguists have been developing theories or practices to address reading and writing skills. How can such important attempts be integrated with extant teaching methodologies so that the literacy skills play more than a supporting role in language instruction?

What promises do recent technological advances—for example, the development of computer-assisted instruction—hold for language teaching? Furthermore, how can the now-languishing language laboratories of Audio-Lingual days be utilized so as to complement the learning that transpires during class time?

What are some ways to exploit the environment outside the classroom? Recognizing that our students spend such a limited time in the classroom and that this country has abundant resources on which to draw, how can teachers prepare their students to learn on their own outside of the class in a manner congruent with what is taking place inside the classroom?

A great deal of responsibility is given the teacher in innovative methodologies for assessing what students are learning. What guidelines can we provide teachers with that will help to make this responsibility more manageable?

Teacher and learner

Modern methodologies make considerable demands on teachers. How can we better prepare teachers through pre-service training or support them through in-service training that will leave them with the resources with which to face these demands?

Many of the methods provide elaborate guidance for teachers who are charged with teaching beginning and intermediate language learners. It is currently incumbent upon teachers to determine how to apply the principles of the method to students who are more advanced. It would be very helpful to teachers dealing with advanced learners if we could be more explicit as to how the principles could be manifest in actual techniques and class activities.

We have also invested teachers with the responsibility for addressing learners who bring with them different learning styles. We have been remiss, however, in giving guidance to teachers in how actually to accomplish this. We have also not been prescriptive in suggesting that certain methods or techniques might be more useful for younger than for older learners.

Language and culture

Are the methods described here equally applicable for the teaching of all languages? Some of the so-called uncommonly taught languages may not be amenable to the methods outlined here.

Does a built-in learner syllabus exist?[24] It has been maintained that learners pass through a series of stages in their acquisition of a particular foreign language, regardless of the native language they speak. Is this true and, if so, what are the methodological implications?

We have said that methodologies should address learner needs. Should we be preparing language learners for general language proficiency or for specific purposes? What are the trade-offs and the implications?

24. S. Pit Corder, "The Significance of Learners' Errors," *International Review of Applied Linguistics*, 5(4) (Dec. 1967).

Finally, it appears that the teaching of culture has not received nearly the attention it deserves. A major assumption seems to be that knowledge of culture should follow from language acquisition or should be dealt with via culture capsules, which give brief glimpses into the foreign language culture. Would we not serve this very important area better if we had more clarity on the whole and some well-articulated philosophy for dealing with culture in its own right?

IMMEDIATE OBJECTIVES FOR A NATIONAL AGENDA

It seems to us that a national agenda should promote endeavors in the areas of both research and development.

Research

Language teaching methodologists have been rightfully criticized for being nonempirical, or at least not assessing themselves in understandable and comparative terms. Over the years, large-scale studies comparing methods have been notoriously unrevealing. It appears that when one deals with the comparison of methodologies, wholesale, the differences do not become apparent. Still the issue of accountability, of having students reap the maximum benefit in the minimum time, is a test to which all methods should be subjected.

There are two ways to redress this deficit. First, we need basic classroom-centered, qualitative research to be conducted. We must understand how the various facets of methods are manifest and how they interface. We need to comprehend the needs of beginning language learners versus the needs of advanced language learners; how language learners differ in their learning styles; how language learners differ according to their ages; how general-purpose instruction differs from specific-purpose instruction; how language methodologies work for different languages—those that are commonly taught and those that are uncommonly taught. Concurrently we need to expand our understanding of the acquisition process. Is there such a thing as a built-in syllabus? How precisely do tutored and untutored acquisition differ? What are ways to facilitate and accelerate the acquisition process? Such research could be conducted in the field by teams of researchers associated with a national foreign language resource center.

Second, we need multivariate comparative quantitative research—not comparing entire methodologies, but describing how features of extant methodologies best serve the learners according to the research parameters just outlined. For example, does the teacher's modeling of pronunciation with student repetition work better for older learners than the students' practicing the pronunciation on their own with teacher guidance? Which error-correction techniques are most efficacious for advanced learners in the long run? Should reading and writing be worked on concurrently with the development of speaking and listening skills for learners of the uncommonly taught languages? Is focusing students' attention on linguistic form a more efficient means of achieving accuracy than having students use the language?

We may discover that there is no appreciable difference between these and other permutations—that any differences that result are dependent upon the teacher. Nevertheless, this would be important to know. Such research could be most easily conducted in experimental classrooms or schools administered by or affiliated with a national foreign language resource center.

Development

Concomitantly, we need to embark on the development of techniques and procedures that specifically address the immediate needs previously detailed:

—techniques for teaching the pragmatics of the language;

—training students to learn more effectively in the classroom and on their own;

—activities that provide structured practice without accompanying ennui;

—integrating reading and writing research findings into extant methodologies;

—revitalization of the language laboratories and integrating new technology;

—out-of-class activities that exploit the environment;

—assessment guidelines teachers can follow;

—guidance for teachers who deal with advanced-level learners;

—guidelines for working with different learning styles; and

—an approach to teaching culture.

Teams of methodologists and materials developers associated with a national foreign language resource center could have responsibility for working on these ten areas.

The challenges are formidable; they are not, however, impossible. If we are to best serve the profession and consequently to best serve the language learning needs of the country, our agenda must be broad and clear.

The Language Teaching Curriculum and a National Agenda

By DALE L. LANGE

ABSTRACT: The language teaching curriculum is found to be predominantly focused on grammatical content. Several designs related to curriculum development are examined: systems-behavioral, communicative, and content. The need for the integration of the several contents of language programs is developed. A national agenda for a different direction, the language learning curriculum, is offered.

Dale L. Lange (Ph.D., University of Minnesota) is professor of second languages and cultures education. He served for seven years as the editor of the American Council on the Teaching of Foreign Languages Annual Bibliography of Books and Articles on Foreign Language Pedagogy. *He also edited volumes two and three and coedited volume four of the* American Council on the Teaching of Foreign Languages Annual Foreign Language Education Series, *and several of his articles are found in this same series. He has written, with Bela H. Banathy, the book* A Design for Foreign Language Curriculum.

THE second language curriculum serves as the major determinant of the outcomes of language instruction. Second language curricula are examined here with respect to what exists, and what could be, to give focus to a national agenda for such development. In this article, the reality, theory, and necessity of the language teaching curriculum are presented.

THE REALITY: THE TEXTBOOK AS CURRICULUM

A second language curriculum, whether on the secondary school or college/university level, ordinarily exists in the text and any supplementary materials connected with it. The observation of and the practice of secondary teachers, teaching assistants, and college professors support this claim. In his well-documented review of the text as an element of curriculum, Ariew uses the phrase "the text as curriculum."[1] Hammerly suggests that text materials are "a harmful factor" in language programs due to an excessive reliance on them to fulfill all curricular and instructional needs.[2] Medley indicates the importance of the text as a substitute for the curriculum itself.[3] And Joiner

shows how the curriculum is directed toward "covering the text" and not toward the development of language competence.[4] These statements demonstrate the reality of the assumption that the curriculum and the text are nearly synonymous.

If this situation is reality, it is a painful one. In the context of the textbook, the curricula of foreign language programs are limited to basically one content, grammar, the one content that teachers expect to teach and students expect to learn. This reality, however, is not the only one. There are scholars who are creating a broader outline for learning beyond the textbook. To understand this broader reality, a discussion of curriculum and its design, content, and orientation provides a basis for further elaboration.

What is curriculum?

From a review of general and second-language-specific definitions of curriculum, there are two aspects of the definitions that answer the question of what a curriculum is: content and process. Content is the stated outcomes of the curriculum toward which instruction is directed, containing those competencies that students are expected to demonstrate in listening and reading comprehension, speaking, writing, and cultural understanding. Process is the means by which the contents are determined and organized for instruction. It is a series of steps that establishes the needs for a program, from which its goals, out-

---

1. Robert Ariew, "The Textbook as Curriculum," in *Curriculum, Competence, and the Foreign Language Teacher*, ACTFL Foreign Language Education Series, ed. T. V. Higgs (Lincolnwood, IL: National Textbook, 1982), pp. 11-33.

2. Hector Hammerly, *Synthesis in Second Language Teaching* (Blaine, WA: Second Language, 1982), p. 201.

3. Frank W. Medley, Jr., "Designing the Proficiency-Based Curriculum," in *Proficiency, Curriculum, Articulation: The Ties That Bind*, Reports of the Northeast Conference on the Teaching of Foreign Languages, ed. A. C. Omaggio (Middlebury, VT: Northeast Conference, 1985), p. 13.

4. Elizabeth G. Joiner, "Listening in the Foreign Language," in *Listening, Reading, and Writing: Analysis and Application*, Reports of the Northeast Conference on the Teaching of Foreign Languages (Middlebury, VT: Northeast Conference, 1986), p. 56.

comes, objectives, and tasks are derived, for which materials, time, the ordering of tasks, teaching approach, equipment, evaluation procedures, and personnel are determined.

In addition to content and process, Crawford-Lange adds a third category: instruction. She argues that instructional alternatives as determiners of curriculum cannot be ignored because of the major impact some of them have upon language curricula.[5] As a result, content, process, and instruction are used here to indicate the means by which curricula are determined.

Curriculum for what?

In general, curriculum statements relate the goals, objectives, outcomes, content, and means of evaluation in programs to students, teachers, administrators, and the general public. The picture given is a schema of the development of language competence that the program offers. The curriculum demonstrates, then, a relationship of the structure of the language to the four language modalities—listening, reading, speaking, writing—processes for and practice in the learning and acquiring of language, and opportunities to become aware and understand the cultural base or bases. It also offers students an awareness of what is known about the processes of language learning itself. The breadth of this content is not found in any one single source, such as a course text.

Foreign language curriculum design: the possibilities

There are three main categories of curricular design used in foreign lan-

guage programs: process, content, and instruction. Each is examined briefly.

Process. It is clear that, by mass common practice, the major curricular development process is labeled systems-behavioral. It is the application of an industrial model to education, creating a system of three basic stages: statement of specific outcomes, choice of learner activities related to those outcomes, and evaluation of student learning as a means of knowing if the stated outcomes have been reached. The entire process is actually more elaborate, including the following ordered elements: needs assessment; statement of purpose; determination of goals, outcomes, objectives; determination of student tasks; choice of materials, equipment, personnel; measurement of learning and evaluation of results; and modification of the program to produce more appropriately the learning desired.[6] Almost all curriculum development in the United States follows this process.

The only real alternative to the systems-behavioral process design seems to be that of a problem-posing orientation. In theory, a problem-posing curriculum is derived from two basic concepts: the real-life situation of the learner, and the student as a decision maker. This orientation was developed in the Third World by Freire, who proclaims that the acquisition of skills and knowledge is a secondary objective of education.[7] For him, the primary

5. Linda M. Crawford-Lange, "Curricular Alternatives for Second-Language Learning," in *Curriculum, Competence, and the Foreign Language Teacher*, ed. Higgs, pp. 86-92.

6. June K. Phillips, ed., *Building on Experience—Building for Success*, ACTFL Foreign Language Education Series (Lincolnwood, IL: National Textbook, 1979). The entire book describes the systems-behavioral curricular development process.

7. Paulo Freire, *Pedagogy of the Oppressed* (New York: Seabury Press, 1970); idem, *Education for Critical Consciousness* (New York: Seabury

intended outcome of education is creative action. This curriculum, then, derives from the life situation of learners as expressed by the themes of their reality. In being aware of these themes, learners acquaint themselves with the information and skills they need in order to act on those themes. The students' perceptions are the most central aspect of a problem-posing curriculum. They form the basis for dialogue and praxis. Dialogue stimulates perceptions, ideas, opinions, and the need to know. The result of this curriculum, praxis, is action upon them to create new perceptions, ideas, opinions, and knowledge in an ever widening understanding of the students' world.

Content. The content of foreign language programs is viewed in several different ways. Although Banathy and Lange are primarily concerned with the decision-making process in the development of curriculum, they are also concerned with its content.[8] Figure 1 displays the content of the language curriculum in a series of overlapping areas that they consider integral to the learning of a foreign language. This conceptualization is a very broad and extensive view of the content of a language curriculum.

Another content approach to curriculum development, a functional-notional approach to curriculum, sees communication as the content of language programs. This approach has been developed by applied linguists in Europe to meet the communicative needs of European Community workers. The re-

sult of this approach to communication is the view of language as function—performance—and notion—expression or reference—taking place within a context. In establishing a functional-notional syllabus, Munby suggests that language needs for communication be determined by asking the question, "Who is communicating with whom, why, where, when, how, at what level, about what, and in what way?"[9] The application of this set of questions to the need for communication has generated what might be called the communicative syllabus. This syllabus has not been widely accepted in the United States, except in materials and curricula for English as a second lanaguge, because it supplies a content and orientation that is not within the experience of most teachers and curriculum developers in the United States. Their experience is basically with grammar.

Cross- or interdisciplinary curricula form another major category of curricular alternative. A cross-disciplinary approach is one in which contents from other curricular areas in which students are currently working are brought into the language classroom. An interdisciplinary program is one in which the actual content of the course is in the target language. In either case, language becomes a tool for learning other contents, rather than the focus of the course itself. One of those contents is in the area of the social sciences, namely, global education. Bragaw, Loew, and Wooster display a description of cognitive and affective processes for students and teaching strategies for integrating language and culture with those processes that

Press, 1973); idem, *Pedagogy in Process: The Letters to Guinea-Bissau* (New York: Seabury Press, 1978).

8. Bela Banathy and Dale L. Lange, *A Design for Foreign Language Curriculum* (Lexington, MA: D. C. Heath, 1972), pp. 67-69.

9. John Munby, *Communicative Syllabus Design* (London: Cambridge University Press, 1978), pp. 34-51.

FIGURE 1
SOME TASK CATEGORIES OF A FOREIGN LANGUAGE INSTRUCTIONAL SYSTEM

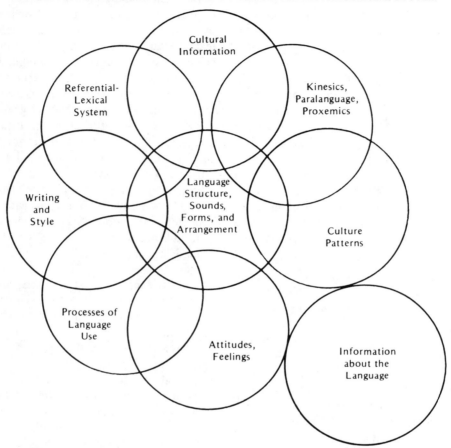

SOURCE: Bela Banathy and Dale L. Lange, *A Design for Foreign Curriculum* (Lexington, MA: D. C. Heath, 1972), p. 68.

bring global awareness and understanding and foreign language learning together in the classroom.[10]

Instruction. Instruction is the interaction of the student and the teacher

10. D. H. Bragaw, Helene Z. Loew, and J. S. Wooster, "Global Responsibility: The Role of the Foreign Language Teacher," in *Foreign Language and International Studies—1981: Toward Cooperation and Integration,* Reports of the Northeast Conference on the Teaching of Foreign Languages, ed. T. H. Geno (Middlebury, VT: Northeast Conference, 1981), pp. 47-89.

with the curriculum, with each other, with other members of the class, and with the environment in which instruction takes place. It plays a role in the development of the desired competencies, but it also influences the curriculum, as the following examples underscore.

The reading method, as described by Bond,[11] deliberately restricted the goals

11. Otto F. Bond, *The Reading Method: An Experiment in College French* (Chicago: University of Chicago Press, 1953), pp. 27-64.

of language learning to reading. This method was at the same time goal and method, created by practical considerations after it was determined that students did not seem to learn a multiplicity of language skills in the short time devoted to language learning in the 1920s. At least two types of reading were stressed, intensive and extensive. Both influenced the curriculum. With intensive reading, all students focused on the same content: the graded readers or a specifically chosen text. Everyone did the same thing, thereby giving a narrow focus to the content. With extensive reading, students could choose the text they wished to read for their own purposes. This aspect of reading allowed the readers to pick materials of their own liking or interest, making the curriculum very broad.

Counseling learning[12] draws heavily upon the affective domain. It is based on student interaction with and trust of the teacher, who is the teacher-counselor-knower. In turn, the teacher's role is that of understanding students by accepting them without judgment, believing they are capable of harmonious integration, and sharing personal experiences and values when appropriate. The method is built upon the concept of security, aggressiveness/attention, reflection/retention, and discrimination. The more secure students are, the more they are ready to risk new learning. Secure learners are courageously aggressive, thereby investing themselves in the learning process by seeking new vocabulary and structures to commit their ideas to expression. In reflection, the instructor mirrors student learning and responses to that learning. Students, on the other hand,

12. Charles A. Curran, *Counseling-Learning in Second Languages* (Apple River, IL: Apple River Press, 1976).

reflect the kinds of content that they pursue. Retention relates to the network of meanings that build up through reflection upon new materials and new contents uncovered by individuals and expressed to others. Discrimination compares new and prior knowledge and implies the integration of new and old knowledge. The description of this method is very sketchy, but it provides enough insight to characterize it as both a curriculum and a means of instruction.

Curricular framework: who decides it?

The decision as to which framework should operate in a language curriculum is generally left to teachers, curriculum experts, and administrators whose decisions are sanctioned by school boards or boards of trustees as representatives of the general public. Because of their preparation, they are entrusted with the necessary authority to make decisions regarding the curriculum. There are, however, elements of a hidden curriculum, decisions about which are made outside of those engendered with the decision-making authority.

Certainly, one example of decisions made about a foreign language curriculum may be found in the thematic material of extant texts, at least for the more commonly taught languages. These decisions are made by publishing houses through less-than-scientific surveys, the data from which supply instructions to authors of texts as to the content and orientation of contracted texts. This process occurs in both secondary- and college-level texts. The resulting materials are, in effect, quasi-censured materials in terms of content.

There are scholars who view curricular decision making in a very broad light. Apple sees curricular decision making tied to social and economic power and ideology.[13] It is in the curriculum of programs that we should see the links to society, the economic system, and the political system, or competing conceptions of these entities. In this light, it is possible to determine what knowledge should be made available and what is not made available to students. But, in this context, questions about the selection of knowledge are required: Whose knowledge is it? Who selected it? Why is it organized and taught in this way? Why to this particular group? Only when these issues are attended to can a clear picture of the intent of the curriculum be understood.

The question of who makes the decisions is not an easy one to answer. If the curriculum is the text, then it appears as though decisions are made more by publishers and text authors than curriculum specialists or teachers.

The orientation of current foreign language curricula

An obvious wealth of curricular directions specific to foreign languages is possible from the categories and examples that have been given. In generalizing from them, however, there appear to be severe limitations to their viability. The traditional orientation toward a grammatical curriculum dominates the scene. That orientation is further supported by lack of adaptation of programmatic and individual needs to almost any curricular process. That lack is manifested in the choice of a text to become the curriculum, indicating

that unknown individuals and corporations may have more influence on foreign language curricula than do field professionals. Further, the systems-behavioral process for curriculum development appears to be the most widely used. Its one major drawback is that it tends to limit language learning to behavioral aspects. In spite of this orientation and these influences, some relatively new proposals may have the power to alter the picture.

THE THEORY: CURRICULUM COMPOSED OF FOUR CONTENTS

There is one curriculum proposal that is particularly important to this discussion, namely that of Stern.[14] He has very carefully defined the four major syllabi of the foreign language curriculum. They are the linguistic, the cultural, the communicative, and the general language education syllabi. A syllabus, as defined by Stern, is the description of each area of learning content, arranged in progressive stages. Stern indicates that, while these four content areas are not new in the history of language teaching, they lead to a more powerful foreign language curriculum through an equal weighting of emphases, a more systematic approach to culture, communication, and language education, and an integration of the four contents. Such a multidimensional curriculum offers a program

13. Michael W. Apple, *Ideology and Curriculum* (London: Routledge & Kegan Paul, 1979), p. 6.

14. H. H. Stern, "Directions in Foreign Language Curriculum Development," in *Proceedings of the National Conference on Professional Priorities,* ed. D. L. Lange and C. Linder (Hastings-on-Hudson, NY: American Council on the Teaching of Foreign Languages, 1981), pp. 12-17; H. H. Stern, "Toward a Multidimensional Foreign Language Curriculum," in *Foreign Languages: Key Links in the Chain of Learning,* ed. R. G. Mead, Jr. (Middlebury, VT: Northeast Conference, 1983), pp. 120-46.

of study that is more educationally substantial and more motivating to both students and teachers. Each of these areas is now examined.

The linguistic syllabus, or knowledge about language

The linguistic syllabus has been associated with the structure of the language—phonology, morphology, syntax, lexicon. Stern argues that these elements are insufficient in the consideration of the linguistic syllabus, that another major aspect must be added to this syllabus, namely, the structure of functional language use, which concerns semantic, pragmatic, or sociolinguistic aspects of language. The functional aspects of knowledge about language come from the shift in language learning and instruction toward the concept of language proficiency or communication.

Stern describes the planning of this syllabus as being crucial to student success. There are at least two ways of ordering the content. One is described by Valdman as being a carefully cyclical gradation that involves the simplification of linguistic structures and lexical content within a deliberate communicative context.[15] Another means of gradation is through steps, related to proficiency levels, with which all students could become acquainted. The American Council on the Teaching of Foreign Languages,

in cooperation with the Interagency Language Roundtable of the U.S. federal government, has developed a system describing the development for all language modalities that could serve that purpose.[16]

The communicative syllabus

The content of this syllabus is the practice of language use. Students are involved in activities in which language is used for authentic communication to indicate a need, to give information, and to express feelings. While there is no clear boundary between the linguistic and communicative syllabi, attention is given to the communicative aspect of language, not its structure. Here, students experience the need for communication strategies that will help them cope with both new situations and an imperfect knowledge of the second language.

While there is no agreed-upon structure of this syllabus, Stern indicates two sets of activities that foster communication: field experiences and communicative situations. In the first category, learners make contact with the second language through travel, residence, work, or study abroad. A second category, the development of communicative situations within the second language classroom, focuses on target language use through classroom management situations as well as any communication in the classroom, whether for instruction or other purposes, with native speakers, in human relations activities, and in specifically created

15. Albert Valdman, "The Incorporation of the Notion of Communicative Competence in the Design of the Introductory Foreign Language Course Syllabus," in *Proceedings of the National Conference on Professional Priorities*, ed. Lange and Linder, pp. 18-23; idem, "Communicative Use of Language and Syllabus Design," *Foreign Language Annals*, 11:567-78 (1978); idem, "Communicative Ability and Global Foreign Language Course Syllabus Design," *Studies in Second Language Acquisition*, 3:81-96 (1980).

16. *ACTFL Provisional Proficiency Guidelines* (Hastings-on-Hudson, NY: American Council on the Teaching of Foreign Languages, 1982) [generic, French, German, and Spanish]; *ACTFL Proficiency Guidelines* (Hastings-on-Hudson, NY: American Council on the Teaching of Foreign Languages, 1985) [generic only].

communication activities: simulations and role plays, games, group discussions, debates, and case studies.

The cultural syllabus

Stern suggests that the cultural syllabus contains elements that can be observed, examined, and analyzed. Here, learners are observers of the culture in both specific and global senses. They acquire knowledge of individuals, institutions, and social relations as they function within the culture or cultures of the particular language. In general, the objectives for this syllabus are cultural awareness, knowledge, and, where appropriate, cultural proficiency.

In the culture syllabus, there is also the question of which knowledge and how it should be ordered. Stern suggests three of four possible approaches. The first one is the adoption of classification schemes of cultural information and behavior.[17] Another system could be developed from those topics said to have "particular educational value," from student interest, or both. A third approach could be the use of mastery levels as suggested in the linguistic syllabus. Cultural topics would then relate to linguistic uses already specified. In this regard, the *ACTFL Provisional Proficiency Guidelines* contains behavioral statements of cultural proficiency that are related to described proficiency levels in each of the four language modalities. A fourth approach—namely, a process approach to language and culture—has been offered by Crawford-Lange and Lange.[18] This suggestion allows cultural topics to arise from student interest or need and processes them within the target culture, but also compares the results of this process with similar content in the native culture. This syllabus is the most difficult to deal with because there is less agreement among teachers and curriculum developers as to its content.

The general language education syllabus

Rarely, if ever in the language curriculum, is much time spent on the nature of language, what we know about learning and acquiring it, and how we use it. In order that learning a second language become more meaningful and that appropriate assumptions about learning, acquiring, and using it be made, the content of this area must find its way into language courses and programs. Stern suggests that inclusion can be accomplished in three ways: in preparatory courses that precede second language programs; through incidental observations as students work with the other three syllabi; or through a deliberately developed general language education syllabus.

17. Nelson Brooks, *Language and Language Learning: Theory and Practice*, 2nd ed. (New York: Harcourt, Brace & World, 1964), pp. 82-96; Robert Lado, *Linguistics across Cultures* (Ann Arbor: University of Michigan Press, 1957); Howard L. Nostrand, "Empathy for a Second Culture: Motivations and Techniques," in *Responding to New Realities*, ACTFL Foreign Language Education Series, ed. G. A. Jarvis (Lincolnwood, IL: National Textbook, 1974), pp. 263-327; H. Ned Seelye, *Teaching Culture: Strategies for Intercultural Communication* (Lincolnwood, IL: National Textbook, 1984), among others.

18. Linda M. Crawford-Lange and Dale L. Lange, "Doing the Unthinkable in the Second Language Classroom: A Process for the Integration of Language and Culture," in *Teaching for Proficiency: The Organizing Principle*, ACTFL Foreign Language Education Series, ed. T. V. Higgs (Lincolnwood, IL: National Textbook, 1984), pp. 139-77.

The most complete description of such a syllabus comes from Hawkins, who outlines four themes: the forms of language, the structure and development of language, language in use, and language acquisition, first and second.[19] In the forms of language, issues such as communication without language, dialect, and differences between spoken and written language are presented. Categories such as phonology, morphology, syntax, and lexicon constitute structure. In language use, such topics as how language is produced, how it is used in different social settings and situations, how it is linked to ideas, and how it changes are the content. In acquisition of the first and the second language, the content relates, for example, to how babies acquire their first language, how vocabulary expands in both first and second languages, and the main differences between first language and second language acquisition.

The importance of this syllabus is threefold, according to Stern: creation of a link between first and second language teaching; learning of the process of language learning to be applied to other languages, for students; and sensitization toward both language and society in order to approach ethnic and linguistic differences in an impartial manner.

Stern's outline of these four syllabi is an extremely important contribution to curriculum development in second language education. Without it, there would be little consideration of the necessity to integrate content.

THE NECESSITY: INTEGRATION OF
LANGUAGE LEARNING CONTENTS

While the definitions of the four contents are prerequisite to the develop- ment of foreign language curricula, they require integration, the next step. Common sense suggests it. There are several alternative approaches to this task, which need consideration: systems-behavioral, proficiency-directed, content-oriented.

Systems-behavioral design

The systems-behavioral design has contributed significantly to the development of curriculum in foreign language education. Its impact, however, has almost exclusively been on form, attending largely to the surface features of language. This carefully worked-out process can apply to all aspects of language learning. It needs consideration in the question of integration of the four language contents with the others to be described here.

As described in Table 1 by Banathy and Lange,[20] this design contains five areas of decision making within which there are seven different decision-making levels. The first four areas comprise a taxonomic or classificatory system that becomes more precise as one works from the left to the right. For example, the curriculum domain could contain any of the nine contents displayed in Figure 1. In turn, each content is divided into decision-making areas, possessing system strategies that define the process content of each decision-making area. Then, each system strategy has component processes that determine the specific content for learning. It is in the organizing concepts, the fifth area, where concepts related to the integration of the four contents appear. The statement that comes closest to naming the four contents is the following: "Content is comprised of elements of knowledge, skill, processes, and attitudes." The

19. Eric Hawkins, *Modern Languages in the Curriculum* (London: Cambridge University Press, 1981), pp. 236-39, and app. C, pp. 292-306.

20. Banathy and Lange, *Design for Foreign Language Curriculum*, p. 47.

TABLE 1
THE CONCEPTUAL FRAMEWORK

Curriculum Domain	Decision-Making Areas	System Strategy	Component Processes	Organizing Concepts*
Selection	Identification	Assess need. State rationale and purpose. Formulate performance objectives.	Identify bases upon which to make decisions about the program. Analyze bases and identify their relevant findings. Identify and state purposes of the program in order to clarify the program's content and major components.	In selecting and organizing content, learning is the purpose for which content is designed. Curriculum construction is a decision-making process in need of alternatives, rational bases, structure, and methodology.
	Specification	Specify what has been learned in order to facilitate the attainment of desired performance. Inventory outcome of this specification.	Specify the main components of the program—linguistic, cultural, semantic process; isolate and inventory items relevant to objectives. In selecting items, analyze the content and components into subcomponents to the smallest independent unit—linguistic, cultural, semantic process.	Content is comprised of elements of knowledge, skill, processes, and attitudes. Content alternatives are needed to satisfy variations in goals, changes in the learning environment, and individual differences.
	Characterization	Determine input competence. A difference between the inventory of learning and whatever is known by learner at the input provides a set of actual learning tasks.	Compare and contrast selected items with input repertoire of native language in order to determine similarities and differences between them. Indicate the degree of difficulty of the learning task and the necessary degree of mastery.	There is a need to determine which source discipline is relevant to what area of curriculum decision making. Language is a communication event infused with cultural, referential, and attitudinal phenomena.

80

Organization	Categorization	Identify the type of learning that the particular learning tasks represent. Identify the difficulty of mastering the tasks.	Establish taxonomic categories into which learning tasks may be ordered. Consider the different types of learning these tasks represent. Transform learning tasks into items of content.
	Distribution	Order content units in a logical sequence.	Space categories of content in relationship to each other; distribute items of the different categories in sequence so as to create strands of content. Establish criterion for slicing the strands into segments.
	Arrangement	Determine compatibility of content units—what goes with what.	Stage content strands and their items into segments. Arrange items into groups, determining what goes with what in a specific learning unit, this being the smallest segment.
	Presentation	Evolve learning structure and integrate content units.	Content units for a particular learning unit to be structured, integrated, and presented for further curriculum processing.

The selection of content in the foreign language curriculum should be based on the contractive analysis of the two respective languages and cultures.

The curriculum makes use of learning about communication, moving from the exercise level of language practice to the experience level of language in the real world.

The unconscious processes of language are made conscious for learning purposes and then reinternalized for language use.

There are different kinds of learning involved in learning a foreign language. Discovery and inquiry are preferred ways of learning. The learner plays an active role in selecting content and assumes increased responsibility for his or her own learning.

SOURCE: Banathy and Lange, *Design for Foreign Language Curriculum*, pp. 41-42.
*The organizing concepts may have relevance to several of the decision-making areas or processes.

statement that most closely resembles a statement of integration is that "curriculum makes use of learning about communication, moving from the exercise level of language practice to the experience level of language in the real world."

But integration of the four contents does not appear to be easily accomplished in this system. Decision-making areas, system strategies, and component processes are determined for each domain, making each one separate and conceptually difficult to integrate. Although integration is perhaps the weakest aspect of the systems-behavioral model, it is attempted by associating structure, arrangement, practice, and use of surface features of the language with learning. Integration is accomplished when the learning process is conceptually wound around and through language as the learner progresses from structure to language use.

Although generally not thought of as a systems-behavioral design, the Council of Europe Threshold level is derived from a system that is based on an analysis of language use.[21] The process of determining the language needs of adults, as described by Richterich,[22] is a systematic process that works backwards from the desired outcome of communication to those communicative elements of language that need to be acquired in order to meet the learner's needs. The classificatory system is different from that described in Banathy and Lange. It

is composed of two basic categories: language activities and language learning. Language activities are composed of situations, functions, notions, forms, and uses of language. Learning activities parallel those of language activities in that acts of language learning are composed of situations, functions, notions, and forms, which need to be learned for a particular communicative need. The selection and organization of tasks in this approach to curriculum design is problematic. There are no criteria or guidelines by which to choose and order tasks. And no clear solution to the problem has emerged. Brumfit, however, has attempted to devise a scheme whereby the linguistic and communicative contents of language could be integrated.[23] In Figure 2, the core of the language program is shown as the grammatical structure that moves in progression toward language use with the functions and notions wound around it. Johnson also deals with this same problem by designating units to have a functional, notional, or structural focus that relates to a central structural core.[24] He expects that the communicative focus will gradually be interwoven with the structural emphasis as students move toward the development of language competence.

Systems-behavioral designs appear weak in their ability to integrate contents. While there is specificity in both content and the structuring of that content from initial learning to language use, that specificity appears to inhibit integration. Further, the interweaving of con-

21. Jan A. van Ek, *Threshold Level in a European Unit/Credit System for Modern Language Learning by Adults* (Strasbourg: Council of Europe, 1976).

22. René Richterich, "Modèle pour la définition des besoins langagiers des adultes," in *Systèmes d'apprentissage des langues vivantes par les adultes: Un système européen d'unités capitalisables,* ed. J.L.M. Trim (Strasbourg: Conseil de l'Europe, 1973), pp. 35-94.

23. Christopher Brumfit, "From Defining to Designing: Communicative Specifications versus Communicative Methodology in Foreign-Language Teaching," *Studies in Second Language Acquisition,* 3:1-9 (1980).

24. Keith Johnson, *Communicative Syllabus Design and Methodology* (London: Pergamon Press, 1982).

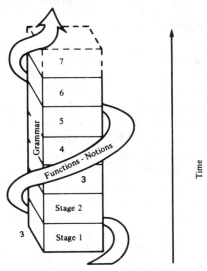

FIGURE 2
BRUMFIT'S COMMUNICATIVE/GRAMMATICAL MODEL

SOURCE: Janice Yalden, *The Communicative Syllabus: Evolution, Design, and Implementation* (Oxford: Pergamon Press, 1983), p. 112.

tents and processes is an extremely difficult matter. Attempts to apply these designs, particularly in the many textbooks that have been published, have been less than fully successful. There are serious doubts about the possibilities of integration with these designs even though the effects of the many developed examples have not been sufficiently researched.

Communicative or proficiency-directed designs

Communicative or proficiency-oriented designs are relatively recent in conceptualization, deriving from philosophical considerations of language,[25] from conceptualization of the role of language in society,[26] and from political, economic,

and practical needs for language use.

Yalden presents a proportional approach to curricular design that rests on the principle of balance.[27] This principle suggests that there should be more focus on form than communicative function in an elementary-level course; in an intermediate course, they should receive equal focus; the most focus on communication should be given in an advanced course. In her conceptualization, Yalden allows some focus on form prior to the development of communication and a return to language features once some ability to communicate has been established. Thus the forms and functions of language can be loosely put together in a progression over the history of a course, allowing

25. John R. Searle, *Speech Acts: An Essay in the Philosophy of Language* (London: Cambridge University Press, 1969), among others.

26. Del Hymes, "On Communicative Competence," in *Sociolinguistics: Selected Readings*, ed.

J. B. Pride and J. Holmes (Harmondsworth: Penguin Books, 1972), pp. 35-71, among others.

27. Janice Yalden, *The Communicative Syllabus: Evolution, Design, and Implementation* (Oxford: Pergamon Press, 1983), pp. 120-37.

communication to be developed exponentially. In this framework, the two contents of function and form can interact reasonably as desired. Clear boundaries are not necessary. (See Figure 3.)

This conceptualization could also integrate the other two content areas: the general language education content and the cultural content. Some of the general language education content could precede and be worked into the learning of some elements of language form, returning when required to prepare students for new understandings about language or different aspects of language learning. Cultural content and communicative situations could also be associated so that some cultural reality and context could surround and interact with the learning of form and function.

Allen, as discussed by Stern and Cummins,[28] offers a conceptualization of a communicative curriculum that is similar to that of Yalden, with some differences. Allen's formulation contains three stages that relate to three aspects of proficiency. Structure, involving building linguistic and communicative competence, is level one. Function, involving the building of intra- and crosslingual skills, is level two. Level three, the instrumental or experimental stage, concerns building language use. In level one, the phonological, morphological, syntactic, lexical, discourse, sociolinguistic, and pragmatic features of language are represented as elements of the curriculum. Level two advances students beyond the phrase and the sentence to a curriculum based on the

functional and discourse aspects in the four language modalities. Level three allows students to apply aspects of learned language in real-life situations, using it in various forms of communication. The purpose of this aspect of the curriculum is for students to experiment with the integration of form and content. In this regard, this proposal responds to much of the criticism of surrounding communicative approaches that focused only on communication, without a grammatical base. (See Figure 4 for an approximation of the Allen model.)

With this model also, two of the four content areas have already been integrated—namely, the linguistic and communicative contents—leaving only the cultural and general language education contents to be accounted for. The general language education content could be developed as part of level one and could be called on again as needed to help explain newly introduced aspects of language and to account for language learning as in the Yalden proposal. Cultural content could most likely be found in all three levels, specifically level three. The integration of cultural content with the other three contents, in this model, is problematic, however. Cultural content would require a conceptualization and organization to fit that of the model itself. There is no conceptualization of culture that fits this model.

Gordon, Lange, and Paradise, in as yet unpublished materials for the teaching of Hebrew in Jewish supplementary schools, describe an approach in which proportional attention to both organization of learning and content directs learners toward the development of language proficiency.[29] In these materials,

---

28. H. H. Stern and James Cummins, "Language Teaching/Learning Research: A Canadian Perspective on Status and Directions," in *Action for the '80s: A Political, Professional, and Public Program for Foreign Language Education,* ed. J. K. Phillips (Lincolnwood, IL: National Textbook, 1981), pp. 202-03.

29. Joel Gordon, Dale L. Lange, and Jonathan Paradise, "Capp Hebrew Curriculum" (Materials

FIGURE 3
YALDEN'S PROPORTIONAL MODEL

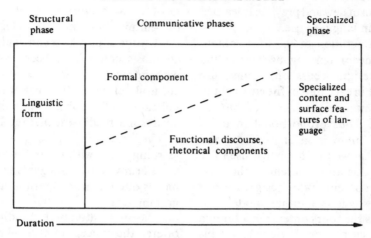

SOURCE: Yalden, *Communicative Syllabus*, p. 124.

FIGURE 4
APPROXIMATION OF ALLEN'S MODEL

Abstract/General → Concrete/Specific

Level 1	*Level 2*				*Level 3*
COMPETENCE	SKILLS				USE
Linguistic competence	(1) Intralingual				Speech acts and Language uses
		receptive	expressive		
phonological grammatical lexical discourse	audiolingual	L	S		Specifications according to role, situation, topic, and function
	graphic	R	W		
PLUS sociolinguistic pragmatic	(2) *Crosslingual: mediating*				*Speech act inventories*
communicative competence	audiolingual: L2 —→ L1 L1 —→ L2 "interpreting" L —→ S L —→ S				
				or	"Terminal behavior"
	graphic: "translating" R —→ W R —→ W				"Behavioral objectives" "Performance objectives"

SOURCE: H. H. Stern and James Cummins, "Language Teaching/Learning Research: A Canadian Perspective on Status and Directions," in *Action for the '80s: A Political, Professional, and Public Program for Foreign Language Education*, ed. J. K. Phillips (Lincolnwood, IL: National Textbook, 1981), p. 203.

each unit is divided into three parts: presentation of the material to be learned, understanding and practice of language,

for the learning of Hebrew, Talmud Torah of St. Paul, MN, 1985).

and language use. This organization parallels the Allen proposal for a language program, but is required for each unit of material to be learned. The purpose of this organization is to give proportional weight to the introduction of new language and cultural material, understanding and practice of the new material, and integration of new and previously learned material in language use.

The integration of the four content areas of the foreign language curriculum in this design occurs on a miniature level, within each unit of the curriculum. It gives some weight to each of the four elements. Thus proportional focus of the curriculum is given to form and function as well as language use. The general education content is the least attended content in this design.

Stern suggests another model that integrates the four contents in a foreign language curriculum.[30] He achieves his model through a display of three main categories—curricular content, objectives, and learning strategies—in a curriculum composed of four contents: linguistics, communication, culture, and general language education. For each of these four contents, Stern outlines objectives that are related to the Bloom-Krathwohl cognitive and affective learning taxonomies. The categories are as follows: (1) proficiency; (2) knowledge; (3) affect, or values and attitudes; and (4) transfer, or learning beyond the language given. The linguistic, cultural, and general education contents in this design are analytical in nature; the communicative content is mainly instrumental, as in the model of Allen's. The selection and ordering of tasks in this system are related to the age and psychological maturity of the learner, differing stages of learning, and differentiation of learning objec-

tives based on needs and purposes for the curriculum. In this framework, the most unsatisfactory accounting is for the cultural content. It is relegated to knowledge about the second culture. Its emphasis could have been associated with intracultural and inter- or cross-cultural activities. In other words, the indication of emphasis in this model needs some readjustment. (See Table 2.)

The selection and sequencing of learning tasks within the four content areas of any of these designs is a potential means of content integration; however, grammatical concepts have received by far the most attention. Valdman has offered the concept of cyclical progression, an additive process that allows for growth of comprehension and use of grammatical features, as aspects of the features are added.[31] Cultural features have not really been analyzed carefully enough to indicate that they could fit into such a process. It is assumed that elements of the general education content could fit into this process.

While Valdman deals with process, Canale and Swain[32] and Swain[33] offer criteria for the selection and sequencing of grammatical, semantic, and social behavior within grammatical, socio-

30. H. H. Stern, "Toward a Multidimensional Foreign Language Curriculum," in *Foreign Languages: Key Links in the Chain of Learning*, Reports of the Northeast Conference on the Teaching of Foreign Languages, ed. R. G. Mead, Jr. (Middlebury, VT: Northeast Conference, 1983), pp. 120-46.

31. Albert Valdman, "Communicative Use of Language and Syllabus Design," *Foreign Language Annals*, 11:567-78 (1978); idem, "Communicative Ability and Global Foreign Language Course Syllabus Design," *Studies in Second Language Acquisition*, 3:81-96 (1980).

32. Michael Canale and Merrill Swain, "Theoretical Bases of Communicative Approaches to Second Language Teaching and Testing," *Applied Linguistics*, 1:1-47 (1980).

33. Merrill Swain, "Large-Scale Communicative Language Testing: A Case Study," in *Initiatives in Communicative Language Teaching: A Book of Readings*, ed. S. J. Savignon and M. Berns (Reading, MA: Addison-Wesley, 1984), pp. 185-201.

TABLE 2
AN INTEGRATED FOREIGN LANGUAGE CURRICULUM MODEL

Content	Objectives				Main Strategies
	Proficiency	Knowledge	Affect	Transfer	
Language syllabus for second language	Suggested MAJOR emphasis	Suggested minor emphasis	Suggested minor emphasis	Suggested minor emphasis	Analytical: study and practical
Culture syllabus for second culture	Suggested minor emphasis	Suggested MAJOR emphasis	Suggested minor emphasis	Suggested minor emphasis	Analytical: study, that is, knowledge about second culture
Communicative activity syllabus for second language and culture	Suggested MAJOR emphasis	Suggested minor emphasis	Suggested minor emphasis	Suggested minor emphasis	Communicative activities: experiential
General language education syllabus	Suggested minor emphasis	Suggested minor emphasis	Suggested minor emphasis	Suggested MAJOR emphasis	Comparative: crosslingual/ cross-cultural

SOURCE: H. H. Stern, "Toward a Multidimensional Foreign Language Curriculum," in *Foreign Languages: Key Links in the Chain of Learning,* Reports of the Northeast Conference on the Teaching of Foreign Languages, ed. R. G. Mead, Jr. (Middlebury, VT: Northeast Conference, 1983), p. 136.

linguistic, strategic, and discourse competencies. They suggest that before grammatical items are chosen they be screened for the following: (1) grammatical complexity, or what must be learned to produce a form spontaneously; (2) transparency in regard to the communicative function of an utterance, or simplicity in relationship to the context in which language is being used; (3) generalizability, or whether the structure can be used in other communicative situations; (4) facilitation in the acquisition of other forms, or the productivity of the structure in the learning of other forms; (5) acceptability in terms of perpetual strategies, or whether the structure supports communicative strategies; and (6) markedness in terms of social and geographical dialects, or how the structures indicate social uses and dialectal differences.

Criteria for the selection and se-

quencing of aspects of the linguistic and communicative syllabus exist, as demonstrated by almost all of the curriculum designs, except for those designs for a general language education and cultural content. They are especially lacking in any conceptualization.

The ACTFL Proficiency Guidelines

One of the most important, recent developments in the evaluation of language competency may have a significant contribution to make in curriculum design. The *ACTFL Proficiency Guidelines* for speaking offer a series of statements that appear developmental in nature from essentially no proficiency to that of superior proficiency. Exponential in their development, the guidelines contain statements of content, function, and accuracy that are related to factors of fluency, grammar, pronunciation, task, vocabulary, and sociolinguistic-cultural functioning.[34] Based on the competence of a well-educated native speaker, the guidelines for oral proficiency serve as the basis for the establishment of guidelines for listening, reading, and writing.

While these guidelines can never perform the specific function of criteria for the selection and sequencing of a curriculum, they do provide a background against which such selection and sequencing can be judged. All of the curricular designs examined here suffer from the lack of a statement or framework of language competence against which progression in the learning of the four language contents can be measured. This framework is the most complete of any general framework in that it appears, on the surface at least, to contain the possibility of the integration of three of the four curriculum contents: linguistic, communicative, and cultural. The language education syllabus is not at all treated. The content that is the least well developed in this system is that of culture, which plays a role in determining proficiency at the advanced level and above, but which the guidelines project as not integral to the development of competence prior to that point. Thus even a proficiency-oriented framework is incomplete in relating to the four contents.

Content-oriented designs

Another means of establishing a curriculum and examining the integration of the four contents of language learning is by means of content-oriented designs. In this approach, content is used as the organizing principle. Other aspects of the curriculum are considered in relationship to it. In these designs, language is a means of learning any content. It becomes a tool, rather than the focus of instruction. Designs for this category are basically two, a process design oriented around cultural content and a framework oriented around knowledge of the world.

In the first model, Crawford-Lange and Lange have developed a process that completely integrates the four contents of the foreign language learning curriculum.[35] The process is derived from the work of Freire.[36] There are eight stages in the process. In stage one, identification of a cultural theme, students and instructor choose a theme of interest that may be taken from existing classroom or other materials. In stage two, presentation of cultural phenomena, aspects of the theme are presented via pictures, bulletin board displays, slides, overhead transparencies, videotape, videodisc, audiotape, and written text. Many different representations of the theme in different forms are presented to students. Dialogue, stage three, focuses on the description of the representations of the theme. Here, students analyze and describe the phenomena presented; then they write their reactions to them. Step four, transition to language learning,

34. Pardee Lowe, Jr., "The ILR Proficiency Scale as a Synthesizing Research Principle: The View from the Mountain," in *Foreign Language Proficiency in the Classroom and Beyond*, ACTFL Foreign Language Education Series, ed. C. J. James (Lincolnwood, IL: National Textbook, 1985), pp. 9-53.

35. Crawford-Lange and Lange, "Doing the Unthinkable in the Second Language Classroom."

36. Linda M. Crawford, "Paulo Freire's Philosophy: Derivation of Curricular Principles and Their Application to Second Language Curriculum Design," *Dissertation Abstracts International*, 39:7130A (1979); idem, "Redirecting Second Language Curricula: Paulo Freire's Contribution," *Foreign Language Annals*, 14:257-68 (1981).

requires students to indicate their language learning needs in order to pursue further information on the theme. Aspects of the general language education syllabus are included as students uncover their need to know and understand language. In language learning, stage five, learners are aware of a need and a thematic content for language learning. The language to be learned is presented here with meaningful, representative cultural phenomena. It is then practiced using various activities that lead to initial opportunities for language use, as the students become ready. In stage six, verification of perceptions in the target or native language are accomplished when students verify their initial perceptions of stage two as they examine as many resources as are available to them. The various pieces of information are brought together, analyzed, described, and compared to the original perceptions of the theme in the native culture as well. Cultural awareness, stage seven, is displayed as learners relate how their perceptions have changed and as they answer such questions as, Why are there cultural differences? What effects have geography, time, and people had on cultural evolution? What caused the learners' perceptions to change? In the evaluation of language and cultural proficiency, stage eight, learners demonstrate the integration of their language proficiency and cultural awareness through the development and presentation of critical incidents, minidramas, culture capsules and clusters, simulations, and dialogues in the target language. It is in this context that they are evaluated on their use of language and their understanding of culture.

The model is a theoretical one only, one without a strong experiential base. The four contents of a foreign language curriculum are integrated in this process.

Yet the design is not without flaws. Without some preliminary language instruction, students may not be able to continue the process in the target language, a concern that is related to both the Allen and the Yalden proposals. This concern is its most serious internal problem. Perhaps the most important external concern is that the model is conceptually 180 degrees from the linear approach to language curriculum, as practiced today, with its emphasis on grammar.

Wallerstein describes an approach to the development of an English-as-a-second-language curriculum that is related to both the Freire and the Crawford-Lange and Lange curricular process.[37] She describes a problem-posing curriculum established on the themes uncovered by researching a community of language learners in California, primarily Spanish-speaking adults. Issues of literacy were built around the themes uncovered. Students were motivated to learn to read, speak, listen, and write because the themes related specifically to them. The students pursued action—praxis—on the themes as they used newly acquired language to resolve problems related to living in another culture. The examples of content relate to culture and conflict, health and welfare, neighborhoods, immigration, and work, among others. It is a curriculum in action that integrates the four contents of language learning in an unconventional, yet motivating, fashion.

In a description of the use of content as a means of organizing foreign language curriculum, Mohan uses a knowledge framework to accomplish the task.[38] He

37. Nina Wallerstein, *Language and Culture in Conflict* (Reading, MA: Addison-Wesley, 1983).
38. Bernard A. Mohan, *Language and Content* (Reading, MA: Addison-Wesley, 1986).

presents any learning activity, related to a topic, as comprised of two basic categories: the specific, practical, or action situation and the general, theoretical, or background knowledge. The specific action situation contains three levels of information: description, sequence, and choice; background knowledge also contains three levels: concepts and classification, principles, and evaluation. (See Table 3.) The specific or practical aspect includes examples of cases within a topic. Description involves the who, what, where, and when; sequence includes the events and their order, processes, procedures, and routines; choice relates the conflicts, alternatives, dilemmas, and decisions of the situation. The general or theoretical aspect of the topic relates to the general concepts, principles, and values of the topic. How concepts apply and how they are related to each other is a matter for classification. Cause and effect, means and ends, methods and techniques, rules, norms, and strategies are the principles that apply to the topic. Finally, the values and standards of behavior constitute the category of evaluation: what counts as good or bad in the choosing of one course of action over another?

There are several steps in the curricular process according to Mohan. The first one is gaining a sense of a topic, which is then divided into specific, particular cases and into theoretical background knowledge. Then specific examples are chosen and presented in some form: demonstration, drama, film, process, or narrative. Related to these examples are aspects of background knowledge presented as charts, tables, reading passages, or short lectures. The particular case is used to illustrate general principles that in turn help students interpret the particular case. Finally, the knowledge structures

of the particular case—description, sequence, and choice—and those of background information—classification, principles, and evaluation—may be used to develop corresponding thinking and language skills.

The process Mohan presents is one that is built on two perspectives of an aspect of knowledge: state of knowledge—expert knowledge and learner's knowledge—and process of using or acquiring knowledge—critical creativity, and learning and development. Expert knowledge is possessed by someone who is competent in the activity. The learner's knowledge is that of someone beginning to learn. What the learner knows requires an analysis of learning stages or what is critical to becoming an expert. Learning and development are the processes that allow the beginner to become an expert. An example of these two perspectives is displayed in Table 4.

The Mohan model, like that of Crawford-Lange and Lange, as well as that of Wallerstein, is probably among the most integrative of the several curricular designs discussed here. The four language contents are intermingled and included in almost every aspect of the design. But the design offers something that the others do not, namely, attention to the nature and structure of knowledge. In this aspect, it provides an ultimate example of the integration of the four language learning contents.

The relationship of instruction to curriculum

In the past thirty years, the foreign language teaching profession has been seeking that method that will best serve its needs. That search has been largely unsuccessful. No panaceas have been found. Circumstances of educational

TABLE 3
GENERAL FRAMEWORK FOR KNOWLEDGE STRUCTURES

	Activity		
	Specific, practical (Action situation)	General, theoretical (Background knowledge)	
Description			Concepts and classification
Sequence			Principles
Choice			Evaluation

SOURCE: Bernard A. Mohan, *Language and Content* (Reading, MA: Addison-Wesley, 1986), p. 35.

TABLE 4
PERSPECTIVES ON AN ACTIVITY

	State of Knowledge	Process of Using or Acquiring Knowledge
Expert	a) Expert knowledge: the grammar of standard English	b) Critical creativity: psycholinguistic processes
Learner	c) Learner's knowledge: a grammar of a child's language	d) Learning and development: the process and strategies of language acquisition

SOURCE: Mohan, *Language and Content*, p. 48.

context, materials, teacher aptitude and motivation, and students have contributed to different results. The monolithic, all-encompassing method has neither been located nor developed. This particular search needs to be abandoned since the quest is unreasonable. Instead, it may be proper to look at instruction as being broader in nature.

Carroll's model of school learning has had a broad impact on the research on instruction.[39] It has led to a generation of research on the effect and effectiveness of classroom teaching that cannot be ignored. Much of this research is summarized in Hawley, Rosenholtz, Goodstein, and Hasselbring.[40] Some of the major

39. John B. Carroll, "A Model of School Learning," *Teachers College Record*, 64:723-33 (1963).

40. Willis D. Hawley et al., "Good Schools:

points of this review can be applied in almost any educational context, not only in the elementary school where the research has been accomplished. Effective teachers do some and maybe all of the following:

—optimize academic learning time by carefully structuring physical space, managing time for instruction, focusing student attention and engagement, and pacing student work to balance performance and progress toward acquisition of skills and knowledge;

—reward student achievement by means that permit students to succeed and that are appropriate to the established learning goals;

—utilize interactive teaching, which gives students opportunities to interact actively and demonstrate their acquisition of knowledge;

—hold and communicate high expectations for student performance about which all students know and which are applied equally to all; and

—select and use a mix of instructional settings, such as groups, the whole class, or the individual, that are appropriate to the learning being pursued.

It may be more appropriate to look in these directions for keys to the link between instruction and curriculum. These principles may be better linked to curriculum than is the search for a single approach to language teaching that does not necessarily relate to student learning. The resolution of the problem may be a

What Research Says about Improving Student Achievement," *Peabody Journal of Education,* 61(4):15-52 (1984).

link between what we discover about student learning processes in second language learning/acquisition and the research on instruction that has contributed to effective teaching. Such an association could be related to any of the curricular designs discussed here, thereby strengthening the relationship between curriculum and instruction.

THE NATIONAL AGENDA FOR A LANGUAGE TEACHING CURRICULUM

One of the major areas of consideration in the development of a national agenda for language education is curriculum design and materials development. The preceding discussion of the reality, theory, and necessity in curricular design leads naturally to considerations of what such an agenda could be. Such an agenda should include the conceptualization of a framework for curriculum design, aspects of curriculum development, research in design effectiveness, and dissemination of the results of such research.

A framework for curriculum development

From all of the previous discussion on the language curriculum, but particularly the issue of the integration of its aspects, it is clear that the language curriculum requires focus, the first priority of this national agenda. There needs to be agreement by the profession on that focus. The following principles are intended to provide the beginnings of a change from a language teaching to a language learning curriculum:

1. In the development of proficiency in a second language, the learner is the center of the language learning curriculum. Learner characteristics, such as personal

background, aptitude, motivation, interests, personality, and age, must become a central consideration given careful attention in the development of any curriculum for the learning of a second language.

2. The development, maintenance, and renewal of proficiency in a second language is the target of the language learning curriculum at whatever educational level and for whatever purpose. The key element is proficiency development, or the ability to use language. All aspects of the language learning curriculum are directed toward that goal.

3. If proficiency in a second language is the target, then the several contents of language proficiency must be included in any specific language learning curriculum design. For the moment, the *ACTFL Proficiency Guidelines* could serve as broad general descriptions of language content, function, and accuracy, to be modified as appropriate with new knowledge and experience, while the aspects of communicative language proficiency—language, strategic, psychomotor—proposed by Bachman in this issue of *The Annals*, could serve as more specific indicators of that proficiency within the broad descriptions. To these two conceptualizations must be added competence in the management of cultural information, including awareness of differences from and similarities to the native culture, and an understanding of the language and the language learning/acquisition process.

4. The design of any language learning curriculum for proficiency development includes the contents of that curriculum and their arrangements at whatever level for whatever purpose. The earlier discussion of the three design types—systems-behavioral, communicative, and content—helps codify them as to major impact and thrust. These designs are not mutually exclusive and may serve different purposes of learning and instruction.

5. The design of any language learning curriculum includes or provides for the tools of access by which proficiency is developed. Here, the contents of proficiency (see item 3) and their arrangements are worked out in detail for whatever level of proficiency or whatever modalities desired. The necessary learning materials, print or nonprint, are constructed for student use for whatever course: regular courses—such as beginning, intermediate, or advanced—or special purpose—such as academic, science and technology. They may be developed for group learning or they may be self-contained.

6. The design of any language learning curriculum for proficiency development includes an integrated system of delivery including role, purpose, and a combination of live and mediated instruction. It is here that the designed and constructed curriculum is interfaced with instructional and learning processes. Any use of live instruction requires knowledge of planning for instruction and effective teaching. The former deals with an understanding of individual student qualities, student progress, the amount of learning that students can handle, and the amount of time available for learning. The latter relates to the implementation of planning. The instructor provides information and instructions as to the desired learning, examples, and models; guides practice; allows for individual practice; and gives feedback to

the learner. In this context, no particular language teaching method is implied. In this framework, there is really no separation of curriculum from instruction.

7. The design of any language learning curriculum for proficiency development includes a system for the assessment of that development that relates to the four contents of the curriculum: linguistic, communicative, cultural, and general language education. It includes achievement, competence, and process measures to evaluate achievement of the organizational aspects of language and language use, to demonstrate competence in using the language in desired modalities, and to reveal the integration of cultural knowledge, similarities, and differences into language use.

8. The design of any language learning curriculum for proficiency development includes evaluation processes for any aspect of the system. The design, the tools of access, the instruction, and the assessment of student learning require continual evaluation to determine their effectiveness, appropriateness, and contribution to the development of student competence in the language.

These eight principles constitute the basic framework in which curriculum development in second languages takes place. Agreement with or modification of these principles is necessary for the improvement of language programs in secondary and college or university programs in this country.

Curriculum development

In relation to the framework for curriculum development, the following practical aspects require attention.

Needs. Some assessment of language needs in this country is necessary in order to categorize those needs. Several questions relating to curriculum design require attention once categories of need have been established. Such questions are as follows: Should all language modalities be included? Which of the designs is appropriate for the general purposes of language learning? What purposes of language learning are to be specially separated from those considered general in nature? When should special purposes be separate? How will that separation affect curriculum and materials design? How are language needs matched with curricular designs? By which criteria should one make decisions for the use of any curriculum design?

Exemplification. The three curricular design categories and their alternatives, as discussed previously—systems-behavioral, communicative, and content—require exemplification. At least one design in each of the three categories should be developed for use in school programs at the elementary, secondary, and college or university levels. Some attention should be given to curriculum development in extra-academic contexts as well. The use of these designs in the teaching of foreign language for special purposes should also be considered.

A team approach to curriculum development. A team approach to the writing of curriculum materials needs to be established. Such a team may include a psycholinguist or specialist in language learning/acquisition, a classroom teacher at the needed level, a native speaker familiar with the language learning/acquisition process, a testing specialist, a linguist interested in the creation of materials, a culture specialist, and a specialist in foreign language curriculum design. Not all of these people would be required to function 100 percent on any project, but could consult and move in or out of a project as needed.

Authenticity of language. The language and cultural content of any curricular design needs to be authentic. Spoken and written texts that exemplify this authenticity must become central to any curricular design. Demonstration of the use of authentic materials in curricular designs could play an important role in the reduction of poorly developed synthetic texts, creating better-quality input for learners.

Publication. Since the finished products of some of the curricular designs could look unfamiliar to publishers, the means by which alternative and experimental curricular materials become published is an extremely important item on the agenda. If they are not published, these newly designed curricular materials may never get into the hands of teachers interested in them, the traditional foreign language publishing establishment being as strong as it is.

Research

At this point, a most important aspect of research would be to verify the effectiveness of the curricular designs and developed materials. Because alternative designs pose problems due to acceptability on the part of teachers, special approaches to the researching of their individual effectiveness have to be determined. Questions about effectiveness relate to the matching of the design and materials with the purpose of language learning, the appropriateness of the direction of the curricular design, as well as the selection and organization of the various contents. This first examination is internal to the curricular design and its purpose.

A second aspect of curriculum research is the effectiveness of any one design in relation to others. While this research is similar to the comparison of the effectiveness of different teaching methods, its value is suggestive and should be considered as such. Qualitative as well as quantitative research methods would have to be employed to give a true picture of comparative effectiveness.

In particular, each of the three designs discussed earlier—systems-behavioral, communicative, and content—requires research as to its effectiveness with learners of different ages in differing contexts.

Dissemination

Conceptually, an extremely important aspect of the national agenda is that of dissemination of information on the development of any curriculum design, concomitant materials, implementation, and any research on the process. The means by which this dissemination could take place are as follows:

1. Workshops could be offered on a short-term, intensive basis on such topics as alternative processes of curricular planning, materials development, test development, assessment of language proficiency, curriculum for language for special purposes, and the like.

2. Demonstration classes also could be available; people in attendance could observe curriculum designs in implementation. Such classes might overlap for instructional purposes as well. In that case, participants could examine the relationship between curriculum design and instruction.

3. Reports of the effectiveness of curricular designs, curricular evaluation procedures, materials, and testing pro-

cedures should be available through publications, workshops, and presentations at state, regional, and national meetings and conferences.

4. Curricular design processes, curricular designs, and curricular materials should also be published and discussed publicly.

This agenda is a healthy one, even in the general form in which it appears here. Its achievements could be of tremendous support in the development of the language resources in this country.

ANNALS, *AAPSS*, **490**, March 1987

The Experimental Classroom

By MICHAEL H. LONG

ABSTRACT: Classroom-centered research on language use surrounding teaching and learning processes can provide much of the information needed to put modern language teaching on a scientific footing. The history of second language classroom research is briefly outlined, and the principal research methodologies are described. A critique is offered of current work, and a proposal made for the next decade. It is argued that priority needs to be given to high-valency, psycholinguistically motivated studies of both a basic and applied nature. Ten topics are identified that meet these requirements and that, it is felt, would merit early consideration in a national research agenda.

Michael H. Long is associate professor of English as a second language at the University of Hawaii at Manoa, where he specializes in second language acquisition, language teaching methodology, and second language classroom research. He is a member of the editorial boards of TESOL Quarterly *and* Studies in Second Language Acquisition *and is coeditor of two books series,* Issues in Second Language Research *and the* Cambridge Applied Linguistics Series.

IF prescriptive pedagogical pieces and anecdotal field reports are to be believed, modern language teaching in the 1980s utilizes a vast array of syllabus types, teaching methods, and materials. Since most would agree that no one syllabus, method, or set of materials could be optimal for every kind of learner, a charitable inference would be that the diversity reflects an attempt by the teaching profession to individualize instruction. More cynical interpretations are possible, however. While individualization has certainly had some effect, the existence of so much variety could equally well be due to teaching still being a laissez-faire, pre-paradigmatic enterprise that as yet lacks the standards of accountability routinely demanded of other professions, such as medicine, engineering, or law. Euphemistically, that is, it is an art, not a science, although, of course, there is a lot more to art than simply not being a science.

THE ART AND SOCIAL SCIENCE OF LANGUAGE TEACHING

For many, teaching should be an art. The artists are really of two kinds, however. On the one hand, there are those who maintain that language teaching is inherently an art and that to try to standardize it would be to inhibit the spontaneity and creativity that characterize so-called good teaching. Good teaching is something proponents of this view claim to be able to recognize, but rarely seem able to define and can almost never agree on. On the other hand, there are those who believe that language teaching is of necessity largely an art now, but will remain one only until knowledge about what makes learning successful increases. At that point, at least part of teaching will be put on a scientific basis.

The latter would appear to be both the rational and the ethical position. It is rational in light of the history of many other fields that began life as art, but that slowly became applied sciences. One assumes, for example, we are all relieved that leeches are now back in the swamps, where they belong. It is ethical, given the importance of efficient and successful language teaching for populations as varied as school-age children for whom proficiency in a second language, the medium of instruction, is the key to educational opportunity, and adults for whom mastery of a new language is vital for their chosen occupation or for life in a new country.

As soon as language teaching is recognized as so important for so many, it becomes unthinkable to leave its outcome to individual whim. We may not be able to define what made da Vinci or Picasso great artists—or even wish to do so—or want to standardize the way millions of amateur artists paint. We cannot escape the fact, however, that while how well Mr. Smith paints affects no one but Mr. Smith himself, how well he teaches a language can determine the life chances of a great many people.

Where, then, should one look for the knowledge that would help give language teaching a scientific basis? Even among those who share this aim, there is disagreement here. For years it was assumed that linguistics held the answer, and countless thousands of learners received instruction based upon structuralist contrastive analyses of their native language and the language to be learned, usually transmitted via neobehaviorist-inspired teaching practices, dialogue memorization, pattern drill, and the like. Research in second language acquisition (SLA) has long since discredited this approach, of course,[1] while not diminishing the importance of linguistic theory in language teaching. That same body of SLA research has also provided considerable insight into the processes by which second languages are learned, both inside and outside classrooms.[2] More recent work has focused specifically on the effects of formal instruction on SLA processes, sequences, rate, and ultimate level of attainment,[3] although this last area is still in its infancy.

In addition to linguistics and SLA, applied linguists have drawn on findings in psycholinguistics, sociolinguistics, education, and anthropology, among other disciplines. Most pertinent of all in the long run, however, must be second language classroom research (SLCR), for this is the area of endeavor the principal and explicit focus of which is classroom language learning and teaching. It is to this work that we now turn.

RESEARCH ON CLASSROOM LANGUAGE LEARNING: A CRITIQUE

The major research on second and foreign language programs in the 1960s and early 1970s took the form of large-scale,

global comparative method studies, audiolingual versus cognitive code, inductive versus deductive, and so on. Typical studies in the United States and Europe involved large numbers of teachers and classes and lasted a year or more.[4] Student test scores—that is, product data—were used to assess the comparative effectiveness of the methods supposedly employed to produce them. While advantages for one program or another were occasionally noted, the differences were usually small and short-lived, and overall results inconclusive. Counterintuitive though it seemed at the time, method appeared not to matter.

As critics have often pointed out, by focusing almost exclusively on product data, the comparative method studies made their findings difficult to interpret. For one thing, due to the paucity of systematic observational data on the lessons taught, there was really no guarantee that method A, B, or C had actually been implemented during the study, or, if so, implemented in the correct classrooms. This would be akin to researchers in a medical study not knowing which patients had received which treatment when attempting to evaluate potential cures for a disease.

The seriousness of this problem has since been demonstrated by several

1. For review, see Michael H. Long and Charlene J. Sato, "Methodological Issues in Interlanguage Studies: An Interactionist Perspective," in *Interlanguage*, ed. Alan Davis, Clive Criper, and Anthony Howatt (Edinburgh: Edinburgh University Press, 1984), pp. 253-79.

2. For review, see Rod Ellis, *Understanding Second Language Acquisition* (Oxford: Oxford University Press, 1985); Evelyn M. Hatch, *Psycholinguistics: A Second Language Perspective* (Rowley, MA: Newbury House, 1983); Diane Larsen-Freeman and Michael H. Long, *An Introduction to Second Language Acquisition Research* (London: Longman, forthcoming).

3. For review, see Michael H. Long, "Instructed Interlanguage Development," in *Second Language Acquisition: Multiple Perspectives*, ed. Leslie M. Beebe (Rowley, MA: Newbury House, forthcoming).

4. See, for example, R. F. Keating, *A Study of the Effectiveness of Language Laboratories* (New York: Columbia University, Teachers College, Institute of Administrative Research, 1963); Mats Oskarsson, "Comparative Method Studies in Foreign Language Teaching," *Moderna Sprak*, 56(4): 350-66 (1972); C.A.C. Scherer and M. Wertheimer, *A Psycholinguistic Experiment in Foreign Language Teaching* (New York: McGraw-Hill, 1964); Phillip D. Smith, *A Comparison of the Cognitive and Audiolingual Approaches to Foreign Language Instruction: The Pennsylvania Foreign Language Project* (Philadelphia: Center for Curriculum Development, 1970).

studies that did include intensive classroom observation and found wide discrepancies between what teachers were supposed to be doing and/or thought they were doing methodologically and what they were actually doing.[5] Indeed, it seems clear that method is too abstract and too general a concept for talking about language teaching practice. Methods overlap at the classroom level, especially over time and as supposedly implemented by teachers and materials. Language teachers think about what they do in other, more specific, more localized ways, such as sequences of activities or tasks,[6] as has also been found to be the case with teachers in content classrooms.[7]

Partly as a reaction to problems of this kind, the focus of much SLCR shifted in the 1970s.[8] Most notably, there was a sharp increase in the number of small-scale, classroom-centered studies, often consisting of micro-analyses of language use surrounding pedagogical processes in foreign and second language lessons. Topics in this second wave of research have varied. A partial list, with representative studies indicated, includes teacher question types and their effects on student production,[9] turn-taking systems,[10] language use in lockstep and small-group work,[11] simplification and elaboration in teacher speech,[12] ethnic styles in classroom discourse,[13] relation-

5. See, for example, Michael H. Long and Charlene J. Sato, "Foreigner Talk in the Classrooms: Forms and Functions of Teachers' Questions," in Classroom-Oriented Research on Second Language Acquisition, ed. H. W. Seliger and M. H. Long (Rowley, MA: Newbury House, 1983), pp. 268-85; Martin Phillips and Clarence Shettlesworth, "Questions in the Design and Use of Courses in English for Specialized Purposes," in Proceedings of the 4th International Congress of Applied Linguistics, vol. 1, ed. Gerhardt Nickel (Stuttgart: Hochschule Verlag, 1975), pp. 249-64; Lorraine Swaffer, Katherine Arens, and M. Morgan, "Teacher Classroom Practices: Redefining Method as Task Hierarchy," Modern Language Journal, 66(1):24-33 (1982).

6. Swaffer, Arens, and Morgan, "Teacher Classroom Practices."

7. See Richard J. Shavelson and P. Stern, "Research on Teachers' Pedagogical Thoughts, Judgments and Behavior," Review of Educational Research, 51(4):455-98 (1981); for review, see Graham Crookes, Task Classification: A Cross-disciplinary Review, technical report no. 4 (Manoa: University of Hawaii, Social Science Research Institute, Center for Second Language Classroom Research, 1986).

8. For review, see Richard L. Allwright, "Classroom-centered Research on Language Teaching and Learning: A Brief Historical Overview,"

TESOL Quarterly, 17(2):191-204 (1983); Stephen D. Gaies, "The Investigation of Language Classroom Processes," ibid., pp. 205-17 (1983); Michael H. Long, Bibliography of Research on Second Language Classroom Processes and Classroom Second Language Acquisition, technical report no. 2 (Manoa: University of Hawaii, Social Science Research Institute, Center for Second Language Classroom Research, 1985); Rosalind Mitchell, "Process Research in Second Language Classrooms," Language Teaching, 18(4):330-52 (1985).

9. Cynthia Brock, "The Effects of Referential Questions on ESL Classroom Discourse," TESOL Quarterly, 20(1): 47-59 (1986).

10. Richard L. Allwright, "Turns, Topics and Tasks: Patterns of Participation in Language Teaching and Learning," in Discourse Analysis in Second Language Acquisition Research, ed. D. Larsen-Freeman (Rowley, MA: Newbury House, 1980), pp. 165-87.

11. Tere Pica and Cathy Doughty, "Input and Interaction in the Communicative Language Classroom: A Comparison of Teacher-Fronted and Group Activities," in Input and Second Language Acquisition, ed. Susan Gass and Caroline Madden (Rowley, MA: Newbury House, 1985), pp. 129-39.

12. Craig Chaudron, "Vocabulary Elaboration in Teachers' Speech to L2 Learners," Studies in Second Language Acquisition, 4(2):170-80 (1982); Vera Henzl, "Foreigner Talk in the Classroom," International Review of Applied Linguistics, 17(2): 159-67 (1979).

13. Charlene J. Sato, "Ethnic Styles in Classroom Discourse," in On TESOL '81, ed. Mary Hynes and William Rutherford (Washington, DC: Teachers of English to Speakers of Other Languages, 1981), pp. 11-24.

ships between practice and achievement,[14] teacher feedback on learner error,[15] relationships between task types and student production[16] and negotiation work[17] and between affective factors and classroom participation.[18]

Most studies in the second wave of SLCR have been small-scale and exploratory, a retreat from attempts at definitive method comparisons. The aim has been to secure reliable descriptions of what actually goes on in second language classrooms, as opposed to what is supposed to go on, presumably a prerequisite for precise manipulation of classroom processes in later experiments.

Such work typically begins with audio or video recordings of lessons, followed by a lengthy and rather tedious transcription process requiring on the order of 10 hours for each hour of data, depending on the detail needed for subsequent analyses, plus time for verification of protocols by independent transcribers. Some standardized transcription systems

and conventions for classroom discourse have been developed, however,[19] usable by novices after about two hours of training, which help to speed up the process as well as to make it more reliable.

Data analysis in these studies continues to show considerable variability. At one extreme, observers code classroom behaviors or events in real time, utilizing a variety of sign and category systems, with about 10 separate low-inference categories being the most a single trained observer can handle reliably in this fashion. Most entries in these systems are derivative of earlier work[20] in content classrooms and tend to emphasize pedagogical, rather than linguistic, features of lessons.

Limitations of this approach are well known and will not be repeated here.[21] Suffice it to say that, while a few relevant low-inference behaviors are what the field as a whole may well ultimately wish to identify for experimental work, selecting a set of them at the beginning of this descriptive stage of the research effort must be somewhat arbitrary unless the selection is clearly motivated theoretically. Being based largely on categories for the analysis of content classrooms, it is certainly limiting, and probably misguided, since it runs the risk of pre-empting new insights into relevant aspects of second language classroom processes.

14. Herbert W. Seliger, "Does Practice Make Perfect? A Study of Interaction Patterns and L2 Competence," *Language Learning*, 27(2):263-78 (1977).

15. Craig Chaudron, "A Descriptive Model of Discourse in the Corrective Treatment of Learners' Errors," *Language Learning,* 27(1):29-46 (1977).

16. Patsy Duff, "Another Look at Interlanguage Talk: Taking Task to Task," in *Talking to Learn: Conversation and Second Language Acquisition*, ed. R. R. Day (Rowley, MA: Newbury House, 1986), pp. 147-81.

17. E. Varonis and Susan Gass, "Non-native/Non-native Conversations: A Model for Negotiation of Meaning," *Applied Linguistics*, 6(1):71-90 (1985).

18. Kathleen M. Bailey, "Competitiveness and Anxiety in Second Language Learning: Looking *at* and *through* the Diary Studies," in *Classroom-Oriented Research on Second Language Acquisition*, ed. Seliger and Long, pp. 67-102; Craig Chaudron, *Second Language Classrooms: Research on Teaching and Learning* (Cambridge: Cambridge University Press, forthcoming).

19. Craig Chaudron, Graham Crookes, and Michael H. Long, "Transcription Procedures and Conventions for Classroom Discourse" (Manuscript, Center for Second Language Classroom Research, Social Science Research Institute, University of Hawaii at Manoa, 1984).

20. Ned Flanders, *Analyzing Teaching Behavior* (Reading, MA: Addison-Wesley, 1970).

21. Michael H. Long, "Inside the 'Black Box': Methodological Issues in Classroom Research on Language Learning," *Language Learning*, 30(1):1-42 (1980).

The purpose of such descriptive work, after all, is precisely to establish the detail of how language lessons are accomplished, with a view to subsequent hypothesis formation and manipulation of selected features in experimental studies.

At the other extreme, various kinds of ethnographic, constitutive ethnographic, introspective, and diary studies have been conducted,[22] work that typically eschews categorization even after data analysis. While undoubtedly holding great potential for hypothesis generation, if not testing, the number of studies of this kind is still surprisingly small, especially in foreign or second language, as opposed to bilingual, classrooms, given the quantity of journal space devoted to advocacy of these approaches in the past decade.

Intermediate between these two extremes exists an approach to analysis that seems to hold the most promise at this stage of SLCR and that I call quantified analysis of discourse. Researchers work from transcripts of lessons, accompanied, needed, by the original audio or video recordings, thereby allowing repeated runs through the data. Language use, as opposed to pedagogical acts, by teachers and students is analyzed using categories the application of which is often too complex for real-time coding—for example, because of the degree of inference involved in some of them or due to the small size or low saliency of the units of analysis involved, such as an utterance or communication unit. There is no attempt to provide an exhaustive account of a lesson or lessons; nor is there necessarily a hierarchical—"consists of"—relationship between categories, that is, two or more levels of analysis.[23] Hence, "analysis of discourse" rather than "discourse analysis." Following coding, quantification is feasible and, in fact, is usually performed.

Examples of categories already used in studies of this kind include open and closed referential and display questions, directed and general solicitations, confirmation and comprehension checks, clarification requests, exact and semantic self- and other-repetitions, prompts, follow-ups, and various kinds of expansion. In addition, such analyses typically employ various measures of linguistic complexity—for instance, sentence node per communication unit—that they apply to the teacher and student speech realizing the categories. Needless to say, the products of these analyses are amenable to subsequent statistical treatment. Again, operational definitions and coding conventions for many such categories and complexity measures have been refined in the course of this second wave of SLCR,[24] and attention given to appropriate procedures for training analysts in their use at acceptable levels of reliability. The results of studies utilizing such procedures are replicable by others and meet traditional standards of scientific work.

22. For review, see Kathleen M. Bailey and Robert Ochsner, "A Methodological Review of the Diary Studies: Windmill Tilting or Social Science?" in *Second Language Acquisition Studies*, ed. Kathleen M. Bailey, Michael H. Long, and Sabrina Peck (Rowley, MA: Newbury House, 1983), pp. 188-98; Andrew D. Cohen and Carol Hosenfeld, "Some Uses of Mentalistic Data in Second Language Research," *Language Learning*, 31(2):285-313 (1981); Mitchell, "Process Research."

23. For requirements on an adequate discourse analysis, see John McH. Sinclair and R. M. Coulthard, *Towards an Analysis of Discourse: The English Used by Teachers and Pupils* (Oxford: Oxford University Press, 1975).

24. See, for example, Craig Chaudron, "Coding Categories and Conventions" (Manuscript, Center for Second Language Classroom Research, Social Science Research Institute, University of Hawaii at Manoa, 1985).

The second wave of SLCR, consisting chiefly of micro-analyses of language use in second language classrooms, has borne considerable methodological fruit, in the form of a rapidly growing set of standardized procedures for data collection and analysis. Further, it has provided a much improved understanding of what actually happens when teachers do things like ask questions, explain vocabulary, correct errors, assign tasks, or perform classroom management activities, and as to the quality of the linguistic performance of students when they respond to soliciting moves of various types, perform different kinds of pedagogical tasks, or work in unsupervised small groups. It has also incidentally identified a wide discrepancy between actual classroom events, on the one hand, and methodological prescriptions and teachers' beliefs, on the other, serious food for thought among those engaged in teacher education and evaluation.

At the same time, unfortunately, little definitive has yet been established about what makes for efficient and successful language learning classrooms. This should come as no surprise. It was not, after all, the immediate aim of this second round of research to provide such information. The avowedly descriptive nature of most of the work, for example, meant that few studies had the kind of designs needed to show causal relationships or the relative merits of A or B.[25] Most, in fact, collected no product data—in the form of student achievement measures— at all, nor were interested in doing so, given their focus on teaching and learning processes. In this regard, they were a complete reversal of the earlier comparative method studies, which focused on

product to the near exclusion of process.

In addition to these inevitable limitations, however, many of the small-scale studies have exhibited some avoidable weaknesses. Among the more obvious and widespread, sampling procedures have tended to be nonsystematic, and, given the labor-intensive nature of such work, n sizes have typically been small, too small even to support the descriptive generalizations made. Further, despite improvement in this regard, many researchers still fail to report— and so presumably to conduct—any kind of interrater reliability study, while often using quite high inference categories in their analyses. These limitations obviously make interpretation and generalization of findings a hazardous undertaking.

More serious in many respects than any of these shortcomings, however, is the apparent lack of psycholinguistic motivation for many studies. Despite the radical changes in linguistic theory and the considerable advances made in SLA research in the last 15 years or so, remarkably few second language classroom researchers seem interested in testing ideas about language learning from either source in their own work, although exceptions do, of course, exist.[26] We return to this issue later in this article. At this juncture, suffice it to say

25. Some process-process studies—for example, Brock, "Effects of Referential Questions"—have been completed, however.

26. See, for example, Susan Gass, "From Theory to Practice," in *On TESOL '81*, ed. Hines and Rutherford, pp. 129-39; Patsy M. Lightbown, "Exploring the Relationships between Developmental and Instructional Sequences in Second Language Acquisition," in *Classroom-Oriented Research on Second-Language Acquisition*, ed. Seliger and Long, pp. 217-43; Manfred Pienemann, "Psychological Constraints on the Teachability of Languages," *Studies in Second Language Acquisition*, 6(2):186-214 (1984); Helmut Zobl, "Grammars in Search of Input and Intake," in *Input and Second Language Acquisition*, ed. Gass and Madden, pp. 329-44.

that, even if applied in orientation, any research that lacks theoretical motivation implicitly chooses to discount relevant existing knowledge and so will almost certainly be inefficient, if not irrelevant—and incidentally misses out on the excitement of theory building. SLCR is no exception.

SECOND LANGUAGE CLASSROOM RESEARCH—THE NEXT DECADE

Reference has already been made to the often noted distinction between basic and applied research. In the present context, it should be expected that in the next decade the third wave of SLCR will push forward on both fronts. There is still a need for detailed descriptive studies, particularly of an ethnographic nature, and with a focus on learners rather than teachers, that suggest new understandings of how language learning lessons work. Basic research of this kind will not be designed to show the effect of particular processes in lesson accomplishment on language learning, although it may help in this regard. Rather, its purpose will be to explore currently unrecognized dimensions of the relationship between language teacher and language student.

Applied SLCR studies, in contrast, will test for relationships between existing variables, along with new ones identified by further basic research, and student achievement. Factors initially identified through description, and then related causally through experimentation to classroom language learning, can finally serve as the basis for prescriptions for teaching and learning. At this stage, there will be a need for another line of applied research, namely, studies of the effectiveness of pre- and in-service training in the processes on subsequent teacher performance in the classroom. As noted earlier,

descriptive studies have already shown the urgent need for research on ways of ensuring that theoretical and empirical advances translate into real, not imagined, changes in classroom practice.

Applied research of this last kind raises interesting and—in our field—hitherto little-explored problems of its own. The typical situation is exemplified by two studies conducted by the Center for Second Language Classroom Research at the University of Hawaii.[27] Those studies each involved tests of (1) the effectiveness of in-service teacher training in questioning patterns, and (2) the effect of increases in the frequencies of certain kinds of open and closed referential questions, as a result of the training, on various linguistic aspects of student production and on the learning of subject matter. The earlier study was conducted in natural intact classes in public high schools in Hawaii, randomly assigned to one of three conditions and using a blend of free and fixed content lessons over a series of four video recordings per class. The later study, by Brock, utilized single-shot encounters between teachers and groups of six adult students created artificially for the purpose of the study, using a randomized block design, with all classes working on fixed lesson content.

Methodological issues raised by such studies include the following:

1. What is the relative generalizability of research findings obtained in the con-

27. Brock, "Effects of Referential Questions"; Michael H. Long et al., *The Effect of Teachers' Questioning Patterns and Wait-time on Pupil Participation in Public High School Classes in Hawaii for Students of Limited English Proficiency,* technical report no. 1 (Manoa: University of Hawaii, Social Science Research Institute, Center for Second Language Classroom Research, 1984).

trived but controlled settings versus relatively uncontrolled but more natural ones? This is a perennial problem in many kinds of research, of course, but surely particularly acute in educational research, given the supposed uniqueness not just of classrooms and teacher-student relationships, but of individual lessons.

2. What steps can be taken to protect the integrity of the treatment—here, the use of increased frequencies of referential questions—given that its delivery to students is in the hands of third parties, the teachers, who are not necessarily part of the research team?

3. What degree of certainty is required or acceptable concerning the persistence of behavioral changes beyond the period of observation, before pedagogical prescriptions are deemed safe?

4. What can be done to counteract the heavier-than-usual doses of both the observer's paradox and the Hawthorne effect in research of this kind?

Few would argue with the notion that SLCR in the next decade should include evaluation studies. In fact, one of the rewards for over a decade of small-scale descriptive studies of classroom processes is that the field is now in a much stronger position to conduct the program evaluations and comparisons to which it was first attracted some 25 years ago. Some decisions will have to be taken, however, as to the appropriate standards for such research and, indeed, as to whether evaluations should be conducted within a research framework at all.

My own view is that evaluation worth the name is research and that the usual standards apply.[28] It is, for instance,

unjustified to claim to show that a program is effective or more effective than an alternative in a summative evaluation without employing a true experimental design, thereby at least potentially protecting the study from the usual threats to internal validity. The only difference is that the purpose, as opposed to the methodology, of an evaluation may differ from that of a pure research study; there may not be any interest, for example, in generalizing the findings beyond the programs evaluated, or in contributing to theory development, although this always seems to me to be a tragic waste of information. Further, data and sources of data may be utilized in an evaluation—particularly a formative evaluation—to help explain the local success or failure of a program in terms of its implementation that would have no interest elsewhere.

Other views are equally strongly held, however.[29] Beretta, for example, claims that it is unreasonable and/or unnecessary to demand the same scientific standards of evaluations because (1) they are conducted in natural classrooms, not the researcher's laboratory; (2) random assignment of students to groups is impossible in most circumstances; (3) the effect of total programs, not isolated parts of them, is of interest; and (4) evaluations should be of long-term, rather than short-term, duration.

Each of these claims seems contestable and/or of dubious status. A brief response to them follows.

28. Michael H. Long, "Process and Product in ESL Program Evaluation," *TESOL Quarterly*, 18(4):409-25 (1984).

29. Alan Beretta, "Toward a Methodology of ESL Program Evaluation," *TESOL Quarterly*, 20(1):144-53 (1986); D. O. Rafter, "Three Approaches to Evaluation Research," *Knowledge: Creation, Diffusion, Utilization*, 6(2):165-85 (1984).

1. Experiments, too, can be and have been conducted in natural classrooms, although unusual problems sometimes arise, as indicated previously.

2. Random assignment is indeed impossible in many cases, but the effect is to preempt causal tests of a program's effectiveness, not to free the evaluator from the usual standards of methodological rigor. In many other cases, random assignment is possible, however, following which the resulting groupings of teachers and students are potentially just as natural as non-randomly formed classes.

3. The experimental paradigm applies as well—or poorly—to complete programs as to parts of them. The difference is simply in the specificity of the findings.

4. To say that evaluations should be long-term is an assertion, not a fact, and one about a relative, not an absolute, concept—duration—at that. It may well be true, but if so, it is an argument in favor of, not against, the true experimental approach to evaluation. Threats to the internal validity of research of all kinds, such as history, maturation, and mortality, are particularly acute with long-term studies. The potential protection against them that the true experiment provides is, therefore, even more necessary if an evaluation is to be long-term.

Needless to say, evaluations of all kinds are useful and will doubtless continue to be undertaken. It seems, however, that a case could be made for encouraging the experimental approach for at least two reasons. First, other things being equal, the findings of an evaluation based on a true experiment are obviously preferable if a choice exists, because they are more likely to be both reliable and valid. Second, findings from evaluations not based on true experimentation, by definition, may not be reliable, and if unreliable, will be invalid, as would eventually come to light when subsequent studies were conducted. Other things being equal, therefore, the choice of methodology for evaluations should be clear.

As indicated earlier, one important way in which the scope of SLCR needs to be defined is in terms of its theoretical motivation. Given classroom SLA as the focus of inquiry, it is, surely, quite logical to expect that the major sources of theory governing the research will be those disciplines most directly involved, that is, language sciences in general and SLA in particular.

While this might seem obvious to some, it has not, apparently, been obvious to many classroom researchers to date. Reviews of the SLCR literature leave one with the strong impression that numerous studies are not theoretically motivated psycholinguistically or in any other way. The surface evidence of this includes (1) the absence of reference to SLA theory either in the studies themselves or in the reviews; (2) the scarcity of citations of other SLCR one would expect in a theoretically motivated, cumulative research program; and (3) the weak generalizations with which most research reports finish, suggesting that the studies themselves had little theoretical significance beyond the immediate research setting.

If the atheoretical picture painted here seems overly gloomy, most would agree that more, and more explicitly, psycholinguistically motivated research would be an improvement, at least. Typically, no more or less work would be required than is currently expended on the execution of a study; however, additional care would be required at the planning stage. A simple example might help clarify the point.

Ordinarily, a study might be conducted to test the teachability or learnability of, say, grammatical structure X or Y via one or another procedure. The result, at best, will be a description of the classroom processes involved, data on the relative efficacy of the procedure or procedures, followed by a suggestion as to pedagogic implications. While useful in itself, the study is far less useful than one in which the structure chosen had some theoretical significance.

Suppose, for instance, that control of structure X reflected a stage in an interlingual developmental sequence for a particular grammatical subsystem—negation or word order, for instance—previously established by SLA research, and that this stage was, respectively, one beyond and two beyond those achieved by two groups of learners, A and B, prior to delivery of the instruction. Group A is at stage one, for example, Group B at stage two, and instruction at stage three. Suppose, further, a theory that holds that stages of interlanguage development are determined by underlying processing constraints, and that learning of new structures is only possible when a learner has the processing prerequisites for that stage or structure. A finding that the new structure was learned by students at stage two when the study began, but not by those at stage one, who ended where they began, would have significance not just for the particular pedagogy utilized, nor just for the particular structure taught, but potentially for the teachability of any structure in either a previously observed or predictable developmental sequence, given knowledge of the students' current developmental stage. The implications, in fact, would extend beyond pedagogy to syllabus design and testing. The study would also be a useful contribution to SLA theory building.[30]

A corollary of theoretically motivated research is, in most cases, research findings of high valency, that is, results usable in a wide variety of cases, not just those specific to or limited by idiosyncratic features of the original research site. This is clearly a desirable characteristic of original experimental work undertaken as part of a national research agenda for the simple reason that the research effort would be of greater benefit to larger numbers of foreign language educators, and so more cost effective.

One can imagine, however, potential research efforts that would be theoretically motivated but still of low valency, perhaps because their outcome was partially dependent on particularities of, say, a rarely taught language, an unusual type of learner, and so on. The research findings might be extremely interesting theoretically and of great value to programs of the type represented in the study, but of low generalizability. When establishing a national agenda, a decision would need to be made as to the priority to be assigned studies of this kind, taking into account such matters as the long-term national importance of the language concerned and available funding and human resources. The views of an advisory committee might be called on in such cases.

30. Readers familiar with the SLA literature will recognize the hypothetical study outlined as a schematic representation of one reported in Pienemann, "Psychological Constraints on the Teachability of Languages."

A NATIONAL AGENDA FOR CLASSROOM RESEARCH ON FOREIGN LANGUAGE EDUCATION

In light of the previous discussion of the scope of research for the next decade, the scope of a national research effort in experimental classrooms can now be suggested. The mandate might consist of a charge to conduct basic and applied SLCR and program evaluations, with special attention devoted to high-valency, psycholinguistically motivated studies. The agenda would also include disseminating the findings of that research to all interested parties, including teachers, teacher educators, syllabus and materials designers, and writers of language tests, conducting pre- and in-service teacher training based on the research findings and evaluating the effectiveness of that training.

It would clearly be presumptuous of one individual to suggest SLCR priorities for a national agenda. Wider discussion and input is clearly essential. The following, then, is offered only as a suggestion of some topics in need of study; theoretical motivation exists for each, but is not stated here due to space limitations:

—studies of the comparative effectiveness of foreign language programs the syllabi and methodology of which do one of the following: (1) focus on isolated linguistic forms—grammatical, lexical, and so forth; (2) focus on form, under specifiable conditions, but only in an ancillary fashion, the primary focus and organizational unit for lessons being something else, such as topics, academic subject matter, or tasks; or (3) focus exclusively on something other than the language itself, eschewing a focus on forms or form;

—studies of the teachability or learnability of linguistic structure with reference to learners' current stage of interlanguage development;

—studies of the effect of instruction in linguistic items on the control of other untaught items—for example, the effect of teaching linguistically marked forms on the acquisition of related less marked or unmarked forms;

—studies of the relative contribution of differing proportions and differently sequenced proportions of formal instruction and natural language exposure to ultimate proficiency, with attention to both accuracy and fluency; and

—studies to identify "intervention points,"[31]—classroom processes that teachers, materials designers, or learners can manipulate in ways that theory or resarch in SLA suggest are beneficial for language learning. Emphasis would be given to high-frequency, low-inference behaviors, events, or procedures that SLCR shows to be manipulable by classroom participants. Where materials are involved, they should be those that are readily available or cheap to produce. Examples of potential intervention points include teachers' questions and the design of pedagogic tasks;

—studies of the effectiveness of pre-service and in-service teacher training modules;

31. Michael H. Long and Graham Crookes, "Intervention Points in Second Language Classroom Processes" (Paper delivered at the Regional English Language Center Seminar on Patterns of Classroom Interaction in Southeast Asia, Regional English Language Center, Singapore, 21-25 Apr. 1986).

—studies of the differential effectiveness of teaching strategies with learners of varying ages—particularly pre- and post-sensitive period for SLA—language learning aptitude, and other state and trait characteristics;

—studies of different approaches to the constructive utilization of language learning universals in foreign language education;

—studies comparing programs with differing emphases and sequences of language skills; and

—studies of the relative effectiveness of different approaches to simplification of the target language—in teacher speech, audio material, and reading matter—for comprehensibility and acquisition.

Whatever studies were finally undertaken, it is suggested that, in the interest of comparability and cumulativeness of findings, serious consideration be given to standardization of research methodology and reporting. This would be feasible in such areas as the establishing of parameters for the description of subjects; data-collection procedures, such as elicitation devices, classroom observation systems, proficiency measures; transcription systems; data analysis, including categories, coding procedures, reliability measures, and the like; methods of quantification; and statistical treatments of data. Careful cumulative work of this kind would pay enormous dividends. While the intangibles of the teacher-student relationship would doubtless remain an art, and probably should, a large part of foreign language education would be more efficient for having a firm scientific basis.

Truly Foreign Languages:
Instructional Challenges

By ELEANOR H. JORDEN and A. RONALD WALTON

ABSTRACT: The teaching of a foreign language to any individual necessarily involves the bringing together of two languages and two cultures: the student's native language and culture—the base—and the language and culture being studied—the target. When these are in marked contrast, many special instructional challenges emerge. Students are confronted with totally unfamiliar linguistic patterns and cultural concepts, which require analysis that will be meaningful specifically to them. In the foreign language classroom, serious attention must be paid to the learners and their particular mind-set, through which they will inevitably filter the target language. A recommended approach to this pedagogical challenge is the use of a team of professionally trained instructors that includes target-natives who, as authentic models of the target, actively and with linguistic sophistication, interact with the students in the target language—the act component—and base-natives, who concentrate on the analysis of the target—the fact component.

Eleanor H. Jorden, the Mary Donlon Alger Professor of Linguistics and director of the year-long, full-time intensive Japanese FALCON program at Cornell University, is currently visiting professor of Japanese language and culture at Williams College.

A. Ronald Walton, associate professor of Chinese language and linguistics at the University of Maryland, College Park, is director of the campus-wide Foreign Language Initiative.

THE difficulty associated with any attempt to divide the languages of the world into groups is clearly reflected in the shifting terminology that has been used over the years. We have had "world" and "non-world languages," "hard" and "soft," "neglected" and might we say "coddled" languages, "critical" and might we say "not-to-worry" languages, and, more recently, the "commonly" and "less commonly taught." Given the performance of Japanese in the Modern Language Association's polls, we might assign that language to an "increasingly commonly taught" category. A twofold division made on the basis of student interest, institutional administrative commitment, and monetary support can, of course, be determined for each institution, but this will be unrelated to linguistic questions.

In the discussion that follows, the languages being examined are, in fact, those that are linguistically unrelated to English—that is, they are non-Indo-European—and spoken within societies that are culturally in marked contrast to our own. We will call these the truly foreign languages (TFLs) and will focus on two we believe to be representative of the group—Chinese and Japanese. While the details we discuss may apply specifically to these languages alone, they are typical of a large group of languages that give rise to problems Americans encounter much less commonly in the Spanish language classroom.

LANGUAGE AS CULTURAL BEHAVIOR

Every foreign language learning situation, by definition, brings together two languages and two cultures: the foreign language and culture being studied—the target—and the student's native language and culture—the base. When these are in sharp contrast, the challenge is enormous, for the base filter that is automatically and unconsciously operative is a constant impediment.

The student who assumes that foreign language learning is fundamentally a matter of finding answers to the question, How do you say x in the target language? —and most of the students who come to us from a background of European language classrooms seem to reflect this syndrome—undergo immediate linguistic culture shock. It is not enough that the purely linguistic code is itself so difficult. The cultural code, which pervades the linguistic code at every level— phonological, morphological, syntactic, and discourse—is even more complex. It must be an integral part of a good teaching program from the first hour of instruction. Imagine a language—Japanese, to be exact—that has no neutral speech style; every speech act reflects choices involving the in-group/out-group membership, status, age, and gender of the participants. Learning to ignore features that are crucial in one's base language, and becoming aware of features of the target that have thus far been ignored, are much more demanding of a student than memorizing irregular verb forms, time-consuming though that may be.

We can assume that every foreign language presents some phonological challenges, but the tones of Chinese, the rhythm and intonation of Japanese, the implosives of North Vietnamese—these are particularly difficult for the Westerner. When we examine lexicon, the phenomenon of semantic mismatch constantly impedes students' attempts at creativity. Examples of this phenomenon occur when any two languages are contrasted, but the frequency of occurrence in the case of culturally unrelated languages presents another learning hurdle. In addition, there is the further problem of sociolinguistic deviance on the lexical level. Without an understanding of the target culture, it is impossible to determine whether concepts are positive or negative. To base one's judgment on one's native culture is at once naive and dangerous.

Imagine the despair of Americans, looking for a Japanese equivalent of "if," when they find they must, in fact, inflect every verb and adjective and copula to achieve a conditional. And then comes a further blow: there are two competing conditional forms, the choice between them determined by complex semantic and discourse features.

Complicated syntax becomes even more difficult for the student because of cultural requirements. Aside from the previously mentioned difficulties of politeness and formality levels, there are further sociolinguistic questions. Students may have learned how to request, refuse, complain, compliment, and so forth, but are they aware of the circumstances in the foreign culture that make these speech acts appropriate? It is perfectly possible to translate English literally into Japanese, but this does not produce the Japanese that native Japanese actually use. Compare the usual style of posted American apartment house rules and regulations, for example, with the Japanese "Let's turn off our stoves before we leave our apartments"! The American surgeon general's warning turns up in Japanese as "Let's act in such a way as not to smoke too much." The underlying pattern of these examples reflects an important feature of Japanese culture that should be given as much emphasis in the language classroom as verb paradigms. Both will determine the extent to which foreigners can communicate effec-

tively in the target language. The crucial question relates to whether foreigners can make the target-native comfortable when they speak the foreign language.

UNFAMILIAR LINGUISTIC CONCEPTS

English and the Indo-European language (IEL) family may well share many, perhaps all, linguistic features with the TFLs at some abstract level. For example, case grammar was developed, in part, by examining the inflectional systems of Latin and Greek, but because the functions defined by case markers are fairly universal, it has been applied to Chinese with some success, in spite of the fact that Chinese has practically no inflectional system. However, at the level of surface structure—that level consisting of the raw language data that the language learner must internalize to form hypotheses and eventually create novel utterances—there are often few features shared between the IELs and the TFLs. Number, tense, gender, surface case, agreement, and the like are not concepts that necessarily have transparent counterparts in the TFLs.

There is an assumption that unfamiliar concepts are problematic to learners and, therefore, to teaching. Since the term "unfamiliar" is vague and refers to a continuum at best, it may be more useful to identify concepts with the following features as difficult or most unfamiliar: (1) the feature takes longer to acquire than others; (2) even though the feature is pervasive in speech—not like the subjunctive in German, for example—and drilled extensively, learners continue to make errors, or they passively comprehend the feature but fail to use it actively; and (3) the feature is prone to attrition. The Japanese system of overtly marked formality and politeness levels is a prime example of a conceptual framework lacking in the IELs. The learner is not simply confronted with mastering the appropriate markers and vocabulary, but with mastering an entirely unfamiliar system of socioverbal behavior. Because there is no such thing as neutral speech in Japanese, foreigners must learn to categorize a speech event in terms of the social status, familiarity, sex, age, and other characteristics of both speaker and addressee, long before the execution of speech itself.

Aspect in Chinese is another example. The event of completing the purchase of two magazines is bounded since there is an end point to the purchasing, but the completion of buying magazines is unbounded since there is no inherent end point. Both Chinese utterances could correspond to something in English called a past tense, but only the former could take an obligatory perfective aspect marker.

There is no doubt that thousands of such examples could be provided for the TFLs. The focus here is on (1) problems in teaching and learning such linguistic concepts; (2) pedagogical approaches to internalization of the concepts by the learner; and (3) the integrating of explanations and internalization strategies. Problems occur in text materials and in the classroom, as well.

In some instances, grammatical explanations resemble a linguistic analysis, often somewhat technical, with pedagogical material added on. This is not too surprising since base-language linguists have often had to do field research on the less common TFLs. If the analysis follows a particular theory, it may not only be unfamiliar to teachers and students alike; it may become dated rather quickly. Depending on the nature of the corpus and how it was collected, it may

be devoid of situational, pragmatic, and cultural factors that influence the selection—as opposed to the delivery—of grammatical features in interactive communication. Again, this is to be expected since the linguists in question may not have had pedagogical goals in mind when collecting the data.

At the other extreme, there can be a long-standing base-language tradition that has never been subjected to critical analysis. Chinese textbooks, for example, continue to rely on limited explanations developed during and just after World War II, even though linguistic research has progressed significantly. To this time, no textbook has sorted the notions of old and new information and presupposition as they relate to subject versus topic and to definiteness, even though linguistic research has clarified the situation considerably.

Since learning the unfamiliar via the familiar is a standard approach in learning generally, there is naturally a fairly pervasive tradition of using English linguistic concepts as a frame of reference in approaching the target language. While this approach may be useful—and is probably inevitable—it can create a good many problems. In some instances, direct equivalents simply do not exist in the TFLs and more harm than good can come from pushing for similarities. In other cases, linguistic concepts reflect partial overlap between the base and target language, but unless such overlaps are presented accurately, learners tend to digest only that portion of the concept found in the base language. Perfective aspect in Chinese and past tense in English are good examples of this. Depending on how perfective aspect is explained, students often mistakenly equate it with the English past tense.

If linguistic explanations are dense

and technical, learners will focus on bilingual examples of the concepts. When such examples rely on translation rather than equivalents, serious problems can arise. If we use Chinese as an example, we find that practically no textbooks provide examples that include discussions of the discourse constraints and pragmatic, situational, and sociolingistic factors that shape the production of a given example in natural speech.

In addition, the explanations of grammatical concepts are often presented from a strictly receptive viewpoint: construction in the target language is equivalent to construction in the base language. This may assist learners in interpreting a grammatical concept when it occurs in the language of target-native speakers, but it gives no guidance on when and how to use the construction actively in speech production. For example, most Chinese textbooks explain two different presentative constructions as if from the listener's viewpoint, without indicating when one is to use one construction or the other.

Explanations coming from the native paradigm are problematic as well. The range can be from the overly linguistic to the overly simplified-for-the-foreigner. Moreover, unless the foreign author or teacher has a high level of proficiency in English and extensive experience in an English-speaking culture, it will be impossible to state target-base equivalents. The result is often a bookish and quite literal direct translation that may be misleading or even unintelligible. In some cases, the presentation of the target language has been based, purely and simply, on English, with contrastive information on usage, particularly sociolinguistic factors, completely lacking.

How concepts are presented for internalization by the learner is equally prob-

lematic. Standard vehicles for such internalization are dialogues, drills, and exercises—provided in print, on tape, and in the classroom. Yet how often one finds dialogues without sociolinguistic or pragmatic parameters spelled out; dialogues far too long for internalization; dialogues with so many new vocabulary items that the presentation of grammatical concepts becomes obscured; isolated sentences for memorization and drill—the list goes on.

Particularly worthy of comment is the gap between linguistic explanation and pedagogical implementation. This gap becomes obvious when one reads the articles in language teachers' publications on specific languages. The contributions by linguists often seek to prove the validity of a particular theoretical approach with little or no reference to pedagogy. Teachers with no formal training in linguistics are expected to translate these analyses into pragmatic practice. In contrast, articles by teachers who are not linguists tend toward describing methodologies and approaches devoid of any linguistic explanation. The same sort of dichotomy is reflected in materials development. All too often, the approaches of the two groups are in contrast rather than mutually supportive. The needs of the learner—a balance of explanation and pedagogical implementation—simply fall between the cracks.

The preceding observations are intended to demonstrate that the teaching of unfamiliar linguistic concepts, at least for some of the TFLs, seems to have no consistent pedagogical philosophy. Between the target language and the learner, there is a scarcity of gatekeepers for the TFLs: too few linguists, too few qualified teachers, too few materials. Moreover, there is a distinct distance problem: distance between the base and target languages and cultures, distance between the pedagogical attitudes and practices of base-language versus target-language teachers and linguists, distance between the linguists and the teachers, distance between grammatical explanation and pedagogical strategies for the internalization of the linguistic concepts. Unfortunately, though many of these languages have been taught for decades both in this country and in the target countries, there is still little evidence, in the case of a good number of languages, of significant change in the wind.

SOUND SYSTEMS

There is no argument that the TFLs are more likely than the IELs to have so-called exotic sound systems: tones, contrastive vowel and consonant length, implosives, pharyngeals, clicks, and so forth. In those cases where learners are required to produce not just new sounds—true in learning any foreign language—but new types of sounds that utilize completely unfamiliar articulatory gestures, problems naturally arise. The teaching strategies commonly used in presenting the sound systems of the IELs—for instance, comparison with similar English sounds, reliance on repetition and extensive listening—are generally inadequate.

The descriptions found in many textbooks of how to produce sounds such as tones and clicks are often nearly useless. Some training in articulatory phonetics is necessary for teachers, including target-native teachers, who generally do not know just how they produce the sounds, though most do have naive and often quite erroneous impressions of the process. Such training is critical, not just for explanation, but for correction. Teachers lacking such training tend to rely on blind correction: since they cannot ascertain the articulatory source of the error, the last resort is endless repetition, which is often confusing to the learner. Some such training is also necessary for learners. The articulatory gestures required often demand a rather extensive introduction to mouth geography and an understanding of the functions of the various articulatory organs.

Because such sound systems—or at least subsystems—are indeed difficult to acquire, presentation becomes a challenge. In Chinese, for example, all teachers know that tones are a learning hurdle. Since the sound system can be defined in terms of a limited number of syllable types, a common approach is to devote several weeks at the beginning of a course to drilling tones and isolation syllables. Student interest flags and many learners become discouraged as their perceptual and discriminatory abilities are overtaxed. In those cases where such intensive effort is initially expended on the sound system, pronunciation is considered covered and may be subsequently neglected, as the emphasis of the course shifts to vocabulary and grammar.

Implicit in such pronunciation modules is the assumption that there will be a direct transfer from work on isolation syllables to the natural utterances of true speech. Since native speakers themselves show considerable variation between conscious, deliberate pronunciation and unmonitored speech, this assumption seems highly questionable. Yet, because pronunciation has been initially targeted for exclusive attention, the learner has not moved into the language per se. Thus there is no opportunity to practice the transfer between isolation-syllable work and speech. The problem is further aggravated when teachers insist on delivering longer utterances in isolation style with artificially deliberate pronunciation. As a rule, there are few opportunities provided in texts or on tapes for pronunciation practice of longer utterances. For example, there is no elementary Chinese text that introduces dialogues, the most realistic samples of speech in the lesson, in a build-up fashion, though drill sentences, which lack realistic context and context-sensitive intonation, are sometimes presented in this fashion.

If the teaching of Chinese is representative, pronunciation practice tends to rely much too heavily on mimicking rather than self-generation. Teachers are frequently perplexed as to why tone problems persist, sometimes indefinitely, not realizing that learners never internalized articulatory strategies for production.

Requirements for accuracy are also troublesome. Some teachers believe that the sound system is so difficult for foreigners that a crude, intelligible, but heavy-accented delivery is acceptable. This is accompanied by a rationale that improvement will automatically occur later, particularly after residence in the target country. Unfortunately, in the case of Chinese as an example, there is no hard data to support this assumption. There are certainly cases where improvement has occurred, but there seem to be as many cases where students return from even a year or more abroad with pronunciation problems that have definitely not improved. It may be that initial pronunciation remains plastic for some learners but becomes fossilized for others.

On the other end of the teaching spectrum, we find teachers, often inexperienced, who insist on highly accurate pronunciation in the very early stages. Here the demand can be too high and intensive, given the short exposure time

that the learner has had to grapple with the sound system. Overcorrection can intimidate learners and discourage the experimentation necessary to arrive at satisfactory articulation.

Yet another approach now in vogue calls for prolonged periods of listening before speaking. The rationale for this approach seem to come from child acquisition of second languages. The silent period is characterized by "intaking" and the formulation of hypotheses about both pronunciation and grammar/vocabulary. Given that the TFLs share little or no lexicon or grammatical structure with English and that the sound systems may require radically new articulations and use of speech organs, it is hard to imagine that such an approach is efficient. Listening is always a critical component of production, but surely novel articulation requires rather intensive production practice, feedback, and correction for the adult learner.

In sum, an evaluation of TFL programs with regard to the teaching of difficult sound systems would ask questions such as the following: Have the teachers received training in articulatory phonetics? Do they understand how they themselves produce the sounds of their native language? Alternatively, are there base-language teachers with these qualifications involved in the teaching process? Do the teachers rely only on imitation and repetition for correction? Are learners instructed in—and given the opportunity for—the production of the sounds without cues? Is pronunciation practice frontloaded into the program and ignored later? Is practice restricted to deliberate, word- or syllable- or sound-in-isolation production and discrimination? Is the demand for accuracy unrealistically high or unrealistically low? Do text and tape materials provide adequate and carefully structured practice on pronunciation? Working on impressions only, one feels that far too few TFL programs adequately address these types questions.

Some additional problems in the teaching of sound systems are discussed in conjunction with orthography.

ORTHOGRAPHY

Those TFLs that use nonalphabetic scripts create an entirely new learning task for the student. The problems begin at the graphic level, but extend in some cases—as with Chinese characters—to the level of forming a sound-symbol relationship where the symbol may give no clue to the sound and vice versa. All nonalphabetic scripts require training in handwriting—a not necessarily overwhelming task, but often an initially time-consuming one. Extensive training in recognition is also required. Some languages have only a partial sound-symbol relationship, so that the learner must know what missing elements to fill in when reading the writing system. Chinese characters may have at best only a vague indication of pronunciation. As a consequence, the memory load for learners is immense. It must be pointed out that native speakers of these languages suffer a similar memory burden. For example, even though native Chinese—unlike the foreign beginner—know the oral language, there are no cases on record of rapid leaps to literacy, though various campaigns have tried this.

For the teaching of some languages, phonologically based transcription systems are used in addition to the native orthography. Properly done, this approach is extremely effective, but some such systems are not always used to their full potential. They are intended for foreigners or, in some cases, for target-native children, but the average native speaker, including untrained target-language teachers, may not be familiar with them. These systems normally lack cultural legitimacy and are often seen by teachers as artificial and unnecessary. In Chinese, even those teachers who see some utility in transcription systems consider them a temporary crutch, apparently unaware that most English speakers will use a transcription system forever when looking up the pronunciation of unfamiliar characters in dictionaries.[1]

These transcription systems are sometimes abused by teachers who use the symbols in an attempt to teach the sounds rather than teaching the sounds first and the symbols later. When learners fail to decode the symbols properly—for example, in Chinese, *hen* is pronounced with a slightly fricative *h* followed by schwa and then *n*, not like the English word for female chicken—the argument arises that the symbols actually cause poor pronunciation—an interesting argument, since the symbols are not oral but printed. Beyond this, there are often competing transcription systems as in Chinese and Japanese, coming from both the base and native systems. Since different textbooks and dictionaries use different systems, learners can be confronted with a bewildering array of systems.

Some transcription systems are intended to be quasi-morphophonemic rather than phonemic or phonetic. The goal in this case is to promote the

1. It is worth noting that with the advent of word processors to Japan, romanization of Japanese—the use of our alphabet to represent Japanese—is acquiring increased legitimacy.

learning of grammar by setting up spellings that show relationships within the language. For example, the English word "paradigm" could be spelled more phonetically by dropping the so-called silent *g*. This, however, would obfuscate the relationship between the noun and its derived adjective, "paradigmatic," where the *g* is pronounced. Needless to say, teachers not trained in linguistics fail to grasp the rationale for morphophonemic spellings and favor a more phonetic system, even if the latter greatly complicates grammatical explanation.

These are but a few of the more common problems encountered in the teaching of nonalphabetic orthographies. Other factors involving orthography are best left for discussion in the following section, on skill mix.

PROBLEMS IN THE SKILL MIX

In the European language context, the relationship among the speaking, listening, reading, and writing skills is often rather direct. For example, a student working on a textbook dialogue in German is practicing speaking, listening, and reading at the same time. If one can use the dialogue material orally, and if one has been reading the material in the text at the same time, then reproducing the material through writing is not an especially demanding task. Thus the learner can cover the four skills almost simultaneously.

For those TFLs that use nonalphabetic orthographies, the situation is much more complicated, for both native and nonnative learners. The gap between oral mastery and mastery of the native orthography can be immense. Consider China, where everyone presumably speaks, but where traditionally only a tiny fraction of the population has been able to handle characters. Native speakers learning to read and write, however, have at least already acquired structural control of the language plus an enormous lexicon, much of which—but not all, of course—is utilized in the written medium. The elementary foreign language learner, on the other hand, has no such head start in structure and lexicon acquired through speech and may be trying to master all skills simultaneously. The gap between speech and a nonalphabetic orthography creates teaching and learning problems in pacing and in skill sequencing rarely found in the case of European languages.

Taking the Chinese and Japanese language teaching fields as examples, one of the most fundamental problems is the lack of a clear distinction between oral and written language. This is particularly true of target-language teachers, though base-language teachers often share the confusion. To many educated Chinese and Japanese, the written language *is* the language. In program after program, students of Japanese spend the initial weeks learning the Japanese sound system by first learning *kana*, the Japanese syllabic writing system. Inexperienced Chinese tutors nearly always attempt to teach spoken Chinese via characters.

It must be remembered that educated members of the target culture, like educated people anywhere, tend to teach in the fashion in which they themselves learned. But native speakers of any language have little or no recollection of how they learned to speak. What they do remember is how they learned to read and write, since these subjects are the hallmark of formal education. Placed in a teaching position, many native speakers tend to repeat their own learning experience as a teaching approach, completely forgetting that they already knew how to speak their languages before learning to read and write them. This approach is particularly obvious among Chinese and Japanese, where the demanding task of learning to read and write is particularly well remembered.

There are a number of pedagogical consequences of the oral-written confusion. First, phonetic transcription systems are misunderstood as substitutes for the native orthography rather than as systems for representing speech. This contributes to the notion that such systems are unnecessary and culturally illegitimate. Thus in Chinese we find textbooks where individual words are presented in both characters and phonetic romanization, but where dialogues, drills, and examples of grammatical patterns are presented solely in characters. Learners cannot study any of the material, including the example patterns, until they have mastered the characters—in other words, character recognition and reading are prerequisites for speaking, even though the ostensible purpose of the text is not to teach reading. Conversation classes for foreign learners in China sometimes begin with a character dictation test—teacher speaks, students write in characters—even though instruction in reading and writing is supposedly limited to other classes. Moreover, tests of grammar and vocabulary, which could be given in romanization and/or orally, often require the writing of characters.

There are serious curricular consequences of the oral-written confusion as well. For Chinese and Japanese, the time requirements for learning characters, especially the writing of characters, is considerable. If oral language is taught via the native orthography, the entire learning process is greatly slowed, and

in particular, the learning of speech is unreasonably and unnecessarily pegged to the speed with which learners can master an extremely memory-demanding written medium.

Many Western linguists hold that speech is primary and that reading and writing are overlaid skills. This concept has obviously found little support in at least some TFL traditions. Reading research in the West has tended to focus on first-language reading acquisition; indeed, the literature on the psycholinguistic processes involved when adults learn to read a second alphabetic language seems so sparse as to suggest that these processes have never been seen as a problem. Reading research on Chinese, however, indicates that true reading— not decoding or word identification— depends at some stage on the speech code. The hypothesis is that readers do not store long strings of characters in short-term visual or iconic memory while the material is being parsed and sorted, but rather that written material is converted to a speech mode for temporary storage. This hypothesis seems reasonable and, if true, suggests that reading should follow work on speech in the learning process, but not vice versa.

While reading may help increase vocabulary, this is a complex task when characters are involved. Since characters give only limited information about pronunciation, the learner usually must look them up in a dictionary or word list where the romanized equivalent is given. Without reinforcement, items thus acquired rarely become an active component of a student's repertoire. In short, it would seem that learning to speak first can greatly enhance the later acquisition of reading, but there is little evidence to support that reading—a silent enterprise, after all—improves speaking proficiency or that it should logically precede learning to speak.

There is also, at least in Chinese and Japanese, a great deal of confusion about the difference between reading and writing. Native speakers of these languages apparently learn the two skills as one bundle. To many teachers of these languages, it is unacceptable to be able to recognize a word but not be able to write it—"knowing" a word means knowing how to do both. The cognitive effort required for recall, however, as is well known, is much greater than for recognition. Psychologists point to simple examples of this, such as the ability to recognize a face instantly, but the inability to describe even a close friend's face to another person. Reading requires recognition, but not recall, whereas writing—that is, from memory—requires recall. Again, the mixture of these two skills into one has serious curricular consequences. If a program puts equal emphasis on both skills, the pace of instruction must be slowed to the speed at which learners can master the more difficult skill of the two. Since this will obviously be recall, the pace at which one learns to read is unrealistically and unnecessarily reduced to the speed at which one can write characters from memory.

In addition, there seems to be little consideration for the different real-world uses of these two skills. Learners indeed need to be able to write in the target language, but for most this will likely be confined to a small pool of tasks— informal notes, letters, and the like. On the other hand, those concerned with the target culture have multiple reading requirements—from signs and menus to newspapers and specialized materials. Since writing, particularly composition, normally presupposes extensive ability in reading, it would seem reasonable to teach reading and writing as separate skills—both for cognitive and practical reasons—with much more stress, in the early stages, placed on reading.

Overall, there is a need to formulate and justify the sequencing of each of the four skills and to assign the instructional weight given to each carefully. This justification should not come from tradition—either target- or base-language— but from consideration of the psycholinguistic processes involved, the relationships of the skills to each other, and the uses to which the skills will be put after formal instruction.

NATIVE AND NONNATIVE LANGUAGE PARADIGMS

Some of the TFLs have highly developed and articulated language and linguistic traditions going back well over a thousand years. The attachment of the language to the culture can be so strong that language is regarded as a unique and defining characteristic of it. Thus attitudes about the language and the teaching of it to foreigners are often markedly different from those of the foreign linguist who tends to focus on the code and its pragmatic use in communication—minus the deep-seated language attitudes of native speakers.

The difference between the native and nonnative teaching paradigms is ever present in teaching approaches, textbook design, linguistic analysis and presentation of grammar, testing, course content, classroom teaching style, and overall methodology. Japanese presents an interesting example. Traditionally it has been assumed that the Japanese language belongs exclusively to the Japanese people: if one is Japanese, one's language is Japanese, and if one knows Japanese, one should *be* Japanese.

With the increase in the number of foreigners studying the language, this one-to-one correlation is breaking down. Japanese language programs are cropping up everywhere, in many cases taught by native speakers totally lacking in relevant training. Even among some of the most internationally minded, there is often a lingering conviction that foreigners cannot master the Japanese language to a high degree of proficiency. Japanese discuss at great length what kind of Japanese to teach foreigners, and they are even willing to produce textbooks for English speakers with the language altered so as to resemble English more closely. This is obviously misplaced solicitude, guaranteeing linguistic failure. It has been repeatedly pointed out that within their own culture, high-level proficiency in a foreign language is not universally regarded positively, since it can indicate a loss of ethnic purity. Why expose foreigners to a parallel problem by presenting the possibility—remote though it is often assumed to be—that they acquire a superior level of Japanese?

Students of a foreign language are not trying to *become* foreigners. They are studying language in order to be able to communicate with members of a foreign culture through the spoken and/or written target language. The effective language program concentrates on a methodology that suits the mind-set of the learners—that enables them to achieve their goals promptly and efficiently. Nothing is to be gained by regarding foreign adult learners as if they were target-natives studying their native language in a school setting. The program that concentrates from the outset on the writing system is doing just that. It ignores the crucial fact that the native, when introduced to literacy, is already fluent in the spoken language.

It is equally unproductive for target-natives to try to teach their native language to foreigners on the basis of foreign language instruction in their own culture. Yet how often features of the target-native paradigm can be traced to such origins. The temptation is to fall back on one's own experience even though base and target are reversed.

But of course the target-native is absolutely essential to the ideal language program. Who else can serve as the perfect linguistic and cultural model? What, then, is the solution?

First, the nature of foreign language learning must be considered. Unlike the study of history or anthropology or economics, foreign language learning involves both a factual component and a skill component—what we may call a fact-act dichotomy. The fact component, which includes thorough, detailed, objective linguistic and cultural analysis in terms that are meaningful to a foreign language learner, is best handled in the base language, guaranteeing that the student understands and is able to ask questions whenever necessary. The act component requires drill and practice in sufficient amounts to enable students to internalize the fact component—to use it accurately and meaningfully, not simply to talk about it. Both components require highly skilled instruction offered by professionally trained pedagogues.

We are convinced that the ideal foreign language program uses a team of instructors. The fact component is handled by base-natives thoroughly trained in the analysis of the target language and culture and able to describe it in terms that are meaningful to the learners. After all, base-native instructors have followed the exact same route that the student will follow, originally learning the target as a foreign language. Only they know what it is to be a foreigner in the target culture.

The act component is handled by target-natives—who are also professionals thoroughly trained to fill this role. They are the models of the student's target. From them, students are able to observe at close hand—and interact with—living examples of the language and culture they are studying.

These two kinds of instructors work as a team, complementing each other's work, each filling a unique role that cannot be filled equally well by the other. In the early stages of instruction, when more explanation is needed, students require more hours with the base-native than later in the program. However, as they become more proficient in the language, the hours with target-native instructors, who use only the target language in all their teaching, gradually increase, as they handle any necessary explanation in the target language. But even initially, the act component requires a higher percentage of class time than the fact component, simply because of the nature of skill acquisition.

Obviously it is not always possible to have a teaching team, but the concept should be kept in mind as the ideal, with careful compensation for either lacking member through the use of appropriate audiotapes, videotapes, and reading matter. In answer to the question of whether a target-native, thoroughly familiar with the base language and even the culture, through long residence within the base culture, cannot function alone as the ideal teacher, it must be pointed out that there are problems. Such instructors—individuals frequently identified as bilingual and bicultural—are in fact often among our most skilled language instructors, markedly superior to the

less qualified among the team teachers. The danger is that as they become increasingly identified with and able to relate to the base culture, they tend to become less authentic models of the target culture—a fact often not recognized by their students. In some cases, their long experience with students has made them tolerant of a variety of the language that would actually be unintelligible to the average target-native. This is most apt to happen when one instructor vacillates between target and base. What is more, they will always lack the personal experience of having originally learned the target language as a foreign language and of ever having actually been a foreigner within the target culture. If they use both base and target languages in their teaching—as is often the case— they counteract the benefits derived from encouraging students automatically to use the target language exclusively in interacting with a target-native instructor. In other words, they are unquestionably invaluable members of a language staff, but they are not the equivalent of a target-base combination.

TEXT MATERIALS

The lack of high-quality teaching materials is a constant problem in the TFL field. For many of the languages there are few materials to choose from, and those that are available tend to be of poor quality. Parallel to the mistaken assumption that anyone who knows a language is automatically qualified to teach it is the equally mistaken assumption that the same individuals are equally qualified to produce text materials.

For some of the TFLs, new textbooks are being published at a rapid rate, but the overall quality continues to be poor.

Some are produced by linguists who are more concerned with complex linguistic analysis and description than with sociolinguistic or psycholinguistic concerns. The goals of the language student are ignored as is consideration of pacing and mastery, as the materials focus exclusively on a theoretical linguistic model.

Surprising as it may seem, materials stemming from the target-native paradigm often present a distorted version of the target language. This may range from an idealized standard to a special dialect deliberately created to match the students' base language. Explanations tend to be extremely brief and seriously inadequate for the foreign student. For those languages with complex writing systems, there is often immediate emphasis on reading and writing from the outset. After all, what else does one study about one's native language in school? In considering the relation between written and oral skills, two facts must always be kept in mind: (1) the best readers of the target language are the target-natives, and they all acquired oral skills before learning a single written symbol; and (2) speaking ability is a positive factor in the acquisition of reading skills, but reading ability does not improve speaking ability. Teaching materials should reflect a recognition of these facts by stressing oral language before introducing the written symbols that represent it. With this ordering, students can learn to read, whereas initial concentration on written symbols promotes decoding.

Language teaching materials that use vocabulary as the primary unit of instruction should be regarded with deep suspicion. The implied message in such methodology is that students are equipped to engage in foreign language production on the basis of translation of their base language. Even isolated basic sentences create problems. The basic unit must always be a sample discourse. It may be extremely brief, but the student must learn how target-natives construct conversations in precisely defined situations. There is no way for students to predict transition words, intonations, deletions, and the like without a target-native model. The basic dialogue should be the introductory pedagogical unit, subsequently analyzed, drilled, manipulated, adapted, and applied. All vocabulary and structural patterns must be introduced within contexts generated by a target-native. The student with highly developed imaginative skills stemming from the base culture, who creates utterances a target-native would never produce, must unfortunately be squelched!

The development of sophisticated text materials also requires good judgment as to the choice and ordering of vocabulary and structural patterns, and the relative proportion of drills and utilization material to new material. Once again a team of target- and base-natives is recommended. The production of truly authentic language samples requires a linguistically sophisticated target-native, but the base-native linguist, who shares the students' mind-set and who knows through personal experience what it means to be a foreigner in the target culture, plays a vital role in analyzing and explaining, and in making decisions related to situations, pacing, ordering, and levels of difficulty.

When a foreign language becomes sufficiently popular to give rise to the publication of multiple competing texts, an interesting phenomenon can be noted. There will be increasing claims that each new text makes the foreign language easier to learn. For Americans, who always want the fastest and easiest route, the suggestion of simplified language learning is very appealing. The quick and easy textbook deludes the unsuspecting foreigner into thinking there is some magic way to learn a foreign language—just like that miraculous way to lose 14 pounds in one week. Significant language learning under such circumstances is as unlikely as permanent weight loss.

The acquisition of one's native language is undoubtedly the most remarkable accomplishment of anyone's lifetime, and to lure unsuspecting potential learners into thinking they can acquire a second language without extended effort is reprehensible. Of course, we can produce an entire population able to say "hello" and "good-bye" in ten languages, but, to quote the linguist Henry Lee Smith, "nine women each pregnant for a month will never produce a baby." To be sure, we do need continuing research on how to do the job more efficiently, but we must not in any way diffuse or distort the task, which is to bring a significant number of learners to a high level of proficiency in foreign languages, even those languages that are native within markedly contrastive cultures.

ANNALS, *AAPSS,* **490,** March 1987

Training for High-Level Language Skills

By CORNELIUS C. KUBLER

ABSTRACT: The majority of attention in foreign language teaching in the United States has in the past been focused on the lower levels of instruction. While many students begin the study of various languages each year, only very few continue to the level where they can truly function. This country's interests demand that we train more students to higher levels of proficiency in a greater variety of languages than ever before. To improve high-level language training, steps need to be taken to (1) coordinate and/or provide advanced-level, intensive language instruction in the United States and abroad; (2) train teachers in the techniques of high-level instruction; (3) catalog, adapt, prepare, and disseminate advanced training materials; (4) conduct research into the most effective training techniques at the higher levels; (5) promote language proficiency testing and certification; and (6) disseminate the knowledge and experience gained from the preceding.

Cornelius C. Kubler holds an M.A. in Chinese literature from National Taiwan University and a Ph.D. in East Asian linguistics from Cornell University. He has taught at the Language Center of National Taiwan University, Eisenhower College, and the Foreign Service Institute. Since 1981 he has served as principal of the American Institute in Taiwan Chinese Language & Area Studies School. He is the author of four books and numerous articles on language learning and linguistics.

BY far the majority of attention and effort in foreign language teaching in the United States has up until now been focused on the beginning stages of instruction. This is true of the types of classes being taught, teaching materials, and teaching methodologies.

Today most Americans studying foreign languages, whether they begin their studies in high school or in college, never progress beyond the elementary or intermediate levels. The normal pattern is to take a year or two of a language and then to drop it, never to pursue language studies again.

Enrollments for practically all languages taught are highest for the first year and then drop drastically with each successive level. For example, according to a recent survey of college and university enrollments in Chinese, there were during 1978-79 a total of 4706 students enrolled in first-year Chinese language classes, 2215 in second-year, 1244 in third-year, and only 882 in fourth-year.[1] And this in a language with a writing system so difficult that the level reached after anything less than three or four years of study is still so low as to leave the student functionally illiterate! As the authors of that survey comment, "While students enrolled in Chinese courses number in the thousands, the number of Americans attaining advanced levels of speaking and reading competence—enough to be able to communicate readily in a variety of social and professional contexts—is very small, probably not more than 200 to 300 per year at the most."[2]

The great majority of students in our language classes today never really attain the levels of competency required to permit genuine use. As a result, aside from the limited value of studying a language as an intellectual exercise and perhaps gaining a vague familiarity with a foreign culture, the initial investment in a language that students, their teachers, and the educational system have made is largely wasted.

While there now exist usable textbooks and effective methods for most languages at the elementary level, materials and methodologies peter out rapidly at the intermediate and advanced levels. Even when available, upper-level language instruction often consists only of reading and translation of literary texts, with very little attention paid to the contemporary spoken language. Ways must be found to encourage more students to continue training through the upper levels and to render those advanced courses that already exist more effective.

American interests, including the national security, demand that we train more of our citizens to higher levels of proficiency in a greater variety of languages than ever before. We must establish clear goals and set high standards for ourselves, adopting a can-do attitude rather than resigning ourselves to the status quo. In many respects, including advances in textbooks, dictionaries, teaching methods, and technology—not to speak of vastly improved international communication and the fact that languages and cultures seem to be moving closer to each other—the study of foreign languages has become much easier than it used to be. We should be able to improve upon the past generation. We can and must do better than we have so far.

1. Peter A. Eddy, James J. Wrenn, and Sophia A. Behrens, *Chinese Language Study in American Higher Education: State of the Art* (Washington, DC: Center for Applied Linguistics, 1980), p. 13.
2. Ibid., p. 42.

WHAT IS HIGH LEVEL?

It will be useful at the outset to be clear about our use of terms. First, what exactly do we mean by "high level"?

At the Foreign Service Institute (FSI) in Washington, D.C., a system whereby language proficiency is described in terms of six distinct levels on a scale ranging from zero to five has been in use since the 1950s. This system, which has of late attracted considerable attention in academic circles, distinguishes between speaking proficiency (S) and reading proficiency (R).

The definitions of the six levels may be paraphrased as follows: S-0 or R-0, no practical proficiency; S-1 or R-1, can cope with the most common survival-type needs and read very simple prose such as in basic textbooks; S-2 or R-2, can handle routine social demands, simple conversations about current events, and limited work requirements and can read and understand the gist of international news articles and simple letters; S-3 or R-3, can discuss current events and professional topics with relative ease and can read newspaper editorials with only occasional use of a dictionary; S-4 or R-4, can speak on and read a wide variety of difficult topics with proficiency approaching, though not equaling, that of a native; S-5 or R-5, proficiency equivalent to that of an educated native. A plus sign can be added to the designation of any level when proficiency substantially exceeds one skill level but does not fully meet the criteria for the next level.[3]

For the purposes of this article, we shall define "high level" as S-3/R-3 or higher proficiency. Beginning at this level, for example, students could enroll for classes at a foreign university, scholars would be able to conduct advanced research in the target language, and businesspeople or diplomats would be competent to engage in substantive business such as conducting negotiations and delivering briefings. Actually, there is nothing particularly high about the S-3/R-3 level, as it represents merely the minimum required to be able to function professionally. In my opinion, however,

---

3. The official Foreign Service Institute language-skill-level descriptions, as recently revised by the Interagency Language Roundtable, follow. For speaking: S-0, no proficiency, means "unable to function in the spoken language"; S-1, elementary proficiency, means "able to satisfy minimum courtesy requirements and maintain very simple face-to-face conversations on familiar topics"; S-2, limited working proficiency, means "able to satisfy routine social demands and limited work requirements"; S-3, general professional proficiency, means "able to speak the language with sufficient structural accuracy and vocabulary to participate effectively in most formal and informal conversations on practical, social, and professional topics"; S-4, advanced professional proficiency, means "able to use the language fluently and accurately on all levels normally pertinent to professional needs"; and S-5, functionally native proficiency, means "speaking proficiency is functionally equivalent to that of a highly articulate, well-educated native speaker and reflects the cultural standards of the country where the language is natively spoken." For reading: R-0, no proficiency, means "no practical ability to read the language"; R-1, elementary proficiency, means "sufficient comprehension to read very simple connected written material in a form equivalent to usual printing or typescript"; R-2, limited working proficiency, means "sufficient comprehension to read simple, authentic written material in a form equivalent to usual printing or typescript on subjects within a familiar context"; R-3, general professional proficiency, means "able to read within a normal range of speed and with almost complete comprehension a variety of authentic prose material on unfamiliar subjects"; R-4, advanced professional proficiency, means "able to read fluently and accurately all styles and forms of the language pertinent to professional needs"; R-5, functionally native proficiency, means "reading proficiency is functionally equivalent to that of the well-educated native reader."

it would be unrealistic at the present time to hope that large numbers of students could be brought to level four and, to be sure, there is some question as to whether certain individuals could ever attain that level in a foreign language.

Most domestic training programs now bring students to the S-1+ or, at most, S-2 level after several years of part-time study. Reading proficiency may be, but is not necessarily, somewhat higher. The main thrust of this article will be on moving students from approximately S-2/R-2 to S-3/R-3.

Although training in all four skills—comprehension, speaking, reading, and writing—is important, I feel that so as to counter the widespread present bias toward the reading of academic materials, special emphasis in the immediate future should be placed on oral training involving practical, job-related language content. Also, although most of my comments in this article are applicable to all languages, I will emphasize training in four of the most important, most difficult, and yet least commonly taught languages—Chinese, Japanese, Arabic, and Russian. This emphasis reflects not only my own particular background, in East Asian language pedagogy, but also the fact that the lack of classes, materials, and appropriate methods at the higher levels for these languages is much more critical than for the more commonly taught ones such as French, Spanish, or German.

OVERVIEW OF EXISTING ADVANCED
LANGUAGE TRAINING PROGRAMS

For the less commonly taught languages, there are at present no truly advanced language training programs offered in the United States. Even for the more common languages, many courses termed advanced may in fact

not be at a level higher than S-2 or S-2+. Due to the lack of sufficient students at the higher levels, many advanced programs are barely viable and amount to being no more than directed reading or tutorial programs in which students laboriously decode written materials through the extensive use of dictionaries.

To be sure, a number of relatively successful intensive training programs in the critical languages exist domestically, such as the Full-year Asian Language Concentration program at Cornell University, which covers Chinese, Japanese, and Indonesian, or the one-year intensive courses given at FSI and the Defense Language Institute. These programs, however, good as they are, can hardly be termed advanced since they do not take students beyond the S-2/R-2 or, at the very most, S-2+/R-2+ levels.

Overseas there are a number of advanced-level training centers, some of which are American-run and others that are entirely local operations. I will list only a few of the more important ones for the less commonly taught languages.

For Chinese there are the Inter-University Program for Chinese Language Studies, the Mandarin Training Center, and the American Institute in Taiwan Chinese Language & Area Studies School, all of which are located in Taipei; Beijing Language Institute and the Center for International Educational Exchange programs in Beijing, Nanjing, and Shanghai; New Asia-Yale-in-China Chinese Language Center and the British Ministry of Defence Chinese Language School in Hong Kong; and Nanyang University in Singapore.

For Japanese there are the Inter-University Center for Japanese Language Studies in Tokyo and the FSI Japanese Field School in Yokohama. For Arabic there are the Center for

Arabic Study Abroad at the American University in Cairo and the FSI Arabic Field School in Tunis. For Russian the U.S. Army operates the Russian Institute in Garmisch, West Germany, with a two-year program leading to advanced-level proficiency.

All of these programs offer advanced instruction in speaking, reading, and—in some cases—writing, with small classes and frequent tailoring of programs to the individual needs of the student. They have made a major contribution to language studies in the United States in that the majority of scholars and diplomats today who specialize in these areas and languages have spent some time at one or another of the centers. Most of the programs, however, suffer at least to some degree from various problems, including lack of high-quality training materials; uneven quality of the teaching; relative isolation from new developments in language pedagogy in the United States; and insufficient or uncertain financial support. Moreover, most of the programs have restricted enrollments so that only a limited number of American students can participate in them.

SPECIAL REQUIREMENTS OF HIGH-LEVEL TRAINING

Students studying at the higher levels have to continue learning more vocabulary and grammar, of course, as they did at the beginning level, but there are certain special requirements of high-level training that distinguish it from basic training.

One special requirement at the advanced level is for smaller class size. Whereas beginning drill work can be carried out effectively in classes of five to ten students, there seems to be a consensus that higher-level conversation classes should not be larger than about three students.[4] Indeed, for training in speaking at the S-2+ level or above, there should be a provision for a certain amount of carefully organized tutorial training.

The higher up on the S scale one progresses, the greater is the need for specialization and individualization of the training, depending on the student's particular strengths and weaknesses, learning style, interests, and job needs. Training content must be increasingly professionally oriented at the higher levels, and there is a requirement for some instructors with both expertise in language teaching and special knowledge of various fields.

At the advanced level, it is essential that students undertake at least part of their training in the target-language country. Indeed, it is doubtful if students can reach advanced levels of proficiency any other way. But to be effective, such programs must be carefully planned and implemented. It emphatically cannot be assumed that a year, or even two or three years, spent in a foreign country will necessarily result in the acquisition of high-level language skills.

THE ROAD AHEAD

It is clear that although a great deal of useful work has already been done, the present situation leaves much to be desired. The keys to ensuring future success are careful short- and long-term planning, tight organization, and close

---

4. At the FSI field schools in Taipei and Yokohama, advanced conversation classes are limited to three students per section. The interuniversity programs in Taipei and Tokyo restrict conversation classes to two to four students. In addition, at all of these schools, students have one or more hours a day of tutorials.

cooperation—not duplication of efforts—among the various institutions involved. Therefore, the national foreign language agenda should include providing, coordinating, researching, and generally supporting advanced language training both domestically and abroad. The rest of this article concerns specific recommendations for what that agenda should include in the immediate future.

LANGUAGE INSTRUCTION IN THE UNITED STATES

A detailed survey should be made of advanced language courses presently offered in the United States with indications of weak areas and needs. Depending on the results of such a survey, there should be established full-year as well as summer-only advanced intensive language programs for college and university students, business people, government personnel, and the general public.

It is essential that in the future there be more centralized planning so that the various institutions complement rather than duplicate each other. Scant resources must be combined. The smaller colleges and universities often have insufficient numbers of students to justify offering advanced courses in all languages. By pooling students and staff from several institutions, such courses could be offered. There must be more cooperative agreements among institutions such as those now existing in the case of a few special summer language programs. The government language schools, which have considerable experience in teaching at the advanced levels, should be included in any agreements to the extent possible.

While the language training programs will need to be large enough to be viable at all levels from beginning through advanced, they should not be so large that quality suffers due to quantity. Assuming for the moment that sufficient qualified applicants, staff, facilities, and funding were all available, the ideal size for a two-year intensive program leading to S-3/R-3 competence in one of the critical languages might be 30 students for the first year and 20 for the second year.

Special emphasis in instruction should be given to developing genuine communicative competence in students. How are invitations, requests, refusals, offers, acceptances, compliments, complaints, and criticism handled in the foreign language? There is a great need for developing job-related exercises requiring performance of prescribed tasks within—and, in some cases, outside of—the language classroom.

Training programs at the higher levels should utilize current materials from the target-language culture—such as newspapers, magazines, and radio and television programs—as early as possible. Such materials are essential for the success of advanced training programs.

Special courses need to be developed in the comprehension of television and radio broadcasts, interpreting, translation, public speaking, comprehension of dialectally influenced speech, and reading of cursive script. With the recent interest in language for special purposes, we need to prepare materials to teach students the language of international trade, banking, travel industry management, diplomacy, the health professions, engineering, agriculture, and other fields. We must try harder to tailor instruction to the future job needs of our students.

More thought also needs to be given to selection criteria for students applying for advanced programs. Selection criteria, while important at all levels, are especially important at the higher levels if the goals of the course are to be met. Candidates for advanced training should be highly motivated, outgoing, aggressive, and preferably young and single. They should have a good record in learning at least one other foreign language and should have already attained within less than the normal amount of time S-2/R-2 proficiency in the target language. It will also be of benefit if they have some prior area studies background in the culture of the country the language of which they are studying.

Languages are hard to learn and easy to forget. The problem of maintaining high-level language skills once achieved is most deserving of our attention. We need carefully thought-out language maintenance programs for persons who have already reached advanced levels of proficiency and wish to maintain their language skills. These need not, of course, be full-time courses, but research should be undertaken on the type and intensity of training required for students to be able to maintain existing levels of competency.

Refresher courses designed for people who attained high levels of proficiency in the past but have become rusty, or for those who wish to upgrade previous skills, should also be available. The problem of language skill attrition is one only now beginning to be addressed. Once we gain a better understanding of exactly what skills are lost, we will be able to devise more efficient ways to restore and add to them.

LANGUAGE INSTRUCTION OVERSEAS

There is a real question of whether so-called advanced conversation can be taught effectively anywhere other than in the target-language country. Upper-level language training cannot be done entirely in the United States, a period of residence in-country being essential if students are to attain advanced levels of proficiency. Once the student has a good grasp of basic vocabulary and grammar and is at the point where he or she can use the language for most daily needs, being in the target-language environment will lead to faster progress than being in any other environment.

For the more commonly taught European languages, students who already have a solid background in the language may be able to attain high-level skills by living on their own in the country for a year or two. A much more systematic approach, however, is called for in the case of the less commonly taught languages due to their inherent difficulty as well as greater cultural differences. Just living overseas for a period of time is not enough! In-country training programs must be carefully planned and executed and should consist of a total-immersion program combining several hours daily of advanced language classes, auditing of courses at local universities, research projects requiring extensive contact with the society, and, if possible, residence with a local family or other local citizens.

Existing overseas training programs in the various languages should be identified, described, and evaluated by both professionals and past participants. A survey should be made of requirements for additional overseas facilities, and new centers should be established in areas of the world where they are needed.

It is in our own interests that we make every effort possible to assist overseas institutions in improving the quality of their instruction and in keeping up-to-date on developments in language teaching in this country. Perhaps some of the staff of overseas schools could be brought to teach at the centralized collaborative institutions for a year or two and then return to their home institutions. Such an arrangement would be most beneficial to both sides.

These institutions should make recommendations to students' home universities concerning credits to be awarded for overseas study, based on the reputation of the particular program and on students' proficiency levels as tested on their return.

Country-specific handbooks should be prepared for students planning to go overseas with detailed suggestions on how to go about their studies. A handbook with recommendations for running successful language training programs *in situ* could also be written for educators and administrators.

It is important that there be improved coordination and integration between domestic and overseas language training programs. Those responsible for domestic programs need a better understanding of overseas programs and vice versa.

As has already been mentioned, refresher courses need to be provided for those whose language skills have weakened. Since they offer the chance not only for classroom training but also for the use of the language in everyday situations and for research, the overseas centers would seem to be the ideal location for most refresher training.

Refresher courses overseas should provide a combination of accelerated review of the basics, some individual work with a tutor who is a specialist in the student's field, and residence in the target-language environment. The Inter-University Program for Chinese Language Studies in Taipei currently runs two refresher programs along these lines. One, in the summer, consists of language study only, and one, during the academic year, includes both language study and research.

One of the best ways to learn language beyond the elementary level is in everyday-life situations where language is used to accomplish tasks rather than studied for its own sake. Since working in the native society can be of great benefit to language learning, we need a clearinghouse on overseas work programs available for American students who have some knowledge of a foreign language. Although English teaching will probably always offer the most opportunities, efforts should be made, for obvious reasons, to locate work in other areas as well.

TEACHER TRAINING

Greatly strengthened teacher training is vital if we are to improve our teaching of foreign languages. Courses should be offered concentrating on foreign language pedagogy at the advanced levels. Teachers in training should do extensive observation of advanced classes themselves. They also need to be trained in administering and rating language proficiency exams.

Bilingual teachers' guides to instruction in the various languages should be prepared and possible curricula for advanced language courses drawn up and made available. Videotapes of successful upper-level classes taught by experienced teachers, with both English and target-language commentary, should be produced to be disseminated throughout the country.

A centralized resource must be created to facilitate the exchange of teachers between the United States and foreign countries. It could serve, for example, as a clearinghouse for language instructors from abroad wishing to apply to teach in the States for two- or three-year periods. Similarly, programs could be developed that would take American foreign language teachers, whether native speakers who have lived in the United States for many years or Anglophones, to the target-language environment so that they can bring their knowledge of the language and culture up to date.

Finally, a teacher certification program should be begun including official FSI-type proficiency ratings in the target language and English. A separate certificate could be awarded indicating pedagogical training and experience. Job descriptions of the future would include these as part of the requirements.

MATERIALS COLLECTION AND DISTRIBUTION

Advanced language teaching materials compiled in the United States and overseas during the past few decades need to be surveyed and cataloged. Bibliographic information should be entered in computer files for periodic updating; it should be published and disseminated widely.

We need a central collection point and clearinghouse for advanced language training materials of all kinds, including language textbooks. Such materials would also include materials from the target-language culture such as books, newspapers, magazines, government documents, audiotapes of radio broadcasts, videotapes of television programs, movies, and relevant computer software. At present, access to such live materials—which are indispensable for successful advanced language training programs—often presents problems, especially for smaller institutions that may have limited resources or few contacts overseas.

Of considerable use would be the reprinting of materials that are no longer available elsewhere.

MATERIALS PREPARATION AND ADAPTATION

A survey of advanced-training needs should be conducted with input from language instructors, supervisory staff, students currently in training, recent graduates of training programs, and employers of graduates.

Based on the results of the survey, new, up-to-date, practical, job-related training materials meeting high linguistic and pedagogical standards should be prepared. To the extent possible, these should be integrated and cumulative, building on each other so as to take the student sequentially through the entire range of skills from the elementary through the advanced levels. One of the biggest problems now facing teachers of the less commonly taught languages is lack of continuity in materials.

Supplementary materials such as student workbooks, teacher's guides, classroom charts, tests, flashcards, audiotapes, videotapes, and computer software should be available for each new textbook produced.

Improved communication and coordination among the various institutions is essential if we are to make the most efficient use of limited resources. At present, materials writers are often unaware of related projects that others in the field may have in progress. By promoting contact among language training personnel throughout the United States and overseas, wasteful duplication of efforts would be avoided.

Existing advanced training materials should be adapted and improved if possible. There exist in a number of the less commonly taught languages tentative, in-house versions of materials that are worth updating and adapting into permanent editions. The wise use of resources requires that we build on previous work where feasible, rather than always starting out anew.

General vocabularies at three levels—basic, through the 1+ level; intermediate, through about 2+; and advanced, 3 to 3+—for the various languages should be prepared and published for use by students, teachers, and textbook writers. The same could be attempted for grammar constructions, sociolinguistic situations, and cultural information. These materials, which will need to distinguish carefully between speaking and reading usages, could also serve as useful reference points in testing.

We earlier discussed the need for training in language for special purposes. Initially, special vocabularies could be prepared for the various subfields, such as business, medicine, and diplomacy, with comprehensive textbooks on these topics—including conversations, vocabulary and grammar notes, and exercises—to be put out as time and resources permit.

A capacity to disseminate the new materials produced will also be essential if we are to achieve our goal of influencing language training throughout the country.

TESTING

Independent testing teams composed of trained faculty members from several of the institutions should be established to travel around the country to administer language proficiency exams. The testing teams should be composed of both native-speaking and non-native-speaking testers who have high proficiency in the target language and English and who are familiar with the problems facing the American student of the language. A less expensive, but less ideal, alternative to on-site testing would be taping the oral exams and sending them to a centralized location for rating.

Sample tape recordings and written copies of proficiency examinations in the various languages and English at the S-1/R-1 through S-4/R-4 levels should be prepared for distribution to testers, teachers, and students. Periodic in-service training sessions should be held to ensure that uniform testing standards are maintained.

One excellent way to promote high-level training would be the institution of a system whereby specific proficiency ratings are required for certification for various language-related occupations. For instance, a graduate student might be required to attain S-3/R-3 proficiency in a particular language to qualify to conduct research abroad; a business-person sent for training by his or her company might be required to reach S-3/R-2 to be eligible for an overseas assignment; a scholar could be required to have S-3+/R-3+ proficiency for certification in his or her area; and an advertisement for an assistant professor of Russian could include a statement requiring attainment of S-4/R-4 proficiency as a prerequisite for employment. To this end, ways must be found to publicize and gain general acceptance for the FSI rating method.

RESEARCH

Research should be conducted into the particular instructional techniques that are most effective at the higher levels. Naturally, this will depend to a considerable degree on the students involved—their ages, educational backgrounds, motivation for learning, and specializations—as well as on the location of the training—in the United States versus overseas—and, not least, on the particular language.

There is a great need for scientific experimentation in different methods and materials. Discussions of the relative merits of different materials and approaches have in the past tended to be long on polemic, but short on empirical evidence. Experimental classrooms should be established as laboratories for testing various hypotheses about language training. Much useful work could be done, particularly on the development of new training methods for advanced students utilizing videotapes, movies, and computer technology.

Some of the questions that need to be answered are: What is the best and/or fastest and/or most cost-effective way to achieve advanced proficiency in a particular language? Can students be trained to advanced levels of proficiency in only one skill when required—for instance, only speaking or only reading? Which techniques work best in which types of learning situations for which kinds of students? Which techniques result in the best retention over time and in easier reacquisition later? What are the relative merits of part-time and intensive instruction? Should these two instructional modes in some cases be combined? In intensive instruction, what is the ideal number of contact hours per day? At what point in the program should overseas training begin? What is the ideal balance between domestic and overseas training? What does the ideal overseas program consist of? Should there be a finishing course back home? These are all important questions that have in the past not been dealt with as

objectively or in as much detail as they deserve.

DISSEMINATION

Ways must be found to share the knowledge and experience gained with as many people as possible.

Articles in appropriate magazines and journals both for the general reader and for the specialist could heighten awareness of problems and publicize work in progress. Workshops and teaching demonstrations could be held around the country to familiarize teachers with new techniques and orientations. These should be recorded on videotape for later viewing by those unable to attend the meetings. Broadcasting on public television would, of course, be another possibility. It is important that appropriate and sufficient follow-up be conducted to gauge what effect the workshops and other activities have had; any necessary adjustments should be made as soon as possible.

A series of national conferences that include personnel from both academia and government should be convened on an annual basis for each of the major language families to share information about problems and suggest solutions. As Lambert and his colleagues suggest, hosts could be the Interagency Language Roundtable on the government side and on the academic side one or more of the national organizations such as the Center for Applied Linguistics, the American Council on the Teaching of Foreign Languages, the Modern Language Association, or the professional organizations of the teachers of the various languages.[5]

5. Richard D. Lambert with Elinor G. Barber, Margaret Merrill, Eleanor Jorden, and Leon I. Twarog, *Beyond Growth: The Next Stage in Language and Area Studies* (Washington, DC:

FINANCIAL SUPPORT

Financial support for the activities outlined in this article, including scholarships and fellowships for students in intensive courses, should be secured from U.S. and foreign governments, foundations, and corporations.

So as to serve as an incentive to promote advanced instruction, the bulk of the financial support should in the future be concentrated at the upper levels. Consideration should be given to a system in which the amount of government financial support provided is linked to the training results of a program. For example, as is the practice in many government training programs, bonus payments could be made to students for achievement of, say S-3/R-3 proficiency as determined by independent, outside testers. Similar bonus payments could be made to an institution for each student brought to a predetermined level.

For its own sake, the national government should increase the number of government-sponsored scholarships and fellowships for students going abroad for advanced study of a foreign language. A part of the financial support could be withheld—or in the form of a loan—until testing on the return of the student confirms that he or she has reached a required minimum level of proficiency.

Possibilities for funding from foreign governments and organizations should also be explored. Sufficient financial support must be secured for the better overseas training centers that lack resources of their own. Moreover, to encourage long-term planning and stability, financial support for all of these activities should be guaranteed to institu-

tions for longer periods than at present—perhaps periods of five years at a time.

Although additional funding will be essential, we must be realistic and understand that these are financially difficult times for all concerned—government, business, universities, and individuals. It is necessary that we examine closely our present use of funds and achieve economies wherever possible. Certainly there is some waste now going on that could be reduced. We should reexamine our priorities and present practices to see what improvements could be effected with existing funds.

A CALL TO ACTION

It is painfully obvious that in spite of the considerable effort and resources that have been expended, far too few Americans are currently reaching the levels of proficiency needed to be able to function in foreign languages. The level of usable foreign language skills among our general population today is dangerously low. We are simply not getting a good enough return on our investment as too many students terminate their language studies before they reach the point where they can put the skills they have acquired to real use.

Certainly, the recommendations in this article will need to be revised and refined in the course of time as further experience is gained. But let us begin somewhere and let us begin now! As an important member of the international community, our country must ensure that a much larger number of our citizens than in the past be trained in foreign languages to levels where they can truly function. The time has come to address our national need in this area. If we as a nation set our minds to tackling the problem, there is no reason why we should not be able to succeed.

Association of American Universities, 1984), pp. 31-32.

ANNALS, *AAPSS,* **490,** March 1987

Language Teaching in the Federal Government: A Personal Perspective

By RAY T. CLIFFORD

ABSTRACT: Historically, communication between foreign language schools in the federal government and academic foreign language programs has been extremely limited. Typical government and academic programs are compared on the 11 significant program characteristics of instructional goals, student characteristics, class size, curriculum, instructional staff, assessment criteria, program length, skill modalities emphasized, instructional methodology, results attained, and supporting empirical research. This series of comparisons reveals a striking contrast in instructional objectives and procedures that has served to reduce cooperation between government and academic foreign language programs. It is argued, however, that these significant differences should be viewed as complimentary, rather than divisive. The combined assets of both foreign language teaching communities provide heretofore untapped resources for empirical research into national foreign language issues. Options are then described for cooperative research ventures to address these issues.

Ray T. Clifford received B.A. and M.A. degrees in German from Brigham Young University and a Ph.D. in second language education from the University of Minnesota. He has taught German at elementary, high school, and college levels, as well as preservice and in-service courses for foreign language teachers. Since 1978 he has been involved in foreign language program administration and is currently provost of the Defense Language Institute in Monterey, California.

ORMAL language training in the federal government began in the 1940s and has been expanding ever since. The first formal language courses were taught in 1941 when the United States Army started Japanese language classes at the Presidio of San Francisco. In the same year, the United States Navy began teaching Japanese at the University of California, Berkeley. The State Department began teaching language courses at the Foreign Service Institute (FSI) in 1946. Eventually the army and navy language programs were consolidated into a single language school, the Defense Language Institute Foreign Language Center in Monterey, California. For the last 20 years the Central Intelligence Agency and the National Security Agency have also offered foreign language (FL) instruction; however, these programs operate on a smaller scale than the Defense Language Institute (DLI) and FSI.

In 1985 DLI and FSI taught a combined total of over 750,000 classroom hours of FL instruction. By comparison, an estimated 5 million hours of classroom instruction in FLs were taught by colleges and universities in the United States.[1] While it is impressive that fully one-eighth of the post-secondary FL instruction offered in the United States was provided by these two government language schools, the figures shift dramatically when one considers enrollment rather than hours of instruction provided. The academic language programs taught over 900,000 students, whereas the government schools taught only about 7000 students in their standard resident FL programs. These data provide clear evidence that government language schools provide more instruction to a relatively small number of students, while academic programs specialize in large enrollments of limited duration. This sharp contrast is but one of a series of dichotomies that emerge when one compares government and academic language programs. In fact, these programs are often so different that communication and cooperation between the government and academic communities have suffered.

The general attitude of professionals in the academic community concerning government programs has generally been one of indifference. On the other hand, the prevalent perception of government program administrators has been, because of their graduates' superior proficiency, that the academic FL community had nothing to offer government programs.[2]

The fact that there has been no sustained cooperation between government language schools and the academic community in the past cannot be accepted as an argument for allowing this situation to continue. In fact, the differences between government FL schools and academic programs increase, rather than diminish, the benefits possible from cooperative initiatives in areas ranging from practical considerations such as curriculum development and teacher training to more esoteric research initiatives concerning language acquisition, teaching methodologies, trait instability, and learning styles.

1. Richard Brod, personal correspondence, 1986. Data are extrapolated from "Census of Foreign Language Registrations" (Survey, Modern Language Association, 1983) (see *ADFL Bulletin*, 16(2):57-63 [1985]) and "MLA-ADFL Survey of Foreign Language Departments" (Survey, Modern Language Association and Association of Departments of Foreign Languages, 1984-85).

2. Allen I. Weinstein, "Foreign Language Majors: The Washington Perspective," *ADFL Bulletin*, 6(4):18-27 (1975).

The following comparison between government and academic FL programs is provided in an attempt to organize the diversity present in both programs through what could be called a subjective factor analysis. This subjective analysis, as with statistical data reduction techniques, has both advantages and disadvantages. At the same time that it identifies central tendencies for classification purposes, it is also forced to ignore the full range of programs available. FL teaching, both inside and outside of the government, has always been as diverse as the teachers who practice this less than perfectly understood art. Readers with firsthand experience in either academic or government language programs will recognize a lack of precise fit if the following generalizations are applied to any specific course of instruction. Also, exceptions to the following generalizations clearly exist. Middlebury College's intensive summer sessions and Cornell's Full-year Asian Language Concentration program are well-known examples of FL instruction that do not fit standard academic norms. Similarly, in addition to their standard courses, government schools offer introductory classes such as FSI's Familiarization and Short-Term training and DLI's Headstart and Gateway courses. Still, there are identifiable trends that have sufficient validity to be of use in comparing government and academic programs as long as the reader recognizes that these descriptions are not poles on a continuum, but measures of central tendencies the associated ranges of which may indeed overlap.

The following 11 distinguishing features of FL instruction are therefore offered as significant points of departure for describing and comparing the FL programs of the U.S. government and the academic community.

INSTRUCTIONAL GOALS

Differences in instructional goals underlie and contribute to all of the contrasts between government and academic programs. The primary purpose of government FL training is to provide students with sufficient functional language ability to prepare them for future job assignments. Although the appropriateness of the term "training" is often questioned, government FL programs have been generally referred to as training programs rather than education programs. In contrast, the instructional goals of academic language programs have been predominately educational in that language is taught primarily as a means of access to the great literature of the world or as a way to expand students' intellectual horizons. In recent years, however, some educational programs have been moving toward relevant offerings such as FL for business applications and survival courses for tourists. This movement has made these courses more parallel in purpose to government instruction, but it has resulted in the criticism that such courses are vocational rather than academic.

CHARACTERISTICS OF STUDENTS

In government language schools almost all students attending have been screened on language learning aptitude; however, the minimum entry requirements vary from one government school to another. DLI uses as its measure of aptitude the Defense Language Aptitude Battery, and FSI uses the Modern Language Aptitude Test. No direct equivalency between scores on the Defense Language Aptitude Battery and the Modern Language Aptitude Test has been developed, but limited double testing of students has shown FSI students to have higher aptitude scores than do DLI students. FSI students also have higher aptitude scores than the population in general. The average score on the Modern Language Aptitude Test for its norming population was 50 points with a standard deviation of 10. By comparison, the average score of FSI students on this test is now 59.5, or almost a standard deviation higher than that found in the norming population. The average for Foreign Service officers is even higher.[3]

Almost all of the current DLI students are high school graduates and 24 percent have a bachelor's degree or better, but no data are available that would allow a comparison of language aptitude between DLI students and students in nongovernment programs. Students in secondary school and college programs have not been subjected to aptitude testing since the late 1960s, when FL enrollments began to decline and instructional availability exceeded the number of students demanding that instruction. Undergraduate degree requirements notwithstanding, it is likely that self-selection through elective enrollments has generally placed the more motivated and/or gifted students in FL programs.

CLASS SIZE

A major difference between government and academic language programs, which is immediately obvious even to the casual observer, is class size. The maximum class size for beginning language classes at DLI is ten students, and some classes are taught on a one-on-one tutorial basis. Overall, the average class size is fewer than eight students. The maximum class size at FSI is six students, but the average class size is close to one-half that number. In contrast, the Modern Language Association survey of foreign language departments, taken in 1984 and 1985, revealed average class sizes at universities and colleges to be 21 students per class for beginning classes, and 15, 10, and 7 students per class for intermediate, advanced, and graduate language courses, respectively.[4] This trend of decreasing average class size for advanced courses is also evident at DLI, where intermediate and advanced courses are generally half the size of the initial language training courses. This smaller class size, however, is as much the result of administrative realities—such as the availability of students—as of a decision based on pedagogical rationale. Regardless of the level of instruction, the overall pattern is clear—academic language courses are at least twice as large as their counterparts in the U.S. government.

CURRICULUM

There are also significant differences in how academic programs and government language programs approach the problem of curriculum design and development. Academic instructional programs are divided into semesters or quarters, and textbooks are written to cover at most one academic year of study, or about 150 to 160 hours of instruction; but courses in government programs are specifically designed for intensive language instruction ranging from 700 to 1400 hours of classroom lessons. Another difference in course design is found in the relationship be-

---

3. Gary Craford, Foreign Service Institute, personal communication, 1986.

4. Richard Brod, personal correspondence, 1986; "MLA-ADFL Survey."

tween classroom study and expectations for student out-of-class study. Whereas a university class might expect up to two hours of student preparation outside of class for every hour the student spends in class, the corresponding expectation of government language programs, because of the intensive nature of the language courses, is only one-half of an hour of outside work for each hour of classroom instruction. Historically these differences have generally precluded the sharing of instructional materials between academic and government language programs.

Only recently has this picture begun to change. At DLI, commercial textbooks organized around topical or functional approaches to language instruction have been adopted by the German, French, Italian, and Norwegian departments and are being considered by other departments for portions of their beginning courses of language instruction. Although these textbooks were not designed for an intensive instructional environment, they have been found suitable as core curricula around which supplementary materials can be developed.

The major example of government instructional materials that have received acceptance in the academic community can be found in Chinese. A decade ago a cooperative effort through the Interagency Language Roundtable produced *Standard Chinese: A Modular Approach*. It is interesting to note that these materials found less acceptance with the teachers of the agencies that produced them than they did with the academic community. Currently, if these materials are used in government language courses at all, they serve only as supplementary materials. At the same time, interest in *Standard Chinese: A Modular Approach* remains high in the academic community, and these materials continue to be sold through the DLI Nonresident Training Division and the National Audio-Visual Center.

INSTRUCTIONAL STAFF

As with the topics discussed so far, a comparison of the professional qualifications of language instructors in academic settings and in government schools provides an interesting contrast. Whereas instructors in the academic community have to meet minimum certification and/or graduate-degree requirements before becoming professional language teachers, government language schools historically have had no such requirements. Nevertheless, they have placed great emphasis in their hiring practices on the teacher's target language abilities. As a result, teachers in government language schools are predominately native speakers, or near-native speakers, of the languages they teach. They possess therefore, on average, higher target language proficiency skills than their academic colleagues.

The possession of near-native proficiency has definite practical advantages for FL teachers, who must develop authentic teaching materials and model the language for their students. Native speakers, however, often lack the broader theoretical foundation provided by teacher certification and graduate foreign language education programs. Therefore, all government language schools also maintain programs to provide for faculty preservice and in-service training. DLI is currently expanding its teacher in-service program to include formal graduate degree programs for qualified faculty.

STUDENT ASSESSMENT

All government language schools measure the success of their programs against a common language proficiency scale. This scale defines various levels of ability according to the functions to be performed in the target language, the context in which those functions are to be accomplished, and how accurately they must be carried out. With only a few exceptions, academic programs assess student learning through the assignment of norm-referenced grading systems, such as letter grades A through F, assigned on a curve or similar distribution system.

It is probably important to note that the preference in government language schools for proficiency-based grading has not always been universal. Prior to 1982, all major DLI language tests used norm-referenced grading procedures. Even tests that purported to be criterion-referenced included elaborate score conversion procedures to adjust scores according to student performance norms. Thus while all language departments used the same grade categories—in this case, integers ranging from zero to five instead of the letters F to A—there was no functional comparability of grades assigned across language departments. A level-three rating, for instance, communicated only that the recipient graduated in the top of his or her class and not that the student had achieved a functional language ability comparable to students assigned level three in other language departments.

While the shift from achievement to proficiency testing as the preferred form of summative student evaluation at DLI has been as difficult as any other significant change in an educational system, it has brought with it observable benefits.

The availability of common functional standards for measuring language ability across languages has allowed the computation of statistics showing the relative difficulty of various foreign languages for American learners and has justified the lengthening of some courses. Since proficiency tests are aimed at testing integrated language ability, rather than the content of a specific course or the techniques stressed in a particular method, proficiency testing has also allowed more meaningful research on language teaching methodologies and on curriculum options.

This is not to imply that proficiency testing is the only kind of language testing used. Norm-referenced grading continues to be used as the dominant testing and grading method for formative student evaluation in some government schools.

LENGTH OF STUDY

The number of hours in an instructional program is determined by the program's duration and by its intensity. Government language courses are generally more intense and longer in duration than academic courses. The norm for government language instruction is 25 to 30 hours per week of structured classroom activity, which is five to ten times more intense than normal college courses. Of course, some academic programs offer intensive language instruction, and some government language schools offer what is referred to as part-time language courses, which meet only a few hours a week. Each of these deviations from the norm, however, represents a very small portion of the language instruction offered.

The duration of language courses taught at government language schools also distinguishes government instruction from its academic counterpart. While it is true that even within government programs there are language familiarization courses of relatively short duration, the standard basic, or elementary, courses of instruction run from six months to nearly a year and include approximately 700 to 1400 instructional hours.

It is also worthy of note that this variance in basic course lengths is the result of establishing those lengths according to the demonstrated relative difficulty of various languages. This contrasts sharply with the academic practice of two years of undergraduate language courses—usually less than 300 instructional hours—followed by upper-division literature courses, many of which use English as the language of instruction and, therefore, provide only minimal FL exposure. One unfortunate outcome of forcing all academic language programs into the same procrustean schedule of the standard four-year curriculum is that students of more difficult languages, such as Russian or Chinese, are not as well prepared to handle authentic literature as are students of languages such as Spanish or French, which are easier for American students.

SKILL MODALITIES

Historically, another distinguishing feature of government, versus academic, language programs has been the emphasis placed upon teaching particular skill modalities. Because of the nature of future job assignments, listening and speaking skills have always enjoyed a high priority in government instructional programs. Academic programs have been influenced by the perceived literary goals of their clientele, which,

combined with the reality that there has always been too little time to master all skill modalities, has led to an emphasis on reading as the most easily taught and tested FL skill. Furthermore, attempts at developing communicative courses, which emphasized speaking and comprehension, have at times been dismissed as not academically rigorous.

Of course, the problem of trying to teach a foreign language within an unreasonably short time span is not unique to the academic community. In the mid-seventies, DLI offered special aural comprehension courses for personnel whose job assignments would require them to intercept radio broadcasts. The philosophy was that by eliminating all speaking requirements from the course, students would be able to spend more time developing their listening comprehension skills. The courses were abolished in 1981, because the expected results were not attained.

INSTRUCTIONAL METHODOLOGIES

This topic is especially hard to discuss because there is probably more variance in teaching techniques and methods across teachers within either setting than there is between government and academic language programs. Even within government schools—such as DLI, which has proclaimed at various times throughout its history a series of official methodologies, such as the Army Method, the Audio-Lingual Method, the Aural Comprehension Method, Self-paced Instruction, Criterion-referenced Instruction, and, most recently a proficiency-oriented, eclectic approach referred to as Progressive Skills Integration—the actual methodologies employed in the classroom continue to be mostly dependent upon the instructor's own experiences and preferences. One perceivable trend is that within government language schools, the mere size of the instructional program has resulted in more regimentation of class schedules and, therefore, of the teaching process. Thus one observes greater variety and experimentation today within the academic community than in government language schools.

LANGUAGE SKILL LEVELS ATTAINED

The proficiency skill levels attained by students in government language schools are by no means uniform across all programs. The speaking skills of graduates from FSI and the Central Intelligence Agency Language Schools are generally in the range of levels two to three, with reading skills equal to or better than the speaking results. The results attained by students at DLI are lower, attributable at least in part to the lower aptitude scores of students and somewhat larger class sizes. Still, the language proficiency of DLI students graduating from their basic course of instruction is equal to that of language majors graduating from undergraduate programs in the United States.[5]

EMPIRICAL RESEARCH

In this category, neither government nor academic language programs provide a praiseworthy model. Disciplined, empirical research has been almost nonexistent within the government schools, where program evaluation has been con-

5. John B. Carroll, *The Foreign Language Attainments of Language Majors in the Senior Year: A Survey Conducted in U.S. Colleges and Universities*, ERIC Document Reproduction Service ED 013 343 (Cambridge, MA: Harvard University, Graduate School of Education, 1967).

ducted essentially through trial and error. While the research picture looks a little brighter on the academic side, the research projects under way continue to be limited both in number and in scope. Most bandwagon teaching methodologies have never been empirically tested, and almost none have been tested across a significant period of instruction. It is this shared, critical need for meaningful research on FL acquisition issues that provides both the best rationale for cooperative research efforts and the best opportunity for meaningful cooperation between government and academic language programs.

INTERPRETING THE FACTORS

The foreign language profession—a profession that has as one of its highest goals the improved understanding of peoples from different cultural backgrounds—has had an internal communications problem. The cursory analysis of the preceding 11 factors has highlighted some of the differences that have contributed to this cross-cultural communications gap between the government and academic FL teaching communities; however, the differences cited in no way justify the continued segregation of these two groups. Rather, these obviously complementary differences mandate enhanced communication and cooperation if the profession is to be successful in establishing and executing a national agenda.

Language is the most complex of all human behaviors, and learning is the least understood of human activities. What is known about language learning is far less than what we do not know. The breadth and variety of experience, which is a natural outgrowth of the differences between academic and government language programs, actually mandates cooperation if a complete and balanced program of research in the discipline of foreign language learning is ever to become a reality.

PROPOSED PLAN OF ACTION

Recognizing the need for more empirical research to support its instructional program, DLI has created a research office to plan, conduct, and coordinate empirical research on topics related to second language acquisition. DLI is now ready, using options available to all government schools, to expand that program to include cooperative efforts with the academic community.

There are at least three options for government schools to pursue such cooperative research ventures: permissive research, research funded through the Intergovernmental Personnel Act (IPA), and contract research.

Permissive research

The first option might best be called permissive research in that the research topic or question would be proposed by a member of the academic community, but would be carried out in a government school where it would be easier to obtain significant numbers of students receiving sufficient hours of instruction to draw meaningful conclusions. This type of arrangement would especially benefit researchers working with less commonly taught languages because they would otherwise have to set up cumbersome multiyear, longitudinal studies to get equivalent results in an academic setting. Of course, such arrangements would be beneficial to the host school, because at minimal cost—through the contribution of faculty and student time to support a

project—it would benefit from the research results. In summary, the distinguishing features of this program would be that:

—research would be proposed by a member of the academic community;

—specific projects would be approved by the participating government language school;

—the government language school would provide students and research support;

—the researcher would share data with the host school as collected and analyzed; and

—results of the research and any products associated with it would be shared with the host school.

IPA-funded research

The second option for cooperative research is made possible through the IPA. This federal statute provides the most flexible opportunity for government funding of academic research. Because IPA agreements are generally limited to a maximum of two years for a given individual or project, IPA funding can be awarded noncompetitively. A specific research project might be proposed by a member of either the academic or the government language research community. The essential requirement is that the university researcher and a government research office agree that the research project is of sufficient mutual interest to warrant entering into a formal agreement. Funding for the project is then transferred from the government language school to the researcher's university, which continues to pay his or her salary and expenses. Specifically, IPA funding covers full salary, benefits, and travel plus per diem, for short projects, or full moving expenses, for longer projects. The beauty of IPA agreements is their simplicity and their flexibility. Agreements may cover one researcher per project, several full-time researchers for a single project, one researcher for multiple projects, or even part of one or more researchers' time for a project of interest to the government language school, while allowing the remainder of the researchers' time to be spent on other projects of interest to them or their university.

Contract research

The third option for conducting cooperative research endeavors is available through standard governmental procedures of requests for proposals and related contracts. Since these procedures include a lot of administrative work for the contracting agency, this option would normally only be used for larger projects that were of great interest to the government and that had sufficient lead time to allow for proposal preparation, competitive review of proposals, and execution of the funding process.

CONCLUSION

Because of the complementary features of government and academic language programs, it is imperative that both of these communities be considered in establishing a national agenda to improve FL instruction in the United States. The foundation for improvements in the field will be meaningful research. Opportunities for joint research abound, and administrative vehicles exist that allow cooperative research efforts utilizing the strengths of both the academic and government language teaching communities. If we, as a profession, are to improve the national status of second languages, we must work together to take advantage of these opportunities.

ANNALS, *AAPSS*, **490**, March 1987

Foreign Language Teacher Education: Current Practices and an Assessment of Needs

By ALICE C. OMAGGIO and STANLEY L. SHINALL

ABSTRACT: This article describes current practice in foreign language teacher education programs—middle-school through post-secondary levels—and provides recommendations for change that might be facilitated through the development of a national foreign language pedagogical research agenda. Discussion of teacher education practices centers around the following concerns: (1) policies regarding the admission and retention of students; (2) the content of teacher education programs, including core courses in the subject-matter specialization or major, professional education courses, and instruction in methodology; (3) preservice teaching experiences; (4) certification standards; and (5) in-service opportunities and maintenance of professional skills. The qualifications of teacher-training personnel, for both secondary and post-secondary settings, are also discussed. Recommendations for the development of a national agenda are grouped into three categories: (1) research and development activities; (2) in-service development opportunities; and (3) opportunities for leadership training. Such an agenda should aid the profession in its efforts to bring about needed change in the education and development of the nation's foreign language teachers.

Alice C. Omaggio (Ph.D., Ohio State University) is associate professor of French at the University of Illinois, Urbana-Champaign, where she coordinates first- and second-year language courses, supervises teaching assistants, and teaches courses in second language acquisition and methodology. She is the author of several college textbooks for French as well as a recent book on methodology.

Stanley L. Shinall (Ph.D., University of Illinois) is assistant professor of French at the University of Illinois, Urbana-Champaign, where he is coordinator of undergraduate instruction for French, foreign language area coordinator for the Urbana-Champaign Council on Teacher Education, and a member of the University High School faculty. He teaches courses in language and methodology and supervises student teachers.

I T is the purpose of this article to describe current practices in foreign language teacher education and to provide recommendations for change that might be incorporated into a national agenda for the improvement of foreign language education. The national agenda should address the needs of both the preprofessional—preservice—and the professional—in-service—members of the foreign language/second language teaching fields. It should therefore be determined not just by extrinsic pressures, such as those coming from state legislatures and national committees on educational policies, but also by intrinsic need.

The first two parts of this article examine current teacher-training practices within foreign language programs—middle-school through post-secondary—identify and discuss problem areas, and make recommendations for change. The final section suggests how a national agenda might be developed to meet the needs assessed.

SECONDARY SCHOOL TEACHER EDUCATION: CURRENT PRACTICES AND RECOMMENDATIONS

The 1980s have witnessed the formation of national, regional, state, and local committees that have produced numerous reports reflecting the crisis in education. There is universally expressed concern about teacher education in terms of the nature of program participants, delivery systems, and the qualifications of those completing teacher education programs and entering the profession, certificate in hand.

In response to the demands being made of today's teachers, it is clear that the content, methodology, and structure of the teacher-training curriculum need to be reassessed. In order to compare teacher education models and review current practice, the following areas common to most programs can be examined:

—admission and retention of students;

—content of subject-matter specialization—courses in language, grammar, literature, civilization;

—professional education courses;

—methods courses;

—preservice teaching experiences;

—standards for certification and follow-up after certification; and

—in-service opportunities and maintenance of professional skills.

These areas will now be addressed through seven questions. Under each question, current practice will be summarized and recommendations for change will be made.

1. How are students admitted to and retained in teacher education programs?

Current practice. Admissibility to teacher education programs has been an area of grave concern nationally. Individual states are currently setting admission standards of minimum competencies for those who wish to enter the teaching profession. While testing instruments and cut-off minimum scores may vary, most states are demanding that both elementary and secondary education students demonstrate basic competency in the reading and writing of English, speech communication, and mathematics, regardless of the teaching field. A state-by-state summary of entrance-level testing is provided by Draper, Graham, and Johnstone, along with other state initiatives and activities in foreign languages and international studies.[1]

In addition to changing entrance requirements, individual institutions have practiced a range of review procedures of their own to determine retention in teacher education programs. For the most part, however, students tend to be retained on the basis of a general grade-point average with little attention to their performance in specific subject-matter areas.

Recommendations. Entry-level testing for competence in basic skills is a trend that should be universally applied in order to assure that candidates for teacher education meet professional intellectual standards. Retention of candidates should be based on periodic review of their performance on various criteria set by the program and relating to language proficiency, subject-matter expertise, and professional competence. Such a review should ideally include an assessment of language proficiency at various points throughout their program, as well as a consideration of their performance in their major subject and in professional education coursework.

2. What is the content of teacher education programs and who provides the training?

Current practice. Jorstad[2] has outlined the history of the professional prepara-

tion of language teachers in the United States and has pointed to the importance of the Modern Language Association's (MLA's) statement of qualifications for secondary school teachers of modern foreign languages.[3] Jorstad maintained that this statement is fundamentally relevant even in the 1980s, since most programs attempt to comply with state standards that are based on those guidelines.

At the present time, many professional organizations representing subject-matter disciplines are reviewing and revising guidelines for teacher preparation. The American Council on the Teaching of Foreign Languages is currently undertaking a revision of the MLA guidelines in a three-year project funded by the federal government.

The 1966 version of the MLA guidelines states that foreign language teachers should be able to:

—develop their students' control of listening, speaking, reading, and writing skills;

—help students understand another culture through language study and understand how that culture contrasts with U.S. culture;

—help students develop an appreciation of foreign literature;

—choose and use materials, methods, and equipment appropriately;

—diagnose students' difficulties and evaluate their progress in learning a language; and

1. Jamie B. Draper, Elizabeth H. Graham, and Tamara S. Johnstone, *State Initiatives and Activities in Foreign Languages and International Studies* (Washington, DC: Joint National Committee for Languages, 1986), pp. 1-22.

2. Helen Jorstad, "The Education and Reeducation of Teachers," in *Learning a Second Language: Seventy-ninth Yearbook of the National*

Society for the Study of Education, part 2, ed. Frank M. Grittner (Chicago: University of Chicago Press, 1980), pp. 168-85.

3. "Guidelines for Teacher Education Programs in Modern Foreign Languages," *Modern Language Journal,* 50(6):342-44 (Oct. 1966).

—work with teachers of other subjects in the school.

While this important statement has had impact, compliance from program to program has been determined by the availability of staff, staff interest, professional preparation of teacher development personnel, and availability of funding. At the present time, institutional resources are frequently being channeled to programs of high demand, such as engineering, business, and technological sciences. Education has typically not been considered an area high on the priority list for funding.

This diversity in institutional resources explains the great variety in content-area programs. Although a state may specify the minimum total hours in a specialty area, the approved program determines the nature of those hours. Many programs have traditionally been heavy in literature, for example, to the neglect of other important areas such as conversation, civilization, and culture. Jarvis and Bernhardt maintain that there has been relatively little change in the preparation of foreign language teachers in subject-matter content in the past twenty years.[4] Results of a survey of practicing teachers done by Brickell and Paul reveal that only 35 percent of the course work typically taken was in language and linguistics and 15 percent in culture and civilization, while 45 percent of the courses were in literature.[5] In that same survey, it was shown that inattention to the development of language proficiency and cultural understanding is of major concern to many practicing teachers.

The core curriculum—or subject-matter area—of the foreign language teaching major is frequently obtained through a department of arts and letters while the professional education and methodology courses are taken through an education curriculum. Sometimes the degree is awarded through a college of education; sometimes it is taken as a specialization within liberal arts and science. In the latter situation, many faculty view literary scholarship as more prestigious than pedagogical concerns, leading to an unfortunate tradition of separation between the two faculty interests.

Recommendations. Attention must be given to the development of language proficiency and cultural understanding in the preparation of teacher candidates, and a regular assessment procedure must be provided. In the case of teacher candidates whose skills are below professional expectations, opportunities must be provided for remediation and further development. While the importance of literary understanding cannot be discounted, program content should reflect most directly those skills that will be needed in teaching students in the middle and secondary schools.

By the same token, those responsible for the education of preservice teachers should have adequate expertise in second language acquisition and should be aware of the needs of the future teacher in the secondary school context. More is said about this matter under question 5.

3. What professional education courses are included?

Current practice. Imig noted in 1982 that while 41 percent of the program for

---

4. Gilbert A. Jarvis and Elizabeth B. Bernhardt, "Foreign Language Teacher Education," *Eric Digest,* pp. 1-2 (Sept. 1984).

5. Henry M. Brickell and Regina H. Paul, "Ready for the '80s? A Look at Foreign Language Teachers and Teaching at the Start of the Decade," *Foreign Language Annals,* 15(3):169-84 (1982).

aspiring elementary school teachers is devoted to professional study, 30 percent of the offerings for secondary school teachers are designated for generic education courses, that is, non-subject-matter specific.[6] Professional education courses typically present background in the history of education, philosophy of education, school policy, curriculum, teaching skills, educational psychology, teaching resources, learner assessment, and similar content. In the Brickell and Paul study mentioned earlier, these kinds of education courses were rated lowest among four categories of program offerings, which consisted of foreign language courses, studies in a foreign country, education courses, and student teaching.

The percentage of time currently devoted to these courses is a major concern. Because of state mandates, intended to assure that teachers are prepared to handle broad ranges of ability levels and cultural and ethnic diversity, additional hours or course modification may be required. The modification of courses is frequently viewed as a dilution of subject matter and an interference with academic freedom. The creation of new courses either lengthens the program or leads to the deletion of offerings considered important to the program.

Recommendations. The sequence and nature of professional education courses should be carefully assessed. There should be a willingness to abandon or modify courses that are not strictly applicable to the needs of the prospective teacher. Attention should be given to recommendations such as those found in the report of the Holmes Group, which suggests massive streamlining and restructuring of teacher education programs in this country.[7]

4. What is the nature of instruction in methods?

Current practice. Methodology courses may be offered by an education college or within arts and letters, either by specialists or by willing faculty. There is great variation in the nature of such courses and in the approach of the teaching faculty. For example, methods courses may be generic, grouping students from all disciplines, often with close attention to none. Occasionally the courses are designed to accommodate all students majoring in a language, with little attention to the particular needs of specific languages. Sometimes the methods courses are language specific. On occasion there are multiple methods courses that combine features of all of the aforementioned approaches. In addition, methods courses may be heavily theoretical with little opportunity for practical application, or they may be cookbook in nature with a wide variety of how-to handouts and little study of the theoretical underpinnings. Most of the time they deal primarily with beginning levels of language instruction, while approaches appropriate to the advanced levels are barely considered. In all these cases, the total needs of the preservice teacher are neglected, since only the development of the ability to make informed decisions is the goal of instruction in methodology.

---

6. Donald C. Imig, "Oversight on Teacher Education," ED 225 970 (Report given at the Hearing before the Subcommittee on Postsecondary Education, Committee on Education and Labor, House of Representatives, 98th Cong., 1983).

7. *Tomorrow's Teachers: A Report of the Holmes Group* (East Lansing, MI: Holmes Group, 1986).

Student teachers cast into the real world may suddenly find themselves confronted with responsibilities for which they are not prepared. The Brickell and Paul survey referred to earlier revealed that in-service teachers consider their course work in methodology, often studied just prior to or in conjunction with the practicum, as being "too little too late." Many said that well-designed methods courses offering practical ideas for their particular subject matter were essential to their preparation. Some institutions have increased offerings in methodology to accommodate different stages of preprofessional growth and experience. The proper sequencing of these courses with other professional education courses is critically important, but sometimes difficult to manage because of other academic requirements.

Recommendations. The Holmes Group report and other studies reflect concern for the development of critical thinking skills in preservice teacher education experiences. It is unlikely that most individuals are able to develop such skills in a single methods course or in a single student-teaching experience. Methodological instruction should begin early and develop throughout the preservice teacher's academic program. As Lange points out, instruction in methodology should be linked to field observations in language classrooms, microteaching experiences, videotaping of the preservice teacher with self-evaluation, and other clinical teaching experiences that are supervised and evaluated.[8] The recognition that the preprofessional needs a variety of experiences has led many

states to mandate early field experience hours: student observations, parateaching, and the like. Here again, the number of hours varies from state to state. Illinois, for example, requires 100 hours, whereas Ohio requires 300.

Furthermore, it is essential that instruction in methodology be tied to an organizing principle, such as the concept of proficiency. Preservice teachers need a framework within which to make critical decisions on a day-to-day basis in their teaching. A concept like proficiency, as defined in the American Council on the Teaching of Foreign Languages' guidelines,[9] helps in the goal clarification process and allows teachers to design curricula, select materials, and create activities that are appropriate to their students' needs and current level of competence. In addition, teachers can assess student progress more confidently using a nationally accepted standard or measure, or adapting classroom tests to reflect such a standard.

5. What is the nature of preservice teaching experiences?

Current practice. The practicum—student teaching or practice teaching—is another area of diversity among institutions. Such experiences range from eight weeks to a full semester or more. As programs are being reviewed, there is a general trend to lengthen the practice-teaching experience and to provide clinical experiences in a number of settings. The qualifications of cooperating teachers vary from program to program as do efforts to train and involve such teachers actively in the professional development and evaluation

8. Dale L. Lange, "Teacher Development and Certification in Foreign Languages: Where Is the Future?" *Modern Language Journal,* 67(4):374-81 (Winter 1983).

9. *ACTFL Proficiency Guidelines* (Hastings-on-Hudson, NY: American Council on the Teaching of Foreign Languages, 1985).

of the student teacher. Supervision of the practice teacher also varies in terms of the qualifications of the supervisor, the number of visits, the feedback given to the student teacher, evaluative procedures, and grading.

Recommendations. The Holmes report recommends multiple preservice teaching experiences, and it urges a more extensive role for the public school cooperating teachers in the education and evaluation of teacher candidates. Teaching experiences should be planned to achieve specific purposes and should familiarize teacher candidates with various learning environments such as classrooms, laboratories, computer facilities, and the like. In addition, the performance of preservice teachers needs to be evaluated regularly, and they need to learn techniques for self-evaluation as well. Institutions that might find it difficult to provide more clinical experiences might rely on videotaped materials for this phase of teacher development.

Supervisors and cooperating teachers must have qualifications that assure teacher candidates of the most productive and rewarding teaching experiences. Among these qualifications are excellent interpersonal skills, solid academic preparation in foreign language education, and professional skills that reflect an understanding of current theory and practice.

6. *What standards for certification exist and what follow-up is given to teachers after they leave the program?*

Current practice. Many states continue to certify programs rather than individuals. These programs are expected to comply with guidelines established by state boards of higher education. The most broadly accepted standards for program approval are those established by the National Council for Accreditation of Teacher Education, which have just been revised, and programs applying for approval after September 1988 will be expected to meet the new criteria. Some of the most important of these new standards are discussed later, in the recommendations section.

In current practice, an individual applies for certification having completed an approved program requiring a given number of content hours, a given set of professional education courses, a practicum, and perhaps a variety of state-mandated requirements such as constitution exams and the like. Recommendation or endorsement by the institution satisfies certification requirements. Proof of the competency of the individual is a matter of major concern, however, and has prompted movements within the profession to monitor itself. This was the rationale behind the development of the MLA Cooperative Foreign Language Proficiency Tests, formulated in the National Defense Education Act and produced by the Educational Testing Service in 1961. This battery of standardized tests represented an attempt to measure the strengths of candidates in the areas specified in the MLA guidelines. Today the profession is reexamining the question of competency with the development of the American Council on the Teaching of Foreign Languages' proficiency tests, which currently exist for speaking and are being developed for reading. Many states are seriously considering using these and other measures of proficiency in the certification of foreign language teachers.

Recommendations. Included among the National Council for Accreditation of Teacher Education's new criteria for teacher education programs are requirements for entrance-level competency testing, provision of a strong background in liberal arts and sciences, a minimum of 10 weeks of student teaching, involvement of practicing teachers in curriculum and policy development, inclusion of research about effective teaching in the education courses offered, and rigorous academic training in the subject-matter area. It seems equally important that institutions monitor the language competence of individuals presenting themselves for certification, using a standard examination procedure that is widely accepted.

An interesting development in certification practice is the recommendation of the Holmes Group. The recommendation is for a three-tier system of teacher licensing: (1) novice teacher—or instructor—whose nonrenewable certificate would last only a few years and whose teaching must be supervised by a professional teacher; (2) professional, who would have completed a fifth year of academic training, at the master's level, and extensive supervised teaching to be qualified to assume full responsibility for teaching the subjects to students; and (3) career professional, requiring further academic study—normally the earning of a doctorate—in one of several professional areas as well as evidence of outstanding teaching. The recommendations of the Holmes Group may or may not be widely endorsed, but they are bound to affect both program structure and certification practices in the future.

Another group that has potential impact on reshaping the teaching profession is the Carnegie Forum on Education and the Economy, which has just issued a report proposing a national teacher certification system for basic subject-matter competency and for advanced levels of skill and specialization. The report recommends different types of certification that would become the basis for differential pay scales. The national certification process would not be directly linked to a degree in education or to individual state licensing processes, allowing for alternative certification procedures. Some educators feel that there is a risk in nationalizing certification procedures since other public school policy is now the province of the states and local school districts. The two major national teacher unions—the American Federation of Teachers and the National Education Association—have, however, endorsed this report on the condition that teachers dominate the national certification process. The *ACTFL Proficiency Guidelines*, mentioned earlier, and other similar measures could well be included in accrediting foreign language teachers if national certification were to become a reality.

*7. What opportunities exist
for in-service teacher development
activities? How are professional
skills maintained?*

Current practice. Professional training opportunities include in-service days at local schools, attendance at local, regional, state, and national meetings, participation in summer intensive workshops and immersion activities, the reading of professional journals and newsletters, and travel and study abroad. According to the Brickell and Paul survey, about 75 percent of foreign language teachers have had some formal in-service experiences in the past ten years. Only about 65 percent of such experiences, however, were directly related to foreign languages and were typically limited to one day per academic year. The teachers in the survey were particularly interested in opportunities to improve their spoken language proficiency and to learn new approaches to classroom instruction. There is no conceivable way, however, that one in-service day could make any lasting difference in a teacher's performance in these areas.

In a 1983 survey, Wright found that only 25 percent of teacher education institutions gave high priority to initiating or increasing in-service training programs. In fact, 46 percent of the institutions surveyed showed only very little interest in devoting resources to such endeavors.[10] Fisher correctly states that the ordinary way of training teachers in educational institutions is insufficient for the needs at hand, and emphasizes the need for federal support in improving teacher education.[11] It seems clear that while teachers are expressing a need for more in-service opportunities, it is difficult for institutions faced with serious financial constraints and program development needs to devote adequate time and resources to the needs of practicing teachers.

Recommendations. It is evident from this profile of the current situation that there is a tangible need for more in-service educational opportunities for the nation's foreign language teachers, as well as funding to support such efforts. Recommendations for the direc-

tion these efforts might take are made later in this article.

POST-SECONDARY TEACHER
EDUCATION: A SUMMARY OF
CURRENT PRACTICES AND
RECOMMENDATIONS FOR CHANGE

If, in the previous section, the preparation that most secondary-school teachers of foreign languages have obtained before beginning their careers seemed less than adequate, consider for a moment that most teaching assistants (TAs) at the university level have had no preservice preparation at all. Furthermore, in nearly one-fourth of the language departments surveyed by Schulz in 1979, no in-service training whatsoever was provided for TAs during the course of their tenure as graduate students.[12] Yet TAs are often responsible for much of the lower-division undergraduate instruction in language departments across the country. As Ervin and Muyskens point out, "To many undergraduate foreign language students, their TA *is* the foreign language department."[13]

In 1963, the McAllister report, prepared by the MLA, revealed that 60 percent of the institutions using TAs provided no training, offered no course work in methodology, made no arrangements for class visitation by faculty, and provided no effective supervision.[14] Re-

10. Douglas A. Wright, "Teacher Preparation in the Use of Computers," *Bulletin of the Office of Educational Research and Improvement* (Washington, DC: Office of Education, 1986), pp. 1-16.

11. Francis D. Fisher, "Computer-Assisted Education: What's Not Happening?" *Journal of Computer-Based Instruction*, 9(1):19-27 (Summer 1982).

12. Renate A. Schulz, "TA Training, Supervision, and Evaluation: Report of a Survey," *ADFL Bulletin*, 12(1):1-8 (Sept. 1980).

13. Gerard Ervin and Judith A. Muyskens, "On Training TAs: Do We Know What They Want and Need?" *Foreign Language Annals*, 15(5):335 (Oct. 1982).

14. Archibald McAllister, "The Preparation of College Teachers of Modern Foreign Languages," *Modern Language Journal*, 50(6):402 (Oct. 1966).

cent surveys and reports indicate that the preparation of TAs has been improving to some extent over the past two decades. The current situation in college language teacher preparation will now be assessed through five questions, which serve to organize the discussion in this section.

1. Who is responsible for teacher development at the college level?

Current practice. According to the results of Schulz's survey of 370 graduate degree-granting departments of foreign languages, linguistics, and comparative literature, fewer than one in five of the faculty members responsible for TA training and supervision had any formal training in foreign language education. As Dvorak points out, many institutions apparently still prefer the so-called left-handed language program coordinator (LPC). "That is, they hope to hire an individual whose training and research interests lie in another field, but who can be asked to use the left hand to manage part of the language program, plus some TA supervision, on the side."[15] An examination of the MLA job lists from recent years reveals that this is indeed the case in many instances. There are, however, an increasing number of tenure-track positions calling for a language teaching specialist, excluding quite specifically candidates whose primary graduate preparation is in literature. This trend is encouraging, not only because it will undoubtedly improve the quality of lower-division university language programs, but also because it will provide for the training of future teachers at the

university level. The importance of this latter function becomes clear when one realizes that the graduate teaching assistantship may be the only teacher development opportunity future language and literature professors will have before entering into the profession, since no certificate for college teaching, comparable to the one obtained by high school teachers, currently exists.

Even if an increasing number of departments begin employing adequately trained teaching specialists to coordinate lower-division programs and supervise teaching assistants, there are serious problems that must still be addressed relating to the role and status of LPCs in their own departments. These issues will be treated under question 5.

Recommendations. It is clear that the individual primarily responsible for teacher education in a college or university language department in which the TA system is used should be a professional with special preparation for the job. Specifically, the person should be an expert in second language acquisition and learning who can connect theory to practice. This means that the LPC has developed expertise in such areas as applied linguistics, psycholinguistics, language teaching methodology, testing and evaluation, educational research, curriculum design, and supervision, and has done doctoral work in these areas as his or her primary focus.

Dvorak summarizes the task of the LPC as "[translating] what is known about language learning into a coherent and reasoned plan for language teaching, and [implementing] the plan through effective methodology."[16] More specifically, this task comprises at least four steps: (1) articulating curricular objec-

---

15. Trisha Dvorak, "The Ivory Ghetto: The Place of the Language Program Coordinator in a Research Institution," *Hispania*, 69:217 (Mar. 1986).

16. Ibid., 219.

tives; (2) designing a curriculum to achieve these objectives; (3) implementing the program through the selection and creation of materials, designing syllabi, training staff in methodological techniques and strategies, and the like; and (4) supervising and evaluating staff performance, as well as student progress in terms of achievement of course goals and proficiency levels attained. Because lower-division courses taught by TAs are, financially and numerically speaking, the lifeblood of the department in most institutions, it seems evident that both the TAs themselves and the students they serve deserve the highest quality of preparation possible. The use of the left-handed LPC, unfortunately, does not assure this kind of quality in post-secondary education.

2. What qualifications does one need to be a graduate TA?

Current practice. In Schulz's survey,[17] 86 percent of the language departments required only the bachelor's degree as a minimum academic qualification for TA appointment, and none of the departments surveyed required TAs to demonstrate language proficiency before their appointment was made. In some departments, TAs were required to take a test of some type to reveal possible linguistic deficiencies, but few if any departments barred TAs from teaching because of poor results on such tests. In most cases, remedial course work was recommended, but the teaching appointment was still offered the first semester.

The majority of TAs teach the first two years of a language, although some departments report using TAs for third-

and fourth-year courses. They also are assigned to work as discussion leaders, language lab directors or assistants, and instructors in courses in conversation, pronunciation, mythology, classical civilization, introduction to linguistics, language for special purposes, advanced literary readings, advanced composition, introduction to literature courses, and culture.[18] Given this proliferation of responsibilities, one wonders if, in some instances, the TA system is not being abused or exploited by literature departments. As Ervin observed more than ten years ago, it is increasingly difficult to see how a department can afford not to have a language teaching specialist on its faculty, given the needs of the typical foreign language department at the level of its greatest enrollment.[19]

In terms of the requirements for TA performance in the classroom, the picture is currently quite bleak. In most cases, the quality of a TA's performance is of little or no import in the TA's reappointment, a fact that is extremely frustrating to the LPC who expends considerable time and energy evaluating classroom teaching. When enrollments are sufficiently high to require additional appointments, the general trend is to accept anyone who is ambulatory and can speak the language, even if the person has no training at all in language teaching.

Recommendations. Schulz recommends that TAs should not be assigned to full teaching duties during their first term of graduate study, but should first obtain some formal training in pedagogy. Courses and seminars in methodology

---

18. Ibid.
19. Gerard Ervin, "The Role of the Language Teaching Specialist in the College Foreign Language Department," *ADFL Bulletin,* 7(2):15-16 (Nov. 1975).

17. Schulz, "TA Training, Supervision, and Evaluation," p. 3.

and teacher development should carry graduate credit that will count for M.A. and Ph.D. programs.

TAs whose teaching has been evaluated as poor by both their students and supervisors should not be reappointed automatically. Rather, the recommendations of the LPC should be heard and considered seriously by department heads to rectify the situation.

3. What are the components of TA teacher development programs?

Current practice. Pedagogical preparation of TAs varies widely from institution to institution, but some general trends can be identified, according to Schulz's survey. As of fall 1979, 69 percent of the departments responding offered a preservice orientation program for new TAs. Only 38 percent, however, offered or required a methods course. Some departments are currently offering both preservice orientation and in-service training, and a few departments provide more than one semester of methodological training for TAs. As stated earlier, 22 percent of the departments reported having no training opportunities at all for TAs.[20]

Recommendations. Two surveys that were conducted recently reveal the kinds of issues that are of most concern to TAs and that are considered most important to them in their development as teachers.[21] Ervin and Muyskens list seven priorities that over 300 TAs and faculty members

20. Schulz, "TA Training, Supervision, and Evaluation," pp. 1-8.
21. Anne G. Nerenz, Carol A. Herron, and Constance K. Knop, "The Training of Graduate Teaching Assistants in Foreign Languages: A Review of Literature and Descriptions of Contemporary Programs," *French Review,* 52:877-81 (1979); Ervin and Muyskens, "On Training TAs," pp. 335-44.

at institutions across the country identified as a group:

— learning practical teaching methods and techniques;

— teaching the four skills of listening, speaking, reading, and writing;

— teaching conversation;

— making class interesting;

— making the best use of class time;

— teaching grammar; and

— inspiring and motivating students.[22]

Although some of the particular priorities may well change as the field of second language education develops, it is clear from this list that TAs need and want practical, applied training as well as an understanding of learning theory. As we saw in the section on teacher education priorities at the secondary level, there is a greater need for a larger proportion of teacher development activities that relate directly to the planning, organization, and delivery of instruction than for the more generic education courses that are not subject-matter specific. Given the relatively small portion of time that is likely to be allotted to college teacher education programs, this concern seems especially important in the university context.

4. How are TAs supervised and evaluated?

Current practice. Classroom observation is considered the most effective supervisory tool in various surveys of language departments. Yet 13 percent of the departments surveyed in 1979 by Schulz said they provided no direct classroom visits to TAs during their first

22. Ervin and Muyskens, "On Training TAs," pp. 335-44.

term of teaching, and about half of the departments reported observing new TAs either once or twice. TAs who had some experience were observed less often.[23] One obvious problem in supervision is the overload of work carried by the LPC, who might be supervising 60 to 70 TAs in some large departments, often with little or no assistance from anyone else. When other faculty do assist in supervision, there are often disagreements about standards, especially when the helper has had little or no training in foreign language education. Some LPCs experience TA hostility to supervision and a lack of cooperation as well. Because there are few if any rewards for supervisory duties, there is a parallel lack of incentive on the part of many faculty responsible for this function.

Some foreign language specialists report the use of videotaped class sessions for supervisory purposes, while others use a form of self-assessment. In some cases, a variety of supervisory techniques are combined.

Evaluation of TAs may take the form of supervisory reports, the use of evaluation forms, self-evaluation, and student evaluations of teaching. Again, there is some improvement reported in recent surveys in terms of evaluation procedures, but these tend to vary widely from institution to institution.

Recommendations. Schulz recommended, in light of her survey, that supervisors should be given sufficient help, release time, and departmental support to assure that high-quality supervision can be provided to TAs on a regular basis. Dvorak suggests that a hierarchical model for the LPC position might work best, with reasonable release

time from course responsibilities.[24] It has been suggested, for example, that LPCs have one advanced TA for every course supervised who might share supervision duties or who might release the LPC from other coordination duties to do more supervision. Department heads need to support the LPC, involving themselves more directly in the supervisory process by requiring regular evaluations of TAs and using those results to determine reappointment. Schulz suggests that new TAs need to be supervised, ideally, at least three times in the first semester by their primary supervisor and perhaps twice by other faculty. Videotaped class sessions also should be considered, as they have proven quite useful in the supervision process.

5. What is the status of the LPC in the language department?

Current practice. Dvorak characterizes the place occupied by the language coordinator in the department as an "ivory ghetto," located on the fringe of departmental activity—"a small preserve within which [LPCs] spend all their time, but which their colleagues enter only on occasion, and then generally with condescension."[25] Some of the problems faced by faculty in coordinating positions include early burnout, misconceptions about their work on the part of other faculty, and academic failure. "Once LPCs join a department in a research institution, they become members of a group whose most striking characteristic appears to be failure,"[26] since many are denied tenure or drop out to accept a noncoordinating position in another

23. Schulz, "TA Training, Supervision, and Evaluation," pp. 3-5.

24. Dvorak, "Ivory Ghetto," pp. 217-22.
25. Ibid., p. 220.
26. Ibid., p. 217.

university before the tenure decision is made. Even when departments do recognize the need for the LPC position, the lack of awareness on the part of other faculty about current knowledge in the areas of language learning and teaching has often led to the perception that the LPC's activities involve little or no expertise.

One serious problem that undoubtedly relates to the failure of many LPCs to obtain tenure is the fact that the duties they are expected to perform in terms of language coordination and supervision, and that they have been especially hired to perform, are rarely considered in promotion and tenure decisions. The motivation to invest time in coordination and language program supervision is quickly eroded by the awareness that this work, which is quite substantial in terms of the time and energy commitment required, does not cut any ice with the dean's office or with one's own colleagues. Thus, in the current academic climate in many language departments and research institutions, the LPC is forced to choose between doing the job well and getting tenure, or between doing the job well and progressing intellectually and professionally. This situation obviously must be addressed if departments are to improve the quality of teacher development activities at the post-secondary level.

Recommendations. First, it is both senseless and unethical to expect LPCs to devote major amounts of time and energy to tasks that will not help them advance in their career and will probably even hinder such advancement.[27] Tenure committees need to reconsider criteria for evaluating the work of LPCs and need to recognize their work as involving

27. Ibid., p. 221.

the same expertise as that of their colleagues and thus forming a legitimate part of their professional production activities. Many LPCs are involved in textbook writing and material preparation, for example, and are given no credit for such work when decisions are made about tenure and promotion. Because this kind of work is clearly related to their field of interest and expertise, as well as essential to the delivery of sound second langauge instruction, it needs to be considered as a legitimate activity for evaluation by tenure and promotion committees..

Second, there is a need for language departments to support the LPC position in a hierarchical fashion, especially in large departments, so that these individuals are not called upon for tasks that do not require their expertise. At present, most LPCs are asked to do such things as administer and score placement exams, handle student drop/add requests, prepare all course materials and examinations, order books, and carry out other tasks that can and should be handled by secretarial support staff or by trained graduate assistants.

RECOMMENDATIONS FOR A NATIONAL TEACHER EDUCATION AGENDA

The review of current practice in the preceding pages reveals at least three major priority areas for the improvement of teacher education in secondary and post-secondary settings. These areas are research and development activities; in-service development opportunities; and leadership training opportunities. Our agenda for change will now be described, using these three areas as an organizer.

Research and development activities would include the following:

—engaging in research on teacher effectiveness, including an examination of factors such as subject-matter expertise, pedagogical skills, choice of teaching approach, and affective considerations;

—developing and experimenting with various methods of training high school and college teachers, including the design of programs for internship and induction-year experiences;

—developing position papers for the profession at large about the status of teacher education, with recommendations for change and improvement, both at the secondary and post-secondary levels;

—developing prototypical models for instructional systems at the novice and intermediate levels for uncommonly taught languages, and at the advanced levels for commonly taught languages. These models should include a teacher-training component that explores both traditional and nontraditional teaching roles as they relate to various instructional modes and formats, such as computer-assisted instruction, the use of interactive videotapes and discs, intensive instruction, self-instruction, and the like; and

—developing videotaped samples of exemplary classroom practice for distribution to teacher education institutions or training centers.

In-service development opportunities include:

—providing for the maintenance and improvement of professional skills and language proficiency of practicing teachers through immersion and other intensive workshop formats;

—designing and sponsoring study-abroad experiences for both preservice and in-service teachers, as well as research into the effects of these experiences;

—providing training in testing and evaluation procedures, in terms of achievement and proficiency testing of students; and

—developing data banks and networks for sharing information relating to teacher education.

Leadership training opportunities include:

—providing opportunities for teacher trainers and college LPCs to develop expertise in the field of second language acquisition and learning and to keep abreast of developments in that field;

—providing opportunities for teacher trainers to develop skills in supervision, including peer and self-assessment techniques, as well as in program evaluation;

—preparing leaders in the conduct of innovative in-service programs and immersion experiences; and

—providing support for supervisors, program coordinators, college teacher-training personnel, and master teachers to make improvements in the areas of curriculum design, methodological innovations, materials development, and the use of technology—such as computer-assisted instruction, video, instructional television, and the like—all of which might best be organized around the concept of proficiency.

If a national foreign language agenda can be developed that addresses the three areas of activity just outlined, the outcomes of the recommended projects will make a valuable impact on the improvement of foreign language instruction in the nation's schools. Such an agenda, when implemented, will un- doubtedly encourage and motivate foreign language teachers, who will see in the various projects a long-awaited response to their expressed needs.

ANNALS, *AAPSS*, **490**, March 1987

Dissemination and Diffusion of Progress in the Foreign Language Teaching Field: A National Plan

By CLAIRE L. GAUDIANI

ABSTRACT: Excellent teaching methods, improved technologies for teaching and testing, and appropriate materials must reach the widest audience once they are developed by language pedagogy specialists. This article reviews the existing dissemination system and proposes a national plan to assure efficient and effective diffusion of tested innovations in the field to the practitioners at various instructional levels. This plan includes the development of an annual research yearbook and videotape, a National Foreign Language Video Conference Day, a National Board of Consultants, a board qualification certificate for foreign language faculty, a television series of great presentations, a set of surveys, and a national foreign language newsletter along with a major national publicity campaign. Wide dissemination of good ideas is as critical as developing improved practices.

Claire L. Gaudiani is currently assistant director of the Joseph H. Lauder Institute of Management and International Studies at the University of Pennsylvania, where she is also senior fellow in Romance languages. She has written books and articles on seventeenth-century French poetry, foreign language pedagogy, humanities education, and management in higher education. She has held research fellowships from the American Council of Learned Societies and the National Humanities Center. Dr. Gaudiani received her undergraduate degree from Connecticut College and her M.A. and Ph.D. degrees from Indiana University.

SOME Americans are using interactive videodisk materials to learn a foreign language. For others, language teaching technology has barely progressed beyond *la plume de ma tante.* Some teachers stress the development of communication skills and have been trained to teach and test these skills. Other teachers still insist on lengthy pattern drills and memorization of unrelated words in lists. While some teachers doggedly take two points off for each incorrect accent, others help language learners to evaluate the significance of different kinds of errors in spoken and written communication. These teachers perceive error as a part of the learning process. The new national thrust for excellence in language teaching must close gaps in the quality of practice in the field. As the language teaching profession develops learner-sensitive methods to teach English speakers other languages, this progress and additional advances in testing and materials development need to be disseminated widely and efficiently to those teaching foreign languages all over the United States. Like other fields where theories can be tested experimentally and data developed to guide better practice and produce improved outcomes, the language teaching field needs a set of mechanisms to assure that its clients receive the current best in service from practitioners.

The national policy agenda requires a bold plan for dissemination of progress in the field. This plan must make research and tested innovations conveniently accessible to the more than 50,000 teachers of foreign languages in the United States. It should include both new initiatives and systematic improvements in dissemination efforts. Accessibility involves efficiency, cost effectiveness, and incentives. Language teachers need regularly scheduled, well-designed, low-cost opportunities to learn new methods and become familiar with new materials. These opportunities must occur within time frames that are acceptable to widely varying teaching schedules of both school and college faculty. A dynamic national plan for dissemination will also include a set of incentives designed to encourage faculty to stay up-to-date with the best methods, materials, and tests to enhance language learning. Administrators as well as direct supervisors and citizens, particularly parents, need to be sufficiently informed about innovations and good practice in the field so that they can inspire as well as require teachers to use the most productive materials and methods. Unless those in influential positions believe that it is possible for Americans to learn languages efficiently, it is unlikely that they will pressure or support their faculty to this end.

Currently, dissemination efforts involve monthly and quarterly professional publications and workshops and meetings that occur in voluntary organizations as well as during regular in-service programming. These efforts are not, however, of uniformly high quality nor are they generally accessible to the mass of faculty in schools and colleges who require help to improve their methods and materials. In general, the national plan for the future should permit more reliance on videotapes and cable programming to disseminate important information in a high-quality format. The medical profession is already highly reliant on video and audio cassettes that are produced and made available monthly to county medical associations by state and national offices of the American Medical Association. An effective national diffusion and dissemination plan will refocus existing dissemination systems as well as add additional components designed to improve the quality and range of impact on the language teaching profession.

REVIEW OF EXISTING DISSEMINATION AND DIFFUSION SYSTEMS

Dissemination currently occurs both in voluntary association meetings and publications subscribed to by teachers and in various institutional settings where teachers work. No central office exerts control over dissemination. Inadequacies in transmittal of innovation are frequent.

Voluntary

Faculty teaching foreign languages and literatures currently have access to national, regional, state, and local voluntary associations that provide professional development opportunities of widely varying quality. In the 1985-86 academic year, 82 foreign language teacher meetings were presented from 1 October to 28 June. These meetings, announced annually in the October issue of *Foreign Language Annals*, occur at the national, regional, and state levels and cover the commonly and less commonly taught languages.

The national dissemination plan should specifically utilize these meetings to address a wide audience of teachers. At plenary sessions, national leaders, in person or on videotape, should present the latest research findings and their impact on the teaching and learning of foreign languages. Follow-up panels composed of local faculty should assess the relationship of this research to the efforts of students and teachers in the schools and colleges of the region.

National. At the national level, four-day annual meetings of the Modern Language Association (MLA) and the American Council on the Teaching of Foreign Languages (ACTFL) offer faculty opportunities to encounter innovation in their field. This is done not only through sessions regularly scheduled as part of the conference, but also as pre- and post-conference workshops. Language-specific associations such as the American Association of Teachers of French, German, Spanish, Italian and Portuguese also meet annually in conjunction with ACTFL. The American Association of Teachers of Japanese and Chinese meet with the Asian Studies Association.

The Association of Departments of Foreign Languages (ADFL) holds a list of 3000 department chairpersons in the field. Community college, college, and university faculty typically belong to departments with department chairpersons. The ADFL organizes a set of meetings with the MLA and also runs two annual chairpersons' meetings— one in the East and one in the West. Currently these meetings are not well attended due, in part, to the travel costs and the timing of the meetings, which take place in mid to late June. To be a more effective asset to the national dissemination effort, ADFL meetings would have to change in the future. In addition to focusing on the important work of improving departmental management, hiring practices, and program evaluation, these meetings should alert chairpersons to the implications of new research on future classroom practice. In some cases, matching travel funding might have to be provided to enable a larger percentage of the department chairs in each half of the United States to attend the annual ADFL meetings.

Also at the university level, the American Association of Supervisors and Coordinators of Foreign Language Programs holds promise as a vehicle for dissemination. This organization includes the college- and university-level language program supervisors. Group members could serve particularly well as disseminators of innovative programs because they are directly responsible for language teaching and often for the training of new teachers. The organization's German section has already worked with the oral proficiency project to expand the number of German faculty prepared to give oral proficiency tests. The capacity of members of this group to develop additional field testing methods and materials could serve as a bridge between researchers and classroom teachers.

The advanced-placement (AP) program is a national effort that connects high school teachers to the college curriculum. Over 3500 high school foreign language faculty teach the AP curriculum. These teachers offer another opportunity for dissemination of particular innovations in language teaching as they relate to the literary content in the field. Typically, many of these teachers are engaged in the reading and evaluation of the AP exams as well as in their development. The College Board at its national office and regional sites keeps contact with high schools where AP classes are taught. While the College Board does not certify the teachers, it does offer one- or two-day professional development conferences sponsored by the regional offices where experienced college and high school AP teachers meet with faculty intending to teach the AP coursework. In 1985-86, 11 colleges and high schools sponsored one or two week-long seminars for high school teachers in-

tending to teach the AP curriculum. Last year, 1424 high schools offered AP courses in French language, 298 in French literature, 653 in German language, 1599 in Spanish language, and 289 in Spanish literature.

The network of AP teachers should play a significant role in the national dissemination plan because they tend to be teachers whose students are at the most advanced stages. These teachers offer a bridge between college and high school faculty. The plan should encourage colleges to offer adjunct positions to these teachers, invite them to curriculum development meetings, and utilize their support in reviewing new research findings and their implications for classroom practice.

Regional, state, and local faculty associations. The regional divisions of the MLA and language teacher conferences attract both college and school faculty for two-day meetings once each year. Groups such as the South Atlantic Modern Language Association, the Northeast Modern Language Association, the Rocky Mountain Modern Language Association, and the Midwest Modern Language Association typically hold annual meetings that are analogues of the national MLA meetings and tend to give graduate students and faculty from smaller institutions an opportunity to read papers on literary topics. These meetings also involve some focus on language teaching, but are generally more focused on the teaching of literature and literary criticism.

In the last five years a new strand of regional associations has developed. These organizations are more focused on language pedagogy and less on research in literature and criticism. They typically meet once annually in a major city in the region and permit high school and college teachers interested in improving language pedagogy to meet, share their innovations, and hear national leaders report their work. The Northeast Conference is the oldest of the regional associations. Others include the Central States Conference on the Teaching of Foreign Language, the Southern Conference of Language Teachers, and the South West Conference of Language Teachers.

Each state in the Union has a state foreign language teacher association. These associations meet annually, and typically attract a mixed group of faculty from colleges and schools. Depending on the leadership in any given sequence of years, these state organizations function more or less effectively to meet the needs of state teachers. Meetings typically begin with a Friday afternoon session and include a banquet with a keynote address and a series of meetings on Saturday. The state associations typically meet with the various language-specific associations such as the state affiliates of the American Association of Teachers of French, the American Association of Teachers of Spanish, the American Association of Teachers of German, and the American Association of Teachers of Italian. Attendance at these meetings varies widely across the states depending on geography, faculty access to travel funds and released time, as well as the capacity of the association's leaders to build and sustain membership rolls. The state foreign language teachers' associations tend to be led by strong high school teachers, and they lead faculty in state universities that have major commitments to foreign language education.

At the local level, faculty in foreign language and literature have elaborated over 100 local communities of inquiry called Academic Alliances among school and college faculty in the discipline. These local groups meet monthly or bimonthly to address important issues together. The faculty members who belong to an Academic Alliance group usually determine together the subjects they want to hear addressed in the set of meetings that occur each year. The groups typically have from 15 to 60 members, with directorship shared by a school and a college faculty member. Many of the faculty who belong to Alliances also belong to state, regional, and national associations, although many more faculty can attend local alliance meetings because there is no need for released time or financial support for hotel and travel accommodations.

Foreign language Alliance groups have a central office based at Marymount College and are part of a national effort to create communities of inquiry among school and college faculty in all disciplines. The central office of the Academic Alliances serving the elaboration of this concept among faculty in all the academic disciplines is based at the University of Pennsylvania.

FACULTY ASSOCIATIONS AND THE NEW DISSEMINATION PLAN

The new national dissemination plan should examine the national, regional, state, and local meetings held each year and utilize portions of these meetings to present major issues to the profession. Each of the meetings currently attended by language teachers should include a plenary session reviewing these major issues and their practical implications for classroom teachers. This approach would help assure that generally agreed-upon important issues would be examined in the most efficient way by the largest number of teachers in practice in the discipline. Ideally, videotapes and printed materials would be produced by national and regional experts and shown at plenary sessions of national, regional, state, and local meetings. Each time the materials are used, two or more respected leaders from the area should comment on them and link the issues and research implications to local efforts already under way. These efforts would assure dissemination of new information, but also would help create confidence in the evolution of good practice and reassure already burdened teachers about how to incorporate new methods and materials efficiently. Such attempts would also remove some of the unevenness of the quality in the meetings held at various levels across the nation.

Professional or institutional structures

Every faculty member teaching foreign languages and literatures is embedded in an institutional system that has some potential for disseminating innovation in the field. Each state has a foreign language supervisor.[1] The person may or may not be a specialist in the field, but he or she does have an administrative responsibility for the field and usually reports through the state department of education. In the experience of the

1. In a recent article, Carl Johnson and Bobby LaBouve published their survey of results relating to the following question: "What kinds of formal organizations or access do you have in your state to reach local supervisors, department heads of schools and districts, teacher educators, and presidents of language organizations within the state?" This question posed to state specialists indicates that the state supervisors appear to maintain contact with school, but not with college, faculty in the field. *Foreign Language Annals,* vol. 18 (Dec. 1985). For a directory of state foreign language supervisors, see ibid., vol. 19 (Dec. 1986).

Rockefeller Foundation Fellowships for Foreign Language Teachers in High Schools, these supervisors have widely varying work styles and levels of effectiveness. A number of states have more than one individual charged specifically with the responsibility of overseeing the quality of education in foreign languages. Among these are Texas, Virginia, California, and New York. State foreign language supervisors have a national association that calls an annual meeting. Members elect one of their own as president. Depending on the leadership quality of the individual who functions as president, this network could provide substantial support in the dissemination of innovation and research findings to the field.

At the district and school system level, faculty again have a variety of administrative structures that could contribute to a dissemination effort. There is, however, no dependable structure at this level across the whole nation. It would not be effective to try to deal with district- or school-system-level foreign language administrators. This is particularly true because depending on the size of the school system, the administrator to whom the teachers report may or may not be in the foreign language field. It is important to note that the lack of disciplinary specialists in supervisory roles is one of the major reasons why the planning implementation of in-service education for foreign language teachers in the schools is so uneven and generally so unsatisfactory.

At the university level, foreign language education departments exist in education schools in many state universities. These departments are particularly responsible for the development of the next generation of professional in the field and, to some extent, for the maintenance of skills of current teachers.

Through a variety of mechanisms from the simple offering of pedagogy courses in the evening to special summer institutes, foreign language education departments offer some opportunities for dissemination of improved practice in the field. But the last 15 years of falling enrollments in these departments have in many cases left them less able to function as dissemination centers or as lively centers of research in the field.

A revised national dissemination plan should utilize these departments in two major ways. The best of them should serve as sites for experimental classrooms where new research is put into practice. Teachers and students should be videotaped both to analyze new methods and to teach new techniques to faculty at other institutions. These departments should also serve as the sites for regularly scheduled one- to two-week faculty summer institutes where college and school faculty could gather each year for intensive work related to new developments in their field. Ideally, teacher education departments should become the centers where researchers and practitioners could meet to assure an orderly flow of well-planned materials and methods into classrooms to the benefit of both teachers and students. A consortium of leadership teacher education departments in foreign languages could be developed to achieve a dependable system and avoid the haphazard approach to teacher in-service education that currently characterizes the national effort.

A case study: dissemination approaches used by the ACTFL oral proficiency test developers, 1980-86

In 1980, the oral proficiency test moved out of the Foreign Service Insti-

tute and into the academic setting. The dissemination effort relied on interpersonal connections among faculty and researchers initially interested in adapting the Foreign Service Institute's test to the high school and college classroom environment. Presentations on the oral proficiency test were offered at least once in the last five years at virtually all the national, regional, state, and local meetings of foreign language teachers. In "Proficiency Projects in Action," Jiménez and Murphy describe the development of the proficiency movement in the United States.[2] A review of this information indicates that there does not appear to have been any real dissemination plan that guided the development of proficiency training sites. It appears that faculty at certain institutions volunteered to provide the settings for initial experimentation with the oral proficiency tests. Eventually, the Department of Education, the Exxon Education Foundation, and the National Endowment for the Humanities provided funds for training for faculty. Formal workshops occurred at a number of sites including the University of California at Los Angeles, San Diego State, the Twin Cities Campus of the University of Minnesota, and the University of Pennsylvania, as well as Georgetown University, Brigham Young University, George Williams College, the University of Rhode Island, and the University of Texas at El Paso.

ACTFL is currently working under a Department of Education grant with the foreign language teachers' certification procedures throughout the state of Texas. This project involves the state board of

2. Reynaldo Jiménez and Carol J. Murphy, "Proficiency Projects in Action," in *Teaching for Proficiency: The Organizing Principle,* ed. Theodore Higgs (Lincolnwood, IL: National Textbook, 1984), pp. 201-18.

education and 52 teacher-training institutions in public school systems. The organization of this project may provide a suitable dissemination design for other states; however, the ACTFL oral proficiency project is notable for its lack of a structured diffusion plan designed to embed the new approach in teaching and testing in the field.

PROBLEMS IN IMPROVING DISSEMINATION OF INNOVATION

Voluntary professional organizations and activities engage between 15,000 and 20,000 language teachers each year.[3] The professional institution-based structures in which faculty operate have efficient access to all teachers currently responsible for instruction in foreign languages. These two systems ought to operate more efficiently to assure that every teacher in practice utilizes the best in methods and materials. However, the quality of continuing professional development is uneven and, in a number of areas, highly inadequate for several reasons.

1. Despite the fact that in many districts teachers must take courses or fulfill continuing education units to keep their teacher certification, teachers' knowledge and skills in their subject area are often unaffected because teachers take courses in areas outside their teaching fields. They do so because often courses in, for example, educational administration lead to better promotions. When teachers do take course work directly in their field, it is often uneven in quality and designed less to connect teachers to new research in the

3. These figures are based on an average attendance of 200 per annual meeting at the national, regional, and state levels.

field than to permit preparation of immediately usable classroom materials.

2. U.S. education has not firmly established the connection between good teaching and continuous formal and informal learning by teachers. There is little expectation that faculty remain learners in their field and little provision for resources that would permit them to do so. Language teaching is especially adversely affected since faculty must usually go abroad to increase their own language proficiency and to make contact with the culture of the speakers of the language. They also, however, need to study in the United States to keep up-to-date on language pedagogy research and how it affects good teaching practices. Language teachers need more time and sustain higher costs for in-service education than other teaching faculty.

3. Hiring practices doom many language programs. In the schools, some administrators feel that a person who can speak the language can teach it. Others assume that a college degree and state certification to teach imply that a teacher is sufficiently competent in the language to serve as an adequate model for students. University departments have long permitted faculty with Ph.D.'s and no formal instruction in language pedagogy, language acquisition theory, or practice teaching to instruct large numbers of undergraduates each year. Since each of these currently accepted practices is widespread, the quality of language teaching is adversely affected in both schools and colleges.

4. Few foreign language programs focus on outcomes in learners as a way of evaluating the adequacy of instruction and materials. Without a focus on out-

comes for students, teachers and administrators often move through academic years with little direct idea of how best to utilize instructional time for the most efficient development of language skills. They have no means of comparison with successful programs and therefore are insufficiently concerned about how their programs can optimize their students' language competence per hour of instruction. A focus on student outcomes would create a stronger motivation for teachers and administrators to participate in the national dissemination plan.

5. The lack of a generally accepted pattern for how and when to teach Americans foreign languages is a major factor in the uneven delivery of continuing education to faculty in the field. Not only is there currently no best method, but the discrediting of the once highly touted Audio-Lingual Method makes teachers and administrators understandably skittish about throwing themselves into this or that camp of fervent disciples of a new methodology. Research is desperately needed to test current methods and identify the most productive approaches and materials for use with different kinds of language learners. Until field specialists can formulate a reliable paradigm, dissemination of current best strategies may be treated like Madison Avenue marketing of volatile fads unworthy of teachers' time or institutional resources.

SOLUTIONS PROPOSED FOR IMPROVING DISSEMINATION OF INNOVATION

College and school faculty working with administrators and both national and local funding sources can cooperate to reorient the foreign language field and address these problems.

1. A well-designed national dissemination effort should make field-specific in-service education a normal part of the professional year for all faculty teaching languages in schools and colleges. These opportunities to remain in contact with the best thinking in the field should occur both during the academic year and immediately following the close of school. Regularly scheduled institutes should operate as a network of annual programming of high-quality instruction to bring college and school faculty together in a challenging learning environment.

2. Colleges, universities, and school systems need to commit themselves to paid opportunities for language faculty to study abroad at least once every three to five years. The current Rockefeller Foundation Fellowships for Foreign Language Teachers in the Schools serves as a model for faculty study in foreign countries. This program should be expanded and replicated to serve a larger percentage of language faculty.

3. The profession should establish good-practice guidelines for administrators who hire language teachers in schools and colleges. Both a knowledge of foreign language pedagogy as well as reasonable standards for oral proficiency should be established nationwide as guidelines for hiring new faculty.

4. The field needs to produce guidelines for programs to evaluate student language skills and compare student performance with national norms for levels of competence per hours of instruction. These norms would enable both teachers and administrators to evaluate the quality of their programs and aim for higher levels of performance.

5. Research is currently going on and must be pursued at a faster rate in an

effort to evaluate current methods and develop a set of paradigms to guide good practice in the field. This is perhaps the most difficult and yet most important challenge facing the foreign language and literature profession between now and the year 2000.

A NATIONAL DISSEMINATION PLAN: KEY FEATURES

While these five problems are being addressed, a national dissemination plan can go forward with a number of new features designed to improve the diffusion of good practice throughout the field and utilize existing voluntary and institutional structures more efficiently.

The research and development yearbook and videotape

During the summer following each academic year, a team of field specialists should create a yearbook containing reviews of the major developments in the field during the previous year. This publication should not exceed 20 pages and should be accompanied by a 90-minute videotape. The videotape should present a series of interviews with faculty researchers reporting major findings and results of work going on in experimental classrooms. An overview of these developments could be provided by a master of ceremonies who would allude to the existence of the yearbook and other publications for further information. During each academic year, as research data are accumulated and prepared for publication, researchers would send a one-page abstract of their findings to the yearbook development group. Review of these documents would culminate in decisions made by the group about what programs and research projects should be included in the yearbook and videotape.

This yearbook and videotape would afford a convenient and easily assimilated format for use at plenary sessions of national, regional, and state meetings of foreign language faculty in schools and colleges. It could also be used by teachers and administrators in school and college in-service programs and classes on foreign language pedagogy. Chairpersons could use the tape with their departments to conduct ongoing workshops during the academic year. These seminars would focus on improving teaching and learning in the field and also help faculty to design research projects to test the results of innovation at the local level. Academic alliance directors could also use the yearbook and videotape for local dissemination workshops for their school and college faculty members. These materials would have an excellent chance of being used by both the voluntary and the institution-based structures where foreign language teachers can be contacted efficiently.

The yearbook and videotape could be advertised in the professional press, including the *ADFL Bulletin* and the *State Foreign Language Supervisor*, and sent free on demand to faculty and administrators. All sites that receive the free materials should be responsible for producing a short review of the tape's impact on teaching in the field and report any changes in teaching and learning based on innovation or research presented in the materials.

National Foreign Language Video Conference Day

The national dissemination effort should sponsor a nationwide cable network conference day announced sufficiently far in advance so that school systems as well as college and university language departments can arrange to watch programming for a two- to three-hour period. Programming could also be videotaped at local sites around the country and used at convenient times following the live broadcast. The National Foreign Language Video Conference Day programming would offer a series of interviews, classroom demonstrations, and panel discussions on advances in the field. Both researchers and practitioners would participate. This programming would also permit a limited amount of telephone call-in for questions from viewers. Regional, state, and local foreign language teachers could follow up the conference-day broadcast with discussions of topics addressed in the program. These discussions could also utilize cable networks, especially where small face-to-face discussions are impractical. Packets of information should be available to individuals and schools that request additional bibliographical information to help them proceed with local assimilation of the information offered in the televised program. In this single-shot dissemination effort, a large majority of those teaching in the field would come in contact with the best current research in the field in an efficient and cost-effective manner.

The National Board of Consultants

In cooperation with currently existing associations of language faculty, a National Board of Consultants should be assembled to assist the progress of researchers and practitioners in the field. Individuals with special experience in curriculum design, technology, testing, department and program management, teacher education, and instruction and supervision of teaching assistants would serve institutions for long- and short-

term consultancies. These consultancies would help disseminate new information related to teaching and learning in the field and also help to evaluate improvements in learning outcomes. Board members would work on a fee-for-service basis.

National board associates

Board associates should be appointed for a three-year term from among groups of people committed to excellence in foreign language teaching. Associates would receive the annual yearbook and help identify strong programs. The associate network would aim to assure a basic level of familiarity with progress in the field within a wide circle of influential people. Associates would be selected from among chief state school officers and top officeholders in local, state, and national political structures. Influential business executives, lawyers, and journalists would also make excellent members of the board associates group.

Board qualification of foreign language faculty

Foreign language teachers should have the opportunity to demonstrate their professional skills and knowledge by achieving board qualification. This program is likely to create a significant incentive to faculty to pursue advanced study. A committee formed by the National Board of Consultants should be appointed and begin working to develop criteria for foreign language teacher board qualifications. This designation should not separate college- or school-level instruction, but could have general and advanced-level qualifications. Requirements developed in cooperation with school and college faculty would encourage colleges to establish norms for the training of new faculty whether they teach at the college or school level and also encourage better hiring and promotion practices at both levels. Board qualification standards should inlcude, for example, specific oral proficiency levels, proven capacity to explain and reinforce grammar and syntax learning, tested understanding of the theories shaping second language acquisition, and familiarity with the culture and major texts of people who speak the language. Board qualification standards designed at two levels would permit teachers to progress from a general board qualification to an advanced board qualification over a seven- to ten-year period. Provisions should be made for board qualification to last for five to seven years with established requalification terms. The qualification process itself would offer an excellent way to assure diffusion of new research findings and improved methods and materials.[4]

Great presentations

The foreign language teaching field needs a set of ideal models designed to show faculty interesting and intellectually compelling ways to teach foreign language, culture, and literature. A series of one-hour programs to be shown on educational television as well as in formal classroom learning settings could create a substantial base of professional quality resources for teachers, students,

4. The American Council on the Teaching of Foreign Languages has begun to discuss foreign language teacher certification with some members of the profession. Dale Lange and Alice Omaggio, both leaders in the field of foreign language pedagogy, have called for an examination of this issue in recent presentations to specialists in the field.

and intersted citizens. Excellent classroom teachers could be brought together with researchers in this format to help disseminate the results of new links between research developments and improved ways to teach language proficiency and cultural awareness in mutually reinforcing ways. The use of videotapes of model presentations by John Rassias has been shown to be a highly effective method of informing large numbers of professionals about a new teaching technique. Rassias's dissemination efforts should be duplicated in the national dissemination plan's series of hour-long programs.

National surveys

The dissemination effort would be greatly enhanced by three surveys. The first survey would address the profession's need to identify foreign language teachers currently functioning in school, college, and private sector learning environments. The school systems and post-secondary institutions as well as the many language teaching businesses should be asked to identify those persons teaching foreign languages. A second, short survey on adult needs for foreign languages should be sent to a large number of foreign language teachers identified in the first survey. This questionnaire could help researchers understand the needs and interests of teachers and their level of familiarity with current best practices. The third survey would be concerned with the field's need to understand how American adults use foreign languages. Motivation to study foreign languages could be affected significantly by better understanding of how adults in a variety of work contexts are currently utilizing their foreign language skills. In addition, it would be helpful to understand how adults in other countries utilize their second languages.

The national newspaper

The mailing list developed in the survey of foreign language teachers in the United States would enable the National Board of Consultants to send a quarterly national newspaper free of charge to teachers of foreign languages. This newspaper could serve to unite the profession and disseminate new ideas quickly and effectively.

Major national publicity campaign

With the help of large state and private universities such as those in the Ivy Consortium,[5] the dissemination plan should include a major effort to improve the awareness of American citizens of the importance of foreign language teaching capacity. A focused advertising campaign should go forward with the help of a professional agency. Perhaps a multinational corporation should be solicited for support of this advertising effort.

Computerized dissemination

A group of specialists in the computer-assisted learning field should review the ways in which computers can be utilized effectively to enhance the diffusion of good ideas throughout the profession. This study would involve a review of the actual use of the Educational Resources Information Center (ERIC)

5. The Ivy League institutions joined with the Massachusetts Institute of Technology, Stanford, and the University of Chicago to form this consortium. Its aim is to improve foreign language teaching on its members' campuses and to promote the importance of foreign language learning in general.

data file and an analysis of how electronic mail could serve as a connecting network among field specialists. A set of suggestions based on this study would help the field to utilize computers efficiently. Major data banks of teaching resources should be developed only if it becomes clear that teachers are able to access this data efficiently and are willing to utilize this form of dissemination.

An efficient and effective dissemination plan is the link between research in the field and the improvement of practice for learners. This plan must maximize the impact of existing voluntary and institution-based structures. It must also undertake bold initiatives like the production of an annual videotape, yearbook, and newspaper and the establishment of an annual National Foreign Language Video Conference Day. Board qualification of language teachers would also have a major impact on the dissemination of quality teaching and learning in the field. In order to disseminate progress most effectively, the profession must foster collegial leadership and the willingness to take collective responsibility for the quality of learning outcomes for students. Faculty must be willing to share responsibility for achieving excellence in the field and to share ownership of the field with diverse constituents. For instance, school and college faculty need to work together to achieve better articulation. Foreign language pedagogy researchers and classroom teachers need to feel increasingly responsible to each other for the quality of the teaching and learning in the field. Regularly scheduled opportunities to learn must become a regular part of every academic year's activities for teachers. Information on research and good practice must be communicated clearly and inexpensively and reach a wide audience of those who will enter classrooms. A well-designed national dissemination plan can help to assure a more linguistically proficient U.S. citizenry by the year 2000.

ANNALS, *AAPSS,* **490,** March 1987

Language Conservation

By RUSSELL N. CAMPBELL and SUSAN SCHNELL

ABSTRACT: Competencies in a large number of languages brought to our schools by representatives of linguistic minority groups are, through an unspoken policy of subtractive language education, irrevocably lost as national foreign language resources. This occurs in spite of repeated declarations of national leaders in commerce, defense, education, and international affairs that our foreign language resources are in a "scandalous" state. There are promising ways in which our schools can conserve the extraordinarily valuable language resources that are currently being squandered. A description of a model of two-way bilingual education is described that has the potential of providing opportunities for linguistic minority children to develop mature, adult literacy skills in their ancestral language.

Russell N. Campbell is professor of teaching English as a second language and applied linguistics and director of China and Mexico ESL Programs at the University of California, Los Angeles. He is a former president of Teachers of English to Speakers of Other Languages.

Susan Schnell is a graduate student in teaching English as a second language and applied linguistics and a research associate on the Modern Language Projects at the University of California, Los Angeles.

WHILE the majority of the articles in this collection address issues related to the teaching and learning of foreign languages by speakers of English, we will, in this brief presentation, consider the conservation of competence in languages spoken by linguistic minority groups in this country. The term "conservation" is used here in the sense that we have come to associate with our concern for other national resources; namely, "a careful preservation and protection of something; esp: planned management of a natural resource to prevent exploitation, destruction or neglect."[1]

It is our contention that the principles of conservation specified in this definition, especially "planned management" and prevention of "destruction or neglect," have not, in any logical, systematic manner, been applied to the conservation of the extraordinarily valuable language resources that substantial numbers of linguistic minority children bring to our schools. Rather, we regularly, as a matter of unspoken national policy, squander these resources in a manner that is clearly contrary to our own best interests and detrimental to the education and welfare of the minority populations affected.

RESOURCES AND LANGUAGE LOSS

In nearly every major urban center in the United States we find large concentrations of homes in which English is not the dominant language of communication. In these homes, children up to the age of five or six regularly acquire and use the home language for all of their sociocultural and basic physical needs. As a consequence, through natural language acquisition processes found in all human societies, these children, in Chomskian terms,[2] acquire nearly all of the phonological, grammatical, and semantic rules that identify them as native speakers of that language. For example, substantial numbers of preschool-age children in the Korean community of Los Angeles acquire the particular set of generative rules that permit them to produce and comprehend the Korean language. That is, by the time they reach school age, if the natural acquisition of Korean is comparable to the acquisition of English,[3] these children's pronunciation, their ability to form words, phrases, and sentences and to participate in extended discourse in Korean is, for all practical purposes, identical to adult Korean competencies in these same areas. In a word, they are native speakers of Korean.

Obviously there are features of adult speech that children do not acquire by age six since there are many sociocultural domains outside of the home and the community that they do not encounter until later in life. Consequently, many concepts and cognitive processes have yet to be experienced and dealt with linguistically. These later-in-life opportunities in their first language (L1) are precisely those that are typically denied linguistic minority children in our society. The consequences are, of course, predictable:

Even languages at one time as numerically strong as German and Norwegian have followed the familiar pattern of practically every minority language in this country by which the second generation, i.e. the children of immigrants, becomes bilingual and the

1. *Webster's New Collegiate Dictionary* (1981), s.v. "conservation."

2. Noam Chomsky, *Aspects of the Theory of Syntax* (Cambridge, MA: MIT Press, 1965).

3. Carol Chomsky, *The Acquisition of Syntax in Children from 5 to 10* (Cambridge, MA: MIT Press, 1969).

third generation shifts relatively completely to English.[4]

It is this long-standing, societally encouraged pattern of English replacement of other home languages—rather than the provision of opportunities whereby linguistic minority children maintain and develop their L1, including literacy skills, in addition to English—that this article is addressing.[5]

LANGUAGE LEARNING AND NATURAL LANGUAGE ACQUISITION

We return now to the characterization of the linguistic competence in Korean that Korean American children often attain during the five or six years before they enter our schools. We are using Korean as an example of the language resources that most linguistic minority children possess. We could just as well have chosen Japanese, Spanish, Amharic, Tagalog, or any one of dozens of other groups.[6] It is our observation that the high level of language proficiency that these children normally attain is rarely, if ever, matched by those who attempt to learn Korean as a foreign language in our schools, colleges, or language institutes. If it is indeed matched, then it is done only at enormous costs of time and energy, as well as human and financial resources. For example, the Defense Language Institute in Monterey, California, estimates that it takes approximately 47 weeks of instruction with six hours of classroom time and three hours of homework per day for a typical adult to reach a U.S. government proficiency rating of S-2 in Korean. This level of competence is described as follows:

Able to satisfy routine social demands and limited work requirements. Can handle with confidence but not with facility most social situations including introductions and casual conversations about current events, as well as work, family, and autobiographical information; can handle limited work requirements, needing help in handling any complications or difficulties; can get the gist of most conversations on nontechnical subjects and has a speaking vocabulary sufficient to respond simply with some circumlocutions; accent, though often quite faulty, is intelligible; can usually handle elementary constructions quite accurately but does not have thorough or confident control of grammar.[7]

4. Eduardo Hernandez-Chavez, "Language Maintenance, Bilingual Education, and Philosophies of Bilingualism in the United States," in *International Dimensions of Bilingual Education*, ed. J. E. Alatis (Washington, DC: Georgetown University Press, 1978), p. 527.

5. There are other populations for which attrition of foreign language capacities constitutes a serious and, psycholinguistically speaking, very interesting problem, namely, those who study foreign languages formally in classroom situations or those who acquire them as a result of extended contact with speakers of other languages in this country or abroad. These would include, for example, businesspeople, diplomats, Peace Corp volunteers, and educators. Clearly these merit serious consideration. If proficiency gained in Russian, for example, at the Defense Language Institute or any other institution, at a cost of thousands of dollars and months of instruction, is, as a consequence of nonuse of and nonexposure to the language, significantly decreased to the point that it no longer serves any practical purpose, then we might energetically seek means to sustain that proficiency.

6. For demographic information on these populations, see Dorothy Waggoner, "Geographic Distribution, Nativity, and Age Distribution of Language Minorities in the United States: Spring 1976," *National Center for Education Statistics Bulletin* (Aug. 1978).

7. Marianne Lehr Adams and James R. Frith, eds., *Testing Kit: French and Spanish* (Washington, DC: Department of State, Foreign Service Institute, 1979), pp. 13-15, as cited in Pardee Lowe, Jr., "The U.S. Government's Foreign Language Attrition and Maintenance Experience," in *The Loss of Language Skills*, ed. R. D. Lambert

Without counting the expected 705 hours of homework, the Defense Language Institute's program calls for approximately 1410 hours of instruction to reach level two of proficiency, and, although no precise dollar cost for the instruction required to reach this level is available, it is our judgment that a conservative estimate would be in the range of $25,000 to $30,000. The magnitude of the investment of time required to attain this level two can be brought into sharper focus if we consider that the 47 weeks of intensive study is equal to at least three to four years of traditional university coursework.

There is no doubt that there are literally thousands of Korean American children who enter our schools with a level of Korean language proficiency that equals or exceeds the government rating of two described previously. Certainly their "accent" and "control of grammar" would, by comparison, be judged at level three or four of proficiency.

Obviously, this proficiency is attained without direct cost to public institutions. We are struck by the irrationality of our collective behavior regarding the conservation of these language resources. By our inaction, our indifference, or perhaps, in some cases, by our mistaken view of what is most beneficial for linguistic minority children,[8] we contribute to the

loss of very valuable language resources and, ironically, in some instances, find these very children enrolled later in traditional language courses, at public expense, to study the very languages they commanded so well as children.

If we were to follow these Korean children, or any similar group, during their early school years, we would observe first a dramatic reduction and slowing of the L1 acquisition process and, subsequently, an onset of an attrition process that would lead, in many cases, to the loss of the home-language competencies so highly evaluated previously. The position that this article takes is that this is an unnecessary, irresponsible waste at a time when we have been told again and again that our national language resources are in a "scandalous" state.[9] It seems obvious that the magnitude and value of these resources are such that we should dedicate ourselves to their conservation for the multiple benefits that would accrue to our society.

SATURDAY SCHOOLS

It might be expected that the responsibility for conservation of the languages of linguistic minority groups could be left with the minority groups themselves. In fact, as comprehensive studies by Fishman have reported, ethnolinguistic groups have made valiant efforts through the establishment and maintenance of Saturday schools and other part-time instructional programs to provide oppor-

---

and B. F. Freed (Rowley, MA: Newbury House, 1982), p. 189.

8. Jim Cummins, "Empowering Minority Students: A Framework for Intervention," *Harvard Educational Review,* 56(1):18-36 (1986). Cummins has provided persuasive evidence that there are powerful scholastic, educational reasons for providing extended opportunity for linguistic minority children to receive their education in their L1. Not only will children perform better scholastically, but they will with greater efficiency, in a shorter period of time, acquire a higher level of English

language competence. These are clearly powerful reasons for providing opportunities for linguistic minority children to receive substantial amounts of their early education in their home language.

9. President's Commission on Foreign Language and International Studies, "Strength through Wisdom: A Critique of U.S. Capability," *Modern Language Journal,* 64(1):12 (Spring 1980).

tunities for their children to maintain some competence in the ancestral language as well as to develop an understanding and appreciation of their cultural heritage.[10]

To gain some firsthand knowledge of such programs, we visited a Korean community school in Los Angeles. The principal, Sam Lee, when asked to state the objectives, informed us that the aim of the Korean language teaching program is not to achieve the same linguistic and scholastic levels as those of students attending school in Korea, but to enable Korean American students to communicate orally with their families and with their friends in the home country. Literacy skills are deemed important, but there is no attempt to develop high-level language-arts skills. In fact, exposure to the culture is emphasized more than the teaching of the language. Mr. Lee also acknowledged that while Korean-born and first-generation parents send their children to ethnic schools, the effort does not usually extend to the third generation, which is typically monolingual English. If other ethnolinguistic mother-tongue schools are similar to this one, then it is clear that these schools will not make a major contribution to the conservation of minority language resources. This conclusion is consistent with Fishman's belief, as referenced in Levy,[11] that these schools are not successful in maintaining—or reintroducing—the non-English language.

10. Joshua Fishman, "Ethnic Community Mother Tongue Schools in the USA: Dynamics and Distributions," *International Migration Review*, 14(2):235-47 (Summer 1980).

11. Jack Levy, "Policy Implications/Complications Arising from Native Language Attrition in U.S. Ethnolinguistic Minority Groups," in *The Loss of Language Skills*, ed. Lambert and Freed, p. 198.

BILINGUAL EDUCATION

If we cannot, with confidence, look to the efforts of the minority communities to assist in the conservation of these language resources, it might be expected that programs supported by the federal government with the title "bilingual education" would possibly provide the desired results. Motivated perhaps by other issues, some political, some scholastic, the notion of providing linguistic minority children part of their education in their home language has been a concern in American schools for some time. The Supreme Court decision in *Lau* v. *Nichols* argued for initial instruction in children's first language to provide opportunity for access to the school content curriculum while learning sufficient English to enter mainstream classes.[12] For well over a decade, under the direction of the Office of Bilingual Education and Minority Language Affairs, public school programs have been supported that have as their goal equal academic opportunities for minority children. To attain this equality there has consistently been a segment of the syllabus taught in the students' home language. Without attempting to provide a comprehensive review of bilingual education's contribution to the conservation of L1 resources, we find ourselves in agreement with the following assessments:

In a just completed national survey of 37 Title VII bilingual education projects in which the program organization, goals, and effects were analyzed in some depth, the American Institutes for Research (1977) found that most of these claimed language maintenance as a primary goal. Yet the study also found out that, in practice, the majority of the programs quickly shifted the greater

12. *Lau* v. *Nichols*, 414 U.S. 563, 1974.

part of their instruction to English and thus are assimilationist in character.[13]

In a recent national survey of the goals of school districts with language minority students, fewer than 10 percent of the districts cited native language maintenance to be their goal. Furthermore, even in programs with a strong component for the development of native language skills, students are quickly moved into mainstream classes, often after one or two years in the program. For the majority of language minority youngsters who go through the revolving door of bilingual education, what lies ahead is the shift to English monolingualism.[14]

TWO-WAY BILINGUAL EDUCATION

Having discounted both existing Saturday school and bilingual education programs as significant contributors to the conservation of language resources, we turn now to the description of an extremely promising experimental model of education that, among a host of other benefits,[15] would permit substantial numbers of children to make normal progress toward the acquisition of a mature, educated level of proficiency in their home language. Although there are several names given to this model, the most common one is "two-way bilingual education" (TWBE). To our knowledge, there are only two locations where this model has been implemented; namely, in the San Diego (California) Unified School District, in 1975,[16] and, more

13. Hernandez-Chavez, "Language Maintenance," pp. 538, 539.

14. C. Snow and K. Hakuta, "Bilingual Education: What Does It Really Cost?" *Psychology Today* (in press).

15. Esp. those suggested in note 8.

16. "An Exemplary Approach to Bilingual Education: A Comprehensive Handbook for Implementing an Elementary-level Spanish-English Language Immersion Program," no. I-B-82-58 (Unpublished document, San Diego (California) Unified School District, 1982).

recently, in New York State, in 1984. The following definition of a TWBE program is found in the "General Information" section of a request for new applications for New York State support for TWBE programs for the 1986-87 school year:

A Two-Way Bilingual Education Program is defined as one which employs two languages, one of which is English, for the purposes of instruction and involves students who are native speakers of each of those languages. Both groups of students—limited English proficient (LEP) and English proficient (EP)—are expected to become bilingual. They learn curricula through their own language and through the second language, become proficient in the second language, and continue to develop skills and proficiency in their native language.[17]

There are a number of goals of such a program over and beyond the conservation and development of the minority students' L1. The other benefits, including high levels of scholastic achievement, earlier and more efficient acquisition of English language skills, higher self-esteem, and decreased chances of dropping out, individually and collectively are probably of greater importance to the education and welfare of minority students than the language conservation issue being addressed in this article. However, the added benefit of L1 conservation is, as we have seen, an extremely precious byproduct, one that is worthy of careful monitoring over the next few years to provide qualitative and quantitative information on the conditions that provide optimal language development opportunities for children in the programs.

17. New York State Education Department, Bureau of Bilingual Education, *Applications for New Grants for Two-Way Bilingual Education Programs* (Albany, NY: Office of State Printing, 1986).

The basic descriptive features of the TWBE program are as follows, assuming English and Spanish as the two languages involved. First, in terms of student participants, there are roughly equal numbers of English and Spanish native speakers in each class. Second, in terms of language of instruction, Spanish is the primary language of instruction from preschool to second grade, but with some time—say, 20 minutes a day in preschool, 30 minutes a day in kindergarten, and 60 minutes a day in first grade—dedicated to the development of English language proficiency and language arts. In grades two through six, the percentage of the curriculum taught in English is increased until by the sixth grade, approximately one-half of the courses are taught in each of the two languages. It must be noted that only one of the languages is used in any instructional period. Each language is used as the medium of instruction for the full spectrum of school subjects, employing all of the verbal skills, both oral and written, normally associated with each content area. It is therefore necessary for the students to develop linguistic skills in both languages that will enable them to read academic texts, write acceptable essays and test responses, and be able to discuss subject-matter areas—history, science, mathematics, and so forth—in both languages.

The characteristics of the TWBE are, of course, markedly different from the bilingual education programs referred to earlier, which were, typically, designed for linguistic minority children only and seldom provide for the development and maturation of adult-level linguistic competence in the children's L1. TWBE also differs from the highly successful immersion programs, which have provided extraordinary opportunities for linguistic majority children to acquire foreign languages.[18] TWBE would appear to offer both linguistic minority and linguistic majority children excellent academic and language acquisition opportunities and, of relevance here, we see no brighter prospects for the conservation of the valuable language resources discussed earlier than those to be gained through participation in a TWBE program. Evidence for the probable success of this proposal is found in an experimental program reported on by Lambert in 1978. What follows is an excerpt from that article:

We participated in an experiment wherein a random selection of schools in the area [Northern Maine] were permitted to offer a third of the elementary curriculum in French and where a second sample of schools with children of comparable intelligence scores and socioeconomic backgrounds served as a control or comparison in that all their instruction was in English. After a five-year run, the children in the "partial French" classes clearly outperformed those in the control classes on various aspects of English language skills and on academic content, such as math, learned partly via French; at the same time French had become for them a much more literate language (in contrast to mainly audio-lingual) because of the reading and writing requirements of the French schooling.[19]

This research is persuasive. Francophone children clearly emerge from the reported experience with a level of literate competence that will allow them to use French for a multiplicity of real-world purposes.

18. California State Department of Education, Office of Bilingual Bicultural Education, *Studies on Immersion Education* (Sacramento, CA: Office of State Printing, 1984).
19. Wallace E. Lambert, "Some Cognitive and Sociocultural Consequences of Being Bilingual," in *International Dimentions of Bilingual Education*, ed. James E. Alatis (Washington, DC: Georgetown University Press, 1978), pp. 226-27.

A RESEARCH AGENDA

Although the San Diego TWBE project was inaugurated some ten years ago, and in spite of the fact that there have been several very positive evaluation reports prepared and disseminated,[20] there remain a very large number of questions that need to be defined and answered regarding the practical and theoretical aspects of this model. In addition to the obvious and important questions regarding the product in both scholastic and linguistic achievement terms, there are questions concerning all of the human, logistical, philosophical, psychological, and fiscal elements that impose themselves on the processes involved in the design, implementation, and evaluation of a TWBE program. For example, far too little is yet known about optimally appropriate:

—teacher qualifications;

—student—individual or group—characteristics;

—instructional materials;

—language proficiency and scholastic content tests;

—time allocations for instruction in the two languages;

—parental involvement;

—school administration support, local or state;

—location and demographics of the community; and

—social factors in second-language attrition.[21]

20. Charles H. Herbert, *Final Evaluation Report Bilingual Basic Grant Project, ESEA Title VII* (San Diego, CA: San Diego City Schools Planning, Research and Evaluation Division, 1986).

21. R. C. Gardner, R. N. Lalonde, and J. Macpherson, "Social Factors in Second Language

Each of these areas, and others to be identified, suggest a number of separate, but related, research questions, the answers to which could provide guidelines for informed curriculum design and development, teacher training, materials preparation, and test construction as well as parental and community activities that might provide additional out-of-school opportunities for authentic language use. Finally, measures of language proficiency attained by participants in TWBE programs could provide secondary-school and university departments with information useful to them in the development of appropriate and relevant language courses for successful graduates of TWBEs.

CONCLUSION

The issue raised in this short article is basically very simple and straightforward: should we not, given the recognized value of multilingual individuals in our society and given the enormous costs of producing in formal classroom situations individuals competent in a second language, make concerted efforts to conserve and develop the enormous language resources that linguistic minority children bring to our schools? It is hard to imagine anything other than a general positive response to this question. Fortunately, a model of education in two languages has been designed and implemented in public school programs on opposite coasts of this country. Results from formative and summative research need now to be considered to guide in the design of appropriate pre- and in-service teacher-training programs, and material and test development, as well as in the determination of the next level

Attrition," *Language Learning*, 35(4):519-40 (Dec. 1985).

of research to help us better understand students' potential for language acquisition and academic success. Both the research questions and the subsequent activities are issues that could appropriately be addressed for the enhancement of foreign language education in the United States.

ANNALS, *AAPSS*, **490**, March 1987

The Humanistic Basis of
Second Language Learning

By WINFRED P. LEHMANN and RANDALL L. JONES

ABSTRACT: A humanistic approach to language study recognizes the necessity of learning a language in its social and cultural contexts, encompassing the ecology and the material, social, religious, and linguistic cultures of the language studied. The need to teach language in relation to social and cultural values affects educational choices with respect to curriculum, materials, and approaches and should be central to national planning and programs for professional development and the improvement of teaching.

Winfred P. Lehmann is director of the Linguistics Research Center at the University of Texas, Austin, and 1987 president of the Modern Language Association.

Randall L. Jones is director of the Humanities Research Center at Brigham Young University.

T HIS article treats language in the context of the humanities, a perspective shared by the Modern Language Association in its concern for improving the teaching and learning of language. Language in the context of the humanities means language in its social and cultural contexts. While language has many varieties including special sublanguages for technology, the physical sciences, and the social sciences, its basis is the human communication that is central to the formation and interaction of all social groups, from family to community to nation.

During the past several years the language teaching profession in the United States has directed its attention to practical language instruction. Oral proficiency has become the primary goal, and virtually all activities in and out of the classroom are directed toward it. The desired outcome is simply to learn to speak the language sufficiently well to use it to accomplish specific tasks.

While the idea that students in a language program should learn how to speak the language is certainly not new, some recent theories, methods, and movements within the profession have had dramatic impact on almost every aspect of our teaching. Chief among these are notional-functional theories, the communicative competence movement, the natural method of language instruction—based in turn on Krashen's theories of second language acquisition—and the proficiency-based language curriculum.

While recognizing that some language programs may wish to offer instruction primarily directed toward reading skills for specific groups of students, we believe that oral proficiency should be the principal goal for the majority of language programs in the United States.

Language, however, is a complex phenomenon, and its proper use requires much more than the linguistic abilities associated with speaking and understanding. One cannot properly learn another language without learning something about the cultural and social contexts in which it is used and the values of those who speak it, nor can one communicate accurately with a speaker of another language if one filters the information received through one's own monocultural experience.

The intimate relation between language and culture becomes especially clear when representatives of Western culture come into contact with individuals in other cultures. Graphic illustrations of the fundamental importance of a humanistic approach are provided by linguists like the long-time secretary and linguistic adviser to the American Bible Society, Eugene A. Nida, who has worked extensively in other cultures on matters of communication and translation.

Nida classifies problems in equivalence among languages under five rubrics: (1) ecology; (2) material culture; (3) social culture; (4) religious culture; and (5) linguistic culture.[1] For each of these he provides numerous examples that any traveler could extend. The five categories may serve to illustrate basic uses of language that are fundamental for its mastery. Contacts with exotic cultures highlight those uses, which involve more subtle differences between languages relatively similar to one another, such as the languages of Western civilization. For control of these languages as well, whether the English of Britain or the widely studied languages of the European continent—French, Ger-

1. Eugene A. Nida, *Exploring Semantic Structure* (Munich: Fink, 1975), p. 68.

man, Portuguese, and Spanish, in their several varieties—users must be aware of the cultural viewpoints of native speakers, and they must set out to master these viewpoints.

ECOLOGY AND LANGUAGE

To illustrate problems related to ecology, we may take Nida's example of finding equivalents for expressing topographical features in languages of peoples located where those features are not found. For example, inhabitants of some islands of the Pacific and of the Yucatan peninsula have no mountains around them, scarcely even hills. To represent the ecology of other cultures to such peoples, special words and phrases have to be constructed. For "mountain" Nida suggests the phrase "large hill." But in communicating with inhabitants of some of the smaller Pacific islands Nida had difficulty finding equivalents for items like river or lake; with inhabitants of inland areas, similar problems arise describing the operation of a boat. Nida came to face many such problems and to propose sensible solutions to them.

Numerous such ecological differences exist among cultures, many even more subtle. Especially when receiving information about a culture that is not exotic but closely related to one's own, it is easy to fall into the habit of imposing a familiar background upon the data received and thus overlook subtle differences. For example, Americans hearing about life in a typical German community may hear words like "child," "family," "house," "street," and "church" and may picture them in their minds according to American models. In such a process, basic social and psychological differences are overlooked, and the resulting image may be seriously distorted.

Unfortunately, many handbooks for language study fail to make allowance for cultural differences. It may seem invidious to cite examples from such books, yet they are widely accessible and, worse, they are often the only available instructional materials for learning the elements of certain languages. Among such handbooks are the Teach Yourself Books published by English Universities Press Ltd. of London. We quote from *Teach Yourself Samoan* by C. C. Marsack,[2] who cannot be held completely responsible for the shortcomings of this handbook, since the publisher advertises a set of texts from Afrikaans to Welsh as "uniform with this volume and in the same series."

The Samoan handbook consists of 20 lessons. In the ninth, the final exercise requires translation into Samoan of the following eight sentences:

—"There is no food on the table in the dining room."

—"I do not know how to dance."

—"The orator made a very good speech."

—"The man from Lepa is hungry."

—"John does not want to go to Apia."

—"The boy is fed up and is not working well."

—"Don't go to church because it is raining."

—"There are no dresses in Mary's box."

Nowhere is there information on Samoan geography or topography. We may well believe that there are a place like Lepa and a man from there who is hungry, but we are not given any informa-

2. C. C. Marsack, *Teach Yourself Samoan* (London: English Universities Press, 1962).

tion on Lepa's whereabouts or those of Apia. Sadly, this type of language instruction is widespread, even in academic handbooks.

Lesson 9 is entitled "The Negative: Some Useful Phrases." There is no Samoan text, only individual sentences illustrating the grammatical structure under consideration. The first of these reads, in translation, "There is no chair in the room"; the second, "There is no money in the box." The handbook on Icelandic treats the negative in lesson 6, where the final exercise includes eight sentences, none of them involving a negative.[3] We quote only the first two:

—"Now the clergyman has come to find father."

—"She clapped her hands together."

It may be unnecessary to add that nowhere in the handbook is there any information on Icelandic geography. With a few substitutions, such as Lepa for Reykjavik, the exercises could be used for Samoan as well—or for Afrikaans through Welsh. There seems to be a tacit assumption that language consists of positives and negatives, that cultural figures like members of the clergy and orators are alike everywhere, and that there is no need to present language as used by its speakers.

The prevalence of such handbooks may seem to indicate that an introductory text cannot deal with more than the fundamental grammatical patterns of a language, that it cannot present a language as an element of an individual culture spoken in specific surroundings by speakers with a distinctive background. Such a view is totally wrong. It is readily disproved by excellent hand-

books such as *Spoken Norwegian* by Einar Haugen,[4] in the generally admirable series produced during World War II under the auspices of the American Council of Learned Societies. These handbooks also observe a set format, but it is based on cultural, rather than grammatical, topics. The first unit of the series is labeled "Getting Around"; the second, "Meeting People"; the fifth, "Seeing the Sights"; and so on. After completing Haugen's handbook, one knows the general geography of Norway and the location of its major cities as well as the principal grammatical features of the language, which are presented in highly useful patterns for daily use. It should be noted that the basic cultural format found in Haugen's book was used, with modifications, for many other languages.

MATERIAL CULTURE

Nida's four further requirements need less discussion. Material culture, for example, may be the most prominent topic in language handbooks today, and indeed attention to some aspects of it could well be reduced. Virtually every handbook for the Western languages treats the topic of telling time, using both straightforward patterns and relatively complex ones that involve prepositions or sequences like the German Wie spät ist es? (literally, "How late is it?"). Yet these days—when nearly everyone wears a watch or carries other devices that give the time, and when every conference room, railway station, and so on has a large clock in a prominent place—asking locals for the time may be among the least used patterns in the language. Moreover, the handbooks

3. P. T. Glendening, *Teach Yourself Icelandic* (London: English Universities Press, 1961).

4. Haugen, *Spoken Norwegian* (New York: American Council of Learned Societies, 1946).

include the stock terms for meals, but travelers to foreign countries soon discover that meals, especially breakfast, often have totally different names.

Perhaps a realistic presentation of material culture would be of some benefit, at least to many adults with firm, if not preconceived, opinions. It is interesting to compare the comments of the columnist George Will concerning food in Moscow with the opinions on American food of Katya, the young Soviet girl who visited the United States in March 1986. Will returned complaining about the lack of variety and the absence of some of his favorite foods in Moscow restaurants; Katya found that American food had a chemical taste, as anyone who likes tomatoes could have informed her.

SOCIAL CULTURE

The topic of social culture is so complex that the handbooks may be excused from attempting even an elementary presentation. We do not need to look at Nida's exotic examples, though one or two may illustrate how much simpler some problems are in such languages. Typically, handbooks solemnly inform their users that "man" and "men" refer to human beings of male gender, "woman" and "women" to those of the female gender. Yet nonnatives probably see the plural form most frequently on certain doors in public buildings. Without a bit of social instruction, a nonnative might be open to embarrassment if he or she entered one of those doors in search of a person of the opposite sex whom he or she had been exhorted to find.

If there were further need to demonstrate the complexity of instructing nonnatives in social culture, one might pursue the terms for ladies' room and men's room from language to language. In Turkey, any nonnative who used *aptesthane*, the textbook term for bathroom, would be greeted with laughter. At least a few years ago, the common name for this important section of a building was *yüz numera* ("the number 100"). In other areas of the Mediterranean as well, including Europe, one still finds such rooms in hotels labeled with the two ciphers *00*. This labeling convention has enjoyed virtually as much success as have the two letters *WC*.

RELIGIOUS AND LINGUISTIC CULTURE

We will not dwell on Nida's last two topics, religious cultures and linguistic cultures. These, however, are intimately related to language and its use. The token references to the clergy or to churches in the handbooks previously cited are scarcely of much benefit to the language learner. By contrast, the authors of brief handbooks for military personnel going to Ireland during World War II were perceptive in warning against asking natives about their religion, advice that is not obsolete today. Similarly, one does well to know that conversation becomes somewhat chilled in Norway when one brings up the topic of language, regardless of whether the group concerned favors *riksmaal* or *landsmaal*. Linguistic culture clearly involves much more, as George Bernard Shaw informed us in his *Pygmalion* or Gilbert and Sullivan in *The Mikado*. The intricate relationships between language and culture in Japanese and the languages of Southeast Asia are practically legendary, requiring little supporting data. We may recall briefly that Ambassador Reischauer, virtually a native speaker of Japanese and also the husband of a Japanese woman, refrained from speaking the language on official occasions.

TEACHING LANGUAGE IN A
CULTURAL CONTEXT

An obvious question at this point is, How does one teach language in the context of culture? First, it is important that all material used in a language course be authentic and typical of the culture. Contrived sentences may serve well to illustrate points of grammar, but they may actually be counterproductive in the student's efforts to achieve proficiency in the language. Dialogues and example sentences can and should contain a considerable amount of readily usable cultural material. Literature can also provide a way of imparting information about the culture of the language, and properly selected texts can help motivate students to learn the language. For most languages, short simple stories by well-known writers can be found that are suitable even for beginning levels.

Visual material, especially video recordings, can be extremely important in teaching the language in the context of its culture. Skilled and innovative language instructors have begun to use news broadcasts and other video material from foreign countries in their instructional programs, but preparing such material for first- and even second-year students is no small matter. There are also numerous problems associated with obtaining copies of foreign telecasts. To make such facilities available, cooperation within the language teaching profession is essential. The Modern Language Association's Commission on Foreign Languages, Literatures, and Linguistics has recommended the creation of a national center as a permanent structure or institution that would have language education as its central concern. One of the projects proposed for the initial phase of the center's activity would be directed toward the acquisition and dissemination of video materials. Once established, a national center could secure the telecasts, whether from Germany, Iceland, Samoa, or elsewhere, and prepare the requisite scripts. These then could be transmitted to language teaching facilities—colleges, high schools, or business establishments—throughout the country.

The proposal has had adequate preparation. James Pusack, at the University of Iowa, has developed a project for the procurement and use of video material in language programs. The project has received significant funding and now includes four other institutions. At Middlebury College, Kimberly Sparks has succeeded in obtaining telecasts from German and Austrian television networks. He estimates that every half-hour telecast requires 24 hours of attention before it can be presented to an elementary class. This requirement alone illustrates the necessity of a national center concerned with language teaching. We need similar telecasts for all the commonly taught languages—not only German, but also French and Spanish—and for Arabic, Chinese, Italian, Japanese, Portuguese, and Russian. The telecasts must be current, not reruns from the previous year or semester. Clearly, the considerations here cited are sufficient to justify the commission's recommendation of a national center, but the center has other aims, and there are more implications for the steps that it may initiate.

Given the development of modern computer networks, with the ability to transmit not only data, but voice and video images, it may not be long until individuals could subscribe to the center's facilities. Technology is already available to provide adequate language teaching materials to individuals in their homes and businesses as well as in classes. We simply need the administrative arrangements to pursue and expand current possibilities. In the words of a recent report on the work of the National Task Force on Education and Technology, organized by former Secretary of Education Terrel Bell, "Better teaching technology will require wider cooperation."[5]

It should be clear that the proposed activities will involve language training based on a humanistic approach. Students making use of the current possibilities will observe members of other cultures pursuing their daily activities, whether with friends, at work, or in their intellectual and cultural pursuits. When new forms of access to language acquisition are made generally available, it will be possible for students from Des Moines, Denver, or Detroit to step off a plane in Delhi with some knowledge of the people they will encounter. That knowledge will include, but will by no means be limited to, the ecology of the area. Preparation may well be specialized, as in the University of Pennsylvania's Lauder Institute program, but it will certainly include information on the literature and other cultural activities of the country or countries concerned. The individuals one meets in international business contacts, in governmental relations, and in academic circles are scarcely impressed if addressed in pidgin English adequate to buy coconuts or sell computers.

Finally, formal teaching about culture may still be necessary in many cases. While it is impossible to provide complete historical, sociological, cultural, and anthropological information about the speakers of a language, there are certain critical facts that should not be separated from the language. These should be taught directly if it is not possible for students to learn them through the literature, from the texts in the handbook, or from video material.

We have been largely concerned with stressing the humanistic basis of language learning and language teaching, citing only occasional implications for national planning. In meeting the problems we will need to vary our priorities. But it is essential that we take action. We can no longer shortchange students, or the country, by providing obsolete or inadequate language instruction. The control of language necessary in the modern world requires well-trained teachers who have the opportunity to renew and maintain their acquaintance with their languages as those languages change and as they are currently used. That control also requires adequate facilities, such as those that a national center would provide.

One must realize the complexity of language and the difficulty associated with learning and using it properly. One of the most remarkable linguists of recent times was the Yorkshireman and first professor of linguistics in Britain, John Rupert Firth. Firth wrote little, thought deeply about language, and spoke about it with great common sense, based on experience with the use of language among African villagers, Indian fishermen, and the British upper class. In his little book *The Tongues of Men and Speech,* he identified speech as social "magic" and went on to say, "You learn your languages in stages as conditions of gradual incorporation into your social organization, which ministers to your needs and gives you most of what you want. A whole hierarchy of values attaches to various forms of

5. Howard LaFranchi, "Better Teaching Technology Will Require Wider Cooperation," *Christian Science Monitor,* 7 Aug. 1985.

language behavior."[6] Successful language teaching involves presenting language in relation to those values as they are determined by the society in question and by individuals at all levels of that society.

The *Christian Science Monitor* recently reported on the use of videotapes for giving "people in many isolated villages . . . the opportunity to share in problem solving."[7] The problems these people face are how to improve agriculture and health. What surprised the sponsors was that "illiterates can learn to use very sophisticated technologies very effectively."[8] The illiterate villagers not only benefited from the tapes, but produced excellent tapes, although they had never before seen even a television receiver. Pondering this example, even the most pessimistic among us may conclude that there is hope for the high school and college students of today.

Language teachers must be allowed to select the values they will present and the level of language they consider of greatest benefit to their students. To have this possibility, they must be informed. It is one of the aims of the Modern Language Association, through efforts like those of its Commission on Foreign Languages, Literatures, and Linguistics, to make that information available. We look forward to cooperating with other individuals and organizations who share our high goals for language teaching and our students' desire to achieve a mastery rooted in the knowledge of both societies and their individuals.

6. Firth, *The Tongues of Men and Speech* (London: Oxford University Press, 1964), pp. 135-36.

7. Kristin Helmore, "Sharing Wisdom," *Christian Science Monitor*, 3 Apr. 1986.

8. Ibid.

ANNALS, *AAPSS*, **490**, March 1987

Theoretical Linguistics, Second Language Acquisition, and Language Pedagogy

By FRANK HENY

ABSTRACT: For three decades theoretical linguistics has had little impact on language teaching, although sociolinguistics has been employed in curriculum design and test construction. Applied linguistics has been eclectic and has seldom applied pure linguistic research. Theoretical linguists, for their part, have not encouraged attempts to apply their results. Theory and practice were separated largely because the theoretical results were so tentative. However, recent theoretical advances suggest important applications for linguistic theory in foreign language teaching and in the testing of proficiency. The acquisition of a nonnative language is probably subject to biological constraints that are closely related to those factors that guide and control first language acquisition. Methodology and test construction must allow for this. Research must determine precisely what the factors are and how they interact. Theoretical linguists interested in such research should be included in interdisciplinary teams working on foreign language learning and testing.

Frank Heny was born in Zimbabwe. He obtained a Ph.D. in 1970 from the University of California at Los Angeles. He was professor of linguistics and philosophy at Groningen University, The Netherlands, from 1975 until he resigned in 1983 to develop undergraduate linguistics in the United States. He has since held visiting appointments at the Universities of Vermont and Minnesota, Carleton College, and the State University of New York at Albany. He founded and coedits the journal Natural Language and Linguistic Theory *and a companion monograph series.*

THEORETICAL linguistics offers no panacea to language pedagogues. In fact, at the present time it still has few, if any, concrete results that can be effectively applied in second language teaching; and no contemporary linguist would offer a recipe for language teachers in the way that the linguists of a generation ago developed and for a time exclusively defended the audiolingual method. Nevertheless, for the first time in three decades, significant numbers of theoretical linguists are seriously interested in the process of second language acquisition. Their research has taken a turn that permits—and indeed forces—them to undertake systematic comparative work on language structure, and there is reason to believe that current theoretical research on language could, if properly encouraged, yield insights of great relevance to curriculum development, test design, and teaching. To investigate and, if possible, to realize this potential, appropriate research must form a significant component of any attempt to increase national language proficiency.

Although "theoretical linguistics" can be understood to comprehend any pure—that is, non-applied—research on human language, I will generally restrict the term "theoretical" to research intended to yield a rigorous, coherent account of language structure, in particular an explanation of the fundamental principles underlying the organization of human language. To date, the most promising work of this sort seeks to derive those organizational principles directly from evolved, and thus innate, characteristics of the human species. More specifically, the organizational principles are derived from those properties of the species that lead to, and control, the development of language

during early childhood. Such an approach to the study of language is allied more closely to the natural sciences, in particular to theoretical work in biology and evolutionary theory, than to the social sciences. There are other kinds of linguistics that are theoretical in other senses, such as sociolinguistics, which is theoretical in roughly the same way that other social sciences are, but I will not in general be referring to such work when I use the term "theoretical linguistics."

I wish to narrow the focus in this way because it now seems likely that research of the sort just alluded to could, over the relatively short term, yield insights that would contribute significantly to the learning and teaching of nonnative languages. Other pure research on human language—on language use, for example—is also obviously relevant to language pedagogy; this relevance is more generally taken for granted and needs less emphasis. Moreover, there do not appear to have been any very dramatic developments in such areas that might warrant special attention at the present time. Thus my focus will be on recent attempts by theoreticians to map out the structure of the mental structures that guide early language development in normal members of the human species.

It might seem that if there have been significant recent developments in theoretical linguistics, these could simply be applied to pedagogy and testing. This is not so. The theoretical results are suggestive, but a good deal of research remains to be done to bridge the gap between those results and the practical problems of learning a nonnative language. What is needed is practical, empirically tested investigation done by theoretically sophisticated research teams working with second language learners. Such teams will consist of theoreticians, "applied" linguists, and pedagogues.[1]

LINGUISTICS AND LANGUAGE TEACHING: PAST AND PRESENT

Linguistics is a young discipline. The Linguistic Society of America was founded in 1924, and the field only really began to develop a distinct identity in this country in the thirties. From the very start, it has seemed natural, especially to nonlinguists, that insights gained from research on language should be applicable, above all, to the teaching of languages, native and nonnative. Yet it has seldom proved possible to apply the results of such research to language teaching, and over the past twenty years much skepticism has developed regarding the possibility of ever doing so. In particular, it has been increasingly taken for granted by many of those involved in language teaching that pure research on language structure is too abstract or formal ever to have any practical implications. Only research into language use—pragmatics, discourse analysis, sociolinguistics, and language processing—might conceivably be applied to practical problems. For much of the recent past such an assessment was not unreasonable. Pure research

1. These teams will also include, where appropriate, sociolinguists and psychologists. Linguists primarily interested in experimental work on acquisition, or speech processing, rather than in the investigation of the language systems are often called psycholinguists. If the field of theoretical linguistics is identified in the way that I have suggested, it is not clear that there is any real justification for making a sharp distinction along such lines, since all theoretical linguists are psycholinguists in that they have no goal other than that of understanding the innate principles of mental organization that result in the observed structure of language.

on language structure did not appear to be yielding results of any practical importance. But, as I have already implied, the situation now appears to be changing very rapidly.

Three decades of applied linguistics

Linguists engaged in pure research have generally had little professional interest in applying their results to practical problems. This situation will by and large persist: the theoretical physicist is not professionally involved in the development of warheads or the uses of nuclear power. There exists a field that might seem to bridge the gap between pure linguistic research and its practical utility: applied linguistics. "Applied linguistics," however, is a peculiarly inappropriate term. It is not primarily engaged in the application of linguistic research to practical problems and, indeed, throughout most of its history has had far closer links with pedagogy, communication studies, and aspects of psychology and sociology than with linguistics. Moreover, it has been concerned with only a very limited range of problems, mostly having to do with language teaching and in particular with the teaching of English. There are many practical problems to which linguistic research might be relevant that, to date, have simply not fallen under its domain.

Precisely when applied linguistics began to be recognized as a distinct field is rather unclear. In this country the founding of the Center for Applied Linguistics (CAL) in 1959 marked its effective birth. Language teaching—more specifically the teaching of English as a foreign or second langauge—has always been at the heart of CAL's concerns, and in other countries, such as Great Britain, applied linguistics was already more or less identified by that time with research in the teaching of English as a foreign or second language. Thus applied linguists have always been primarily engaged in research related directly to language pedagogy, especially the teaching of English to nonnative speakers.

For most of the period since the emergence of the discipline, applied linguists have, very pragmatically, adopted techniques and ideas from many sources to solve their problems, and they have often had relatively little exposure to pure linguistics. Because the results of linguistic research, especially research on language structure, have had little to say about language teaching, such adoption was perfectly natural. However, it means that, contrary to what is probably a natural assumption, the applied linguist is not necessarily at all well equipped to interpret and apply the results of theoretical linguistics.

This was not always so. For a while—until shortly after the founding of CAL, in fact—there seemed to be some hope of applying linguistics to the problems of language teaching—and perhaps to other areas, too. During the fifties, which saw the first moves toward institutionalizing the field in this country, the most plausible account of human language lent itself very readily to such application. Linguists were confident that they had the key to human language: it was a pairing of hierarchically arranged units of sound together with accompanying patterns of behavior. Every part of language was ultimately constructed out of elements that were directly present in the sound signal. Language learning involved no more than a series of behavioral responses to auditory stimuli. Language in use was a complex of habit patterns linked to the hierarchical sound structures: the produc-

tion habits—speech—which produced the sounds, and the habitual modifications in behavior that those sounds induced in the hearer. This thoroughly behaviorist and positivistic account, deriving in large part from the work of Leonard Bloomfield, had clear implications for the language pedagogue.

If language were no more than hierarchically structured patterns of sound linked to various habit patterns, and if learning language involved making ultimately simple responses to ultimately simple stimuli, then it should have been a simple matter to increase the effectiveness of language learning. At least two things seemed necessary: an accurate description of the hierarchical structure of the language to be learned, and a set of drills based directly on this analysis and designed to function as stimuli that would elicit appropriate responses and hence inculcate the desired habits in the learner. Pure linguistic research would supply the analyses, in addition to justifying the endeavor in the way that I have sketched, and the applied linguist would use these to develop drills. Also, since the habits of the original language might interfere with that to be acquired, contrastive analyses of languages would help to highlight and solve problems arising when the original habit patterns interfered with the acquisition of a new set.

There was no question in those early days but that the field was applied linguistics; it involved the application of research on language structure to the practical problems of teaching nonnative languages. The pure research in question was not theoretical in the narrow sense, for the linguists of the fifties did not concern themselves with trying to account for why language patterns are as they are. They simply described patterns; the patterns resulted from habits—or, better still, were themselves habits. The task of the applied linguist was simply to work out the best way of developing those habits.

Many people who are neither linguists nor involved in language teaching know how this supposedly scientific approach to language teaching, after its apparent successes during World War II, when many linguists became involved in devising crash language courses for the armed forces, began to come under fire. The failure of the audiolingual method and the realization that there is a great deal more to the effective teaching of nonnative languages than the mechanical development of habit patterns mirroring the formal, grammatical properties of the target language led to a rapid change in approach and a loss of faith in the relevance of linguistics.[2] Of course, by the late sixties and early seventies, the positivistic view of science and the behavioristic psychology upon which descriptive, or structuralist, linguistics was based were far less firmly entrenched. But no account of language was available at that time that could replace the earlier one that had provided the initial foundations for applied linguistics, or for the audiolingual method with which it was so closely associated in the early years. It was quite clear that language was not simply a passively acquired set of habits built around a hierarchically structured sound system. Theoretical linguists, at least, were convinced that language was far more complex than this and that aspects of the system were ultimately determined by evolved, innate properties of the human species. But neither they

nor anyone else was able to translate this into terms that had any clear implication for the teaching of nonnative languages.

It was during this period that applied linguistics became quite eclectic. The teaching and evaluation of English as a second or foreign language—or of any nonnative language—have been affected not by contemporary research on language structure, but mainly by work directed to the use of language: pragmatics—including the work of philosophers and linguists on speech acts—discourse analysis, psychology, communication, and sociology—especially aspects of sociolinguistics. From time to time, this teaching and evaluation have attempted to construct independent approaches to problems of language teaching and acquisition, as in the work of Selinker on interlanguage.[3] Most recently, some attempts have been made to use ideas about meaning developed in the context of artificial intelligence.

Concepts that have influenced language pedagogy and testing, a good example being "communicative competence," have sometimes resulted from attempts by sociolinguists and others to extend ideas originating within theoretical linguistics to cover aspects of language use. They have not themselves been a part of any rigorously theoretical attempt to isolate and explain the fundamental characteristics of language itself—those that are narrowly determined by properties of the species.[4] Thus there

2. See, for example, Wilga Rivers, *The Psychologist and the Foreign-Language Teacher* (Chicago: University of Chicago Press, 1964). Rivers was, in fact, ahead of her time.

3. Larry Selinker, "Interlanguage," *International Review of Applied Linguistics*, 10:209-31 (1972).

4. Since the notion of "communicative competence" has played such an important role at times in applied linguistics, it may be worth emphasizing that Hymes himself consciously used the word "theoretical" in his paper introducing the notion—but he carefully pointed out how he intended this to be taken: "This paper is theoretical. One

has been no single source of insight, and there has been much conflicting advice; teaching methods and evaluation have been based hardly at all upon solid knowledge about language but upon ideas drawn from many disparate sources.

Theoretical linguistics in the sixties and seventies

Two years before the founding of CAL, Chomsky's *Syntactic Structures* was published.[5] This work, and the unpublished material from which it was extracted, laid the foundations for the development of the theoretical linguistics of the sixties and seventies. The really important change that Chomsky effected in linguistics was to provide a new goal—and an increasingly specific apparatus for realizing that goal. I referred in the introduction to both: the goal is to provide a completely rigorous explanation for an ever increasing subpart of the structure of human language; the method was, in broad terms, to develop hypotheses about innate principles governing language acquisition, which would be so constructed as to determine the relevant aspects of structure.

Although the goal was reasonably well articulated from the start, the analytical apparatus that was initially proposed, transformational grammar, turned out to be quite inappropriate,

though it laid the foundations for what has followed. Analysis in terms of grammatical transformations was really only well suited to the description of English—the language on which Chomsky worked in developing it—as many field linguists complained bitterly, right from the start. Hence there was in principle no way in which transformational analysis could yield any insight into the fundamental structural relationships between languages. For example, although a long tradition of philological and linguistic work on language has made more or less vague reference to "passive" sentences in many languages, there was no way within transformational grammar of determining systematically for any language whether it included a structure comparable in significant ways to the English passive—or to any other structure in any language.

Obviously such an account of language could yield no scientifically based insight into the similarities or differences between the native and target languages, let alone illuminate the process of second language acquisition in general. It was, moreover, unlikely that an approach to the structure of human language that was so narrowly based on the structure of just one language would provide a useful framework for the investigation of the use or acquisition even of that language, and it predictably proved totally inadequate as a basis for attempts to isolate and explain the general properties of human language.

Because they were well aware of how very tentative their hypotheses were, theoretical linguists like Chomsky warned repeatedly against attempting to apply their results to practical problems, and they pointed out that although their ultimate goal was that of understanding the fundamental nature of language and

connotation of 'theoretical' is 'programmatic'; a related connotation is that one knows too little about the subject to say something practical. Both connotations apply to this." Dell H. Hymes, "On Communicative Competence," in *Sociolinguistics*, ed. J. B. Pride and Janet Holmes (London: Penguin Books, 1972), p. 269. Later in the same piece, Hymes explicitly contrasts his work with theoretical linguistics in something like my sense.

5. Noam Chomsky, *Syntactic Structures* (The Hague: Mouton, 1957).

language development, it was too early to expect this work to yield practically useful results. They felt perfectly justified in attempting to come to grips with the difficult problems they were attempting to solve—for, despite appearances, they were not simply playing abstract mathematical games!—but knew that their results were a long way from solving the really deep problems and warned against overoptimism. A good example of this is the often quoted—and generally misinterpreted—statement of Chomsky's in 1966: "I am, frankly, rather skeptical about the significance, for the teaching of languages of such insights and understanding as have been attained in linguistics and psychology."[6] In retrospect, such caution was well justified. Historically, the principal contribution of transformational grammar to our understanding of language was that it permitted the development of more effective tools for language analysis.

Two specific aspects of linguistic theory in the sixties and seventies made it especially unsuited to the function that it was intended to perform, namely, to characterize those properties of language that resulted directly from innate features of the human species. First, the core analytical units that it employed turned out to be seriously deficient; second, the way in which human language development was represented was at best misleading. These problems sound very abstract, but their effects were concrete—and serious.

Languages were represented as infinite sets of sentences, some sentences of each language being structurally related to others in ways that were significant. In English, any active sentence, such as

6. Noam Chomsky, "Linguistic Theory," in *Readings in Applied Transformational Grammar*, ed. Mark Lester (New York: Holt, 1970; 2nd ed., 1973), pp. 51-60.

"Jane has seen Jim," can be thought of as having a passive counterpart—"Jim has been seen by Jane"—and each has a question counterpart: "Has Jane seen Jim?" and "Has Jim been seen by Jane?" Structural relationships of this sort, and the underlying structures on which they were based, yielded the basic structures of language in transformational grammar. This account of structure differed principally from the earlier view of the structuralists in that transformational relations between sentences permitted a more adequate description of language than was possible under the assumption that the sound pattern of individual sentences contained all that was relevant to their analysis and processing. But transformational analysis offered no possible explanation of aspects of language structure. It was a dead end. This can be seen most clearly by considering the account of acquisition based on it.

The child learning English was supposed to construct a grammar for the language—a finite set of rules characterizing or generating the infinite set of sentences that composed it—making use of such elements as the transformations defining the relationship between active and passive sentences and between declarative forms of these and their question counterparts. The innate knowledge of language that a child brings to bear on the task of learning a language consisted, on this account, principally in the expectation that the language to which the child was exposed would be optimally analyzable in terms of such units. This representation of innate linguistic ability should have depicted the task of constructing a grammar as rather simple—thus explaining how it is that languages come to be learned so naturally by children. Of course, it would also thereby have explained why all human languages exhibit such relationships, as well as accounting for the rapidity and ease of language learning. The construction of a transformational grammar by a child, however, would not be a simple matter.

The most obvious problem with the model was that many languages did not seem to exhibit structural relationships at all analogous to those found in English, on the basis of which the theory had been developed. The underlying and more serious failing was that even for languages closely related to English and apparently extremely similar, it was impossible to determine whether a given transformation in one language was or was not the same as one in another, whether they were similar, or totally unrelated. Comparison of the passive in German, French, and English, or even in two dialects of English, was meaningless. Linguists could simply show how various constructions could be analyzed in transformational terms. But each language, defined by its transformations and other rules, remained an isolated, unexplained entity.

The theory was devised in order to reduce the mystery of initial language learning, but it offered remarkably little in this respect and provided even less insight into the process of second language learning. Whether or not the results of research on language structure could ever be applied, it was certainly unlikely that the results of work in this framework could. Although theoretical linguists repeatedly pointed this out, it is not clear that they always understood the ultimate significance of having to do so.

Research on language use: its relevance and limitations

Quite clearly, other linguists did not understand that significance. Many with sociolinguistic or practical interests would have applied to transformational grammar what Fishman, one of the first serious sociolinguists, wrote about pre-transformational linguistics: "Linguistics, particularly American linguistics during at least the first half of this century, has been primarily a 'formal discipline,' almost along the lines of abstract mathematics."[7] Fishman himself saw clearly, as indicated by the approval he gave to "mentalistic" linguistics in the paragraphs after this quotation, that transformational grammar was something other than "abstract mathematics," but many others, professional linguists and potential users of linguistic results, saw it otherwise. Fox and Skolnick, for example, complained that "some contemporary linguists, seeking to establish the independence and scientific validity of their discipline, have isolated it from the world of non-linguistic events and concentrated on abstract and formal theories about the nature and structure of language."[8] It is clear from the context that they were referring to contemporary transformational linguistics.

The aim of the "abstract and formal" theories of language was not simply to establish the scientific validity of the field. At least that was never the aim of transformational grammar, which constituted the dominant formal approach to language at the time Fox and Skolnick wrote. The aim was precisely that of theoretical linguistics as I have characterized it: to discover those patterns in language that can be attributed to the innate human propensity to learn lan-

7. Joshua A. Fishman, "Introduction," in *Readings in the Sociology of Language*, ed. Joshua A. Fishman (The Hague: Mouton, 1972), p. 6.

8. Melvin Fox and Betty Skolnick, *Language in Education* (New York: Ford Foundation, 1975), p. 6.

guage—and hence to learn more about that property of the species. It is not surprising that this ultimate goal was lost sight of; a substantial number of formal linguists of the period did little more than pay lip service to it. Since the available model was incapable of yielding insight into language development or of permitting meaningful investigation of what constituted the real core properties of human languages—those that resulted crucially from the mechanisms responsible for their development in the child—it might just as well, for all practical purposes, have been "abstract mathematics."

The development in linguistics that has been most important to language teachers up to now is the rise of sociolinguistics and the realization that language is itself open to study as a social phenomenon. Sociolinguistics may be thought of as a subfield of linguistics or, instead, as Fishman has described it, as an "interdisciplinary tool."[9] It has included a number of distinct, but related, strands of research: Fishman's work on the sociology of language and language planning: Ferguson's on patterns of language usage, grounded in the descriptive linguistics of the fifties; the identification by Labov, G. Sankoff, and others of precisely quantifiable covariance between aspects of linguistic structure and the social context of utterances; and attempts by Dell Hymes and others to investigate communicative competence—that knowledge which, presumably as a result of both innate and environmental factors, develops in human beings, enabling them to function effectively in society, in interaction with

other members of the species.[10] Such research has provided a wealth of factual material and insight that have affected curricular developments and that have helped to mold tests aimed at evaluating the ability of language learners to communicate in the target language—the ultimate goal of much contemporary language learning.

Emphasis on the use of the learned language has also very naturally led to attempts[11] to combine those insights yielded by sociolinguistics with ideas derived from speech act theory and discourse analysis.[12]

To the extent that we can increase systematic knowledge about and insight into language usage and precise relationships between linguistic features and features of the social organization and dynamics of the societies in which languages function, this will obviously be of potential significance in teaching, and evaluating success in learning, a foreign language. For the majority of learners, success in learning a foreign language obviously involves functioning in the societies in which it is used. The significance of research on the social aspects of language and its relations to other social phenomena, however, must be seen in proper perspective if this research is to

9. Joshua A. Fishman, *Sociolinguistics: A Brief Introduction* (Rowley, MA: Newbury House, 1970), p. 6.

10. For useful references, see the bibliographies in Ralph Fasold, *The Sociolinguistics of Society* (Oxford: Basil Blackwell, 1984) and Ronald Wardhaugh, *An Introduction to Sociolinguistics* (Oxford: Basil Blackwell, 1986).

11. For example, Evelyn M. Hatch, *Second Language Acquisition* (Rowley, MA: Newbury House, 1978).

12. A good example of relevant pure research is Penelope Brown and Stephen Levinson, "Universals in Language Usage: Politeness Phenomena," in *Questions and Politeness*, ed. Esther N. Goody (Cambridge: Cambridge University Press, 1978), pp. 56-289. For other references, see Stephen Levinson, *Pragmatics* (Cambridge: Cambridge University Press, 1983).

be appropriately used for practical purposes. There is now no doubt at all that the first language—and, to a degree still far from adequately determined, also second and subsequent languages—develop in accordance with innately determined principles, just like physical organs or the complex behavior patterns of other animals. Many aspects of language structure result from the particular mechanisms that control language development, probably in much the same way that the structure of physical body parts is determined by those genetic factors that control physical development. There is no more hope of attributing the entire structure of language to the contexts in which it is used than there is of attributing the entire structure of the eye—the composition of the vitreous humor, for example, or of the retinal artery—to the properties of light.[13]

Sociolinguistics, pragmatics, and other ways of characterizing the patterns of language usage are not likely to provide a reliable basis for practical work such as language teaching, unless they are informed by the realization that a language is more than just its "users and its uses."[14] Applied linguists, after a period in which they either looked to pure research on language use for guidance or developed their own practical approaches, appear to be aware of the need for a more adequate foundation.

For example, the ideas of Krashen[15] have created a great deal of interest and have had considerable influence. Taking off from the observation, or at least the claim, that errors made by second language learners show interesting similarities to errors made by children learning their native language, he suggested that under certain circumstances—those that are relevantly similar to the circumstances under which a first language is learned—there is no real difference between the processes of first and second language learning, no matter how late in life the latter occurs. Analogy with the development of native language skills in infancy led Krashen to suggest, further, that second language acquisition might be most successful to the extent that it progressed without conscious reflection. The underlying implication was that the innate language acquisition capabilities, which, since Lenneberg's research,[16] had been assumed to atrophy during puberty, might in principle still be available. Krashen has not succeeded in articulating his ideas in such a way as to permit fruitful investigation or development, and though they seem to relate, in a number of rather imprecise ways, to contemporary work in theoretical linguistics, no clear links have been made and little direct empirical support has emerged for his claims.

Various other attempts have been made to use research on language structure rather than on language use. Several have been based on the typologies sug-

13. Some contemporary linguists have nevertheless apparently taken it for granted that all aspects of linguistic structure can be rather directly attributed to the functions of language. See, for example, Talmy Givon, *On Understanding Grammar* (New York: Academic Press, 1979); William A. Foley and Robert D. van Valin, Jr., *Functional Syntax and Universal Grammar* (Cambridge: University Press, 1984); Gillian Sankoff and Penelope Brown, "The Origins of Syntax in Discourse," *Language*, 52:632-66 (1976).

14. For a contrary view, see Fishman, "Introduction," p. 7.

15. Particularly as represented in Stephen D. Krashen, *Second Language Acquisition and Second Language Learning* (Oxford: Pergamon, 1981).

16. Eric Lenneberg, *Biological Foundations of Language* (New York: John Wiley, 1967).

gested by Greenberg,[17] and others on such empirical, descriptive work as that of Keenan and Comrie.[18] Some applied linguists have attempted to use aspects of what has been called markedness theory. It has been clear, at least since Roman Jakobson, that certain linguistic structures are less common in the world's languages; some structures tend not to occur in a language unless certain other, more common structures occur; and some structures tend to develop later in children. There is a tendency for all three of these properties to run together, but no clear, general account of what is at issue has yet been given. During the seventies, when it was unclear to many theoretical linguists how to proceed, a fair amount of taxonomic work on markedness was undertaken, and Eckman, among others, attempted to show how use of this work could predict the difficulties that speakers of a given language would have in learning particular structures in another.[19] The results of this work are far from clear; it is not based on any solid theoretical foundations, since the original investigations into markedness were very inconclusive.

Recent developments
in linguistic theory

In the late seventies, while applied linguistics was searching eclectically, and

17. For example, as represented in Joseph Greenberg, ed., *Universals of Language* (Cambridge, MA: MIT Press, 1966).

18. Edward Keenan and Bernard Comrie, "Noun Phrase Accessibility and Universal Grammar," *Linguistic Inquiry*, 8:63-100 (1977).

19. For example, Fred R. Eckman, "Markedness and Degree of Difficulty in Second Language Learning," in *Proceedings of the Fifth Congress, International Association of Applied Linguists*, ed. J.-G. Savard and L. Laforge (Montreal: University of Laval Press, 1981), pp. 115-26.

more or less in vain, for insights into language structure that might be relevant to pedagogy, theoretical linguistics underwent a quiet, but profound, revolution. The basic elements of analysis were radically changed, and on the basis of this a totally new account of language development and the principles that control it began to emerge. This theoretical approach is not static; in fact, the details are changing very rapidly, in part because it has stimulated so much new research. Dozens of languages have been investigated over the last ten years, most within the last five, and the pace of relevant research is still accelerating as more and more non-English-speaking linguists become involved. All the major European languages have been investigated, including the Scandinavian languages, Yiddish, dialects of Dutch, Spanish—including South American dialects—Portuguese, Rumanian, Irish, Welsh, Breton, Finnish, and Hungarian, and so have languages as diverse as Turkish, several dialects of Arabic, Hebrew, Japanese, several dialects of Chinese, Korean, Warlpiri, Navajo, Dogrib, Chamorro, Malayalam, Hindi, Bengali, Persian, and a number of African languages, including Vata and Chichewa. A single descriptive apparatus has been employed. Its use has permitted the development of a theory that is able in principle to deal equally well with a great number of superficially very diverse systems—and to relate them very precisely to each other, thus in effect beginning to extract the essential properties of human language.

The essence of the theory can be understood best by contrasting the account of language development that it supports with the one based on transformational grammar. I suggested earlier that a child faced with the task of learning a language by discovering, and hence learning, its transformational grammar would have a hard time: languages differ from each other in apparently arbitrary ways when viewed from that perspective, and they would have to be learned piecemeal—essentially as the behaviorists thought. Only the inventory of basic structural units would be available to the child as a help. If, on the other hand, the variation between languages results from the fixing of a small number of rather unobvious parameters, which in interaction yield all the possible structural properties of human language, then language development consists largely of setting those parameters. Each setting will determine, in interaction with the others, vast amounts of apparently arbitrary variation. Learning a first language is choosing from the available alternatives those that yield the best fit with the speech in the environment.

The available parameters are, of course, the same for every infant and are constrained, it is supposed, by some part of our inheritance as members of the human species. Each child simply has to learn how they are set for the language or languages he or she hears. Thus the child does not learn the grammar of any individual language, but discovers which values that language exhibits for each of the innately available parameters. The principles constraining that development ultimately derive, if this picture is correct, from the human genotype, just like the principles that control the development of the eye;[20] it is these principles

that make up the innate knowledge of language.

The possibilities for variation in languages are very highly constrained—far more so, it turns out, than is suggested by superficial observation. Much of the observed variation can now very plausibly, and often quite specifically, in detail, be reduced to the interaction of a small number of abstract parameters along which languages, or subparts of languages can vary.

Obviously, the language facts that have to be analyzed by the new approach include those that were successfully dealt with before. The effect of the change in analytical basis is to include a far wider range of facts. Above all, it provides a way of analyzing human language that is equally appropriate to the analysis of English, French, Chamorro, Japanese, Navajo, Arabic—and accounts for a number of hidden dependencies between structures, found in a wide cross section of these languages once the appropriate analytical tools are employed. The essentially English-based descriptive apparatus of the older model has entirely disappeared, and meaningful comparison of languages has become possible and, indeed, forms an essential part of linguistic research. Language description—which, incidentally, is not less, but more, detailed than ever before—now concentrates on those features that appear to be subject to parametric variation, and it attempts to discover how far it is possible to derive the superficially unpredictable properties of individual languages from the interaction of settings of universal parameters.[21]

---

20. Interestingly, it does not seem to have been Chomsky or any of his followers, but Thomas Sebeock in a review in *Language*, 39:466 (1963), who first clearly pointed out how reasonable it would be for the genetic code to play a direct role in determining the structure of linguistic codes.

21. The approach to theoretical linguistics that is discussed in this section is not yet well served by literature accessible to the nonspecialist. It was first developed in detail in Noam Chomsky, *Lectures on Government and Binding* (Dordrecht:

I will end this very brief account of the theory with a programmatic account of one small part of language structure. Consider the fact that some languages optionally leave out the pronominal subject in a sentence like "He will go." If this were an isolated fact about a language it would warrant little attention, and while it was assumed to be one, it received very little. But if the possibility of omitting the subject is a consequence of some unobvious interaction between several independent linguistic features, then the dropping of that pronoun—permitted by Italian, Chinese, and under some circumstances modern Hebrew and Irish, but virtually not at all by English, modern French, or German—becomes part of a structural network of potentially vast complexity, significance, and interest.

Once the child discovers from the speech around him or her that the pronoun in the language in question may be dropped, there will be a great number of automatic consequences. Some of those consequences will not need to be learned, once the fact of pronoun dropping is firmly established; and indeed there is virtually conclusive evidence that some could not in principle be learned from the available data alone. Notice how this account immediately provides a basis for explaining the relatively fixed patterns of language development. If second language learning should turn out to be able to make even limited use of the apparatus whereby the parameters were initially set on the basis of primary language data, then clearly it is of paramount importance to applied linguists and language teachers to discover this apparatus. Moreover, if certain structures are linked in ways that cannot be predicted from superficial observation, as now seems beyond doubt to be the case, then curriculum development and, above all, evaluation cannot possibly ignore such relatedness.

Theoretical research on language acquisition

This analysis of human language in transformational terms had little or nothing to offer those interested in second language learning, but it inspired a good deal of empirical work on child language acquisition during the sixties. At first, this appeared to be quite promising and suggested strongly that acquisition could be profitably viewed in terms of the addition of transformations to a developing grammar, in the sense of grammar then current. But this research never yielded insights to the extent originally hoped for, and just as many linguists—in particular, applied linguists—turned, during the seventies, to attempts to analyze language use, so those concerned with acquisition began to concentrate their attention on child-caretaker interactions during this period, rather than on the internal developmental process.[22]

Foris, 1981). David Lightfoot, *The Language Lottery* (Cambridge, MA: MIT Press, 1982), attempts an argument, intended for the general reader, for the genetic basis for certain language structures. Thomas Wasow, "Postscript," in *Lectures on Contemporary Syntactic Theories*, by Peter Sells (Stanford, CA: Center for the Study of Language and Information, 1986), provides a good, brief summary of recent developments in linguistic theory. See also Frederick J. Newmeyer, *Grammatical Theory: Its Limits and Possibilities* (Chicago: University of Chicago Press, 1983), esp. chap. 5, "The Applicability of Grammatical Theory."

22. For example, see the articles collected in Charles A. Fergusen and Catherine E. Snow, eds., *Talking to Children: Language Input and Acquisition* (Cambridge: Cambridge University Press, 1977).

More recently, it has become clear that, as was originally predicted on theoretical grounds, relatively little insight into the nature of the acquisition process can be gained when language acquisition is viewed solely as a matter of social interaction. Just as in the field of second language acquisition, there has therefore been a renewed interest in the explanatory potential of a theoretical approach to the innate factors determining structure.

The development of a model of language that encourages research on parametric variation between languages derived from innate limits to language development provides a framework that specifically demands research on first language acquisition. Such research is already under way and has yielded some suggestive, if still very tentative, results. A large-scale empirical project at the University of California, Irvine, under the leadership of Kenneth Wexler and including both psychologists and theoretical linguists, is investigating language development in terms of parameter setting, especially in relation to the development of the pronoun system of young children, and through this research it is giving new content to the notion of markedness. Other work on first language acquisition within this framework is being undertaken at the University of California at Los Angeles, the City University of New York Graduate Center, the University of Massachusetts at Amherst, McGill University in Montreal, and many other centers both in the United Stated and abroad.

Of more direct relevance to the present article is the fact that there are some very specific ways in which this language model can drive research on second language acquisition. Such research is in its infancy, but it has begun—at Irvine, among other places. One particularly striking aspect of the paradigm that is developing is that it encourages, and provides a meaningful framework for, the investigation of claims, like those of Krashen, to the effect that there are significant parallels between first and second language acquisition, and those of Eckman regarding markedness. It also provides a precise reinterpretation of the notion of interference—the originally behavioristic hypothesis that led to contrastive studies—which is the claim that the structure of the learner's first language interferes in specific ways with acquisition of a second.

If the development of a first language involves the setting of parameters, then the least marked situation will correspond to the null setting of all parameters, and it should be possible to establish what factors are necessary to induce changes in these basic neutral settings. Once parameters are set, then this constellation of parameter settings constitutes the position from which a learner of a second language sets out. Some questions that then arise are how far adult language learning can or should be a matter of resetting parameters, how the old settings may interfere, how far conscious learning or pattern drilling induces or interferes with the setting of parameters. Now that specific parametric variation between languages is beginning to be understood, these are real issues with specific content. Research has begun to spring up in many centers addressing such issues. Among the researchers and centers most active are Rutherford at the University of Southern California, Flynn at the Massachusetts Institute of Technology, Bickerton at the University of Hawaii, White at McGill University, and Felix at the University of Passau in West Germany. At the University of

California, Los Angeles, Hyams, whose initial work was on first language acquisition,[23] has begun working with graduate students from the applied linguistics program, students of Schumann and Hatch, and this work may well lead to a further blossoming of relevant research there.

It might be worth citing a specific example. Some preliminary work at the State University of New York, Stony Brook, on the use of English reflexives by Korean speakers, undertaken by Finer and Broselow,[24] suggests that at a certain stage during the learning process, a specific error pattern tends to develop in linking a reflexive to its antecedent. The errors are not simply random; nor is the interlanguage a system based either directly on Korean or directly on English—or explainable on the basis of simple conceptions of markedness. It may turn out to be possible to attribute the error pattern, at least in part, to the influence of that same apparatus that leads to the development of a first language—but is affected in specific ways by existing settings in the first language. It is hoped that this research will provide concrete information about how parameter setting in adulthood can proceed.

While it is obviously too early to leap from these very tentative results to conclusions of any real importance, confirmation of these results would clearly have significant implications for language pedagogy and testing. The work of Felix

explores the implications of similar findings. Such research is significant not because it provides evidence that parameter setting is the framework within which first and second language learning takes place—it is far too tentative for that!—but because it permits a remarkably precise formulation of hypotheses about the differences between first and second language learning and about the innately determined controls that may determine aspects of the latter.[25]

Important issues concerning fossilization, the plateau effect, and language attrition can clearly be conducted in such a way as to make use of the emerging knowledge about hidden relatedness between language structures, and the possible influence of this upon second language development, but as far as I know such research has yet to begin on any significant scale. Somewhat related work, not yet explicitly guided by the advances in knowledge about language structure to which I have drawn attention, is being undertaken—for example, by Michael Long and his associates at the University of Hawaii.

THE NATIONAL AGENDA

In the fifties, descriptive linguists thought they had all the answers. After that, theoretical linguists insisted that they had none, but they never excluded

23. Nina Hyams, "The Acquisition of Parameterized Grammars" (Ph.D. diss., City University of New York, Graduate Center, 1985).

24. Dan Finer and Ellen Broselow, "L2 Acquisition of Reflexives," in *NELS 16: Proceedings of the 16th Annual Northeastern Linguistic Society Meeting* (Amherst: University of Massachusetts, forthcoming).

25. William Rutherford makes this point very effectively in his "Grammatical Theory and L2 Acquisition: A Brief Overview," in *Proceedings of the MIT Second Language Conference*, ed. S. Flynn (Dordrecht: Reidel, forthcoming). See also Ellen Broselow, "Second Language Acquisition," in *Linguistics: The Cambridge Survey*, vol. 4, ed. F. Newmeyer (Cambridge: Cambridge University Press, forthcoming). Both these papers contain bibliographies that include the work on second language acquisition in this framework, and both discuss its potential relevance to the field.

the possibility that at a certain stage they might have some. Notice in particular, that when Chomsky said in 1966 that no results up to that date seemed applicable to second language teaching, he was speaking at a time when, according to the account I have given here, he was absolutely correct. But Chomsky did not say, and to my knowledge has never implied, that useful insights would never be available. In fact he went right on to assert, after the passage I quoted earlier, that he thought there would come a time when they would become available. I do not claim that that time is here, but I do believe that there is good reason for thinking it may be just around the corner and that research is urgently needed in order to determine how far hidden relationships between aspects of language structure do, in fact, play a significant role in the process of second language learning.

A significant change in the attitude of theoretical linguists has now come about. The most tangible sign is the recent conference on theoretical linguistics and second language acquisition at the Massachusetts Institute of Technology. This is the first such occasion since the Ann Arbor conference in the late fifties, which led to the founding of CAL—and in this case it was the theoreticians who organized the conference. I, like a significant number of other theoretical linguists, now believe that under the right circumstances we may be able to work out, along with others involved in practical problems, new, insightful ways of approaching those problems, using the currently available ways of thinking about language.

At the same time, I believe, a significant number of applied linguists and perhaps those directly involved in language pedagogy—though I admit to having

less knowledge about that—are actively searching for a more satisfactory theoretical foundation for their work. It has become clear that they cannot rely only on sociolinguistics and other ways of approaching language solely from the viewpoint of its use. To do so ignores the fact that humans do not simply select an arbitrary code and communicate. The fundamental problem and challenge for the language teacher is to bridge the gap between the desire to communicate and the specific structures of language within which we are forced, as members of the human species, to conduct our business. Our inescapable use of specific language structures is why students have to be taught not communication, but Chinese, Japanese, Russian, or French.

From the point of view of evaluation, the significance of this recent work may be even greater than it is for curriculum development and teaching methods. If second language acquisition is in part controlled by innate factors, then any instrument must clearly distinguish between these factors and those that have a social origin and may be subject to far less strict determination from within the organism. Above all, if there are hidden dependencies between virtually all aspects of language structure, evaluation of proficiency based in part on structural criteria must allow properly for dependencies between aspects of the language that are determined by the underlying parameters. Clearly, language testing cannot simply wait for the results of research—any more than curriculum and methods development can be abandoned until all results are in—but the relevant research must be undertaken as a matter of urgency alongside the development of evaluation, curricula, and methods.

Research should obviously be expected to continue in the areas mentioned briefly in the section of this article on theoretical research on language acquisition. It is important not to decrease in any way existing links between sociolinguistics or pragmatics and the national language effort. Proficiency testing and teaching must be geared to the precise needs of society, and, clearly, language is taught in order that it may be used. At the same time, it seems increasingly likely that teaching and testing that fail to take into account the effects of innately determined controls on language development is, at best, of dubious validity and, at worst, useless. It is important that research guided in part by theoretical linguists form a modest but crucial part of any national language effort. Were it not for the unfortunate misunderstandings and rivalries of the past thirty years, that would go without saying, since it is in principle scarcely open to question.

Book Department

INTERNATIONAL RELATIONS AND POLITICS

CHARLTON, MICHAEL. *The Eagle and the Small Birds: Crisis in the Soviet Empire: From Yalta to Solidarity.* Pp. 192. Chicago: University of Chicago Press, 1984. $14.95.

MAULL, HANNS. *Energy, Minerals, and Western Security.* Pp. xvii, 413. Baltimore: Johns Hopkins University Press, 1984. $35.00.

Each of these books deals with the security of the West in its own way: the Charlton volume with Soviet-Western relationships since Yalta; the Maull study with economic and strategic security issues posed by the availability of fuel and non-fuel minerals that constitute the lifeblood of modern industrial societies.

Charlton, an Australian journalist, has introduced a new approach to oral history. He acts as the questioner-narrator, using his sources to carry the argument forward. The argument, briefly, is that since Yalta, Western leaders and diplomats have been too naive and too easy in negotiations with the Soviets. The result of Charlton's approach, because of the selection of those to be interviewed, is to reaffirm basically the hard-line conservative interpretation of East-West relations since 1946. Whether intended or not, this is, I fear, the result of the study. It makes a good television script, but poor history. For Charlton and his friends, we get our security from strength and by our containment of the Red Army, the enforcer of the communist ideology that Charlton and others in the book believe is dead.

The Maull study is an impressively documented analysis of the vulnerabilities of the United States, Europe, and Japan with respect to the availability of fuels and nonfuel minerals. The study culminates in 14 recommendations for the development of economic security policies regarding these materials. The sanity and good sense of these recommendations make this an important book for students of international relations as well as required reading for policymakers.

Maull addresses his recommendations to governments. He abjures the use of the "military option" and urges an effort by the industrialized nations to open a dialogue with the USSR about critical mineral and fuel security issues that might involve them in crisis management. Some of his other suggestions include strengthening international monitoring systems of key mineral markets, including constraints on production and distribution, and real and potential threats to critical fuel and mineral supplies; developing internal controls for substituting, rationing, and stockpiling; and strengthening the International Energy Agency by improving the European Commission's energy activities as well as its crisis management capability.

This is a reference work. There are 54 tables and two figures and 933 footnotes in this 422-page book. Within the parameters of its chosen subject matter, this study may be considered to be definitive.

JACK L. CROSS

Texas A & M University

College Station

KUPER, LEO. *The Prevention of Genocide.* Pp. ix, 286. New Haven, CT: Yale University Press, 1985. $22.00.

"There must surely be unanimity among the members of the United Nations on the primacy of the right to life." With these words, Leo Kuper begins his searching analysis of perhaps the most damnable of crimes ever committed by humanity: genocide. This is the latest book on the compelling subject by one of the leading political sociologists of human rights; it should be read by every member of the species that crawls on earth thinking that he or she is proud to be human.

The central thesis of the book is clear. Despite universal condemnation of genocidal and related crimes against humanity in the voluminous declarations, conventions, and protocols by the United Nations, its performance records on the prevention and punishment of those responsible for "such an odious scourge" are deplorable. The reason is that most genocidal acts are perpetrated by governments or individuals under their protection and that there are structural biases in the United Nations in favor of the primacy of a state's right against the right to life of individuals.

A profoundly disturbing fact is that, for the post-World War II generations of political leaders who grew up witnessing the horrors of the Nazi death camps, the primacy of the state's right and considerations of political alignment still prevails over the urgent task of eradicating so hideous a crime against humanity as genocide and mass political murders. To the extent that there were any real efforts in the world toward the protection of the human rights of ethnic, religious, or other minority groups, they were to be found in the investigative reports, publicity of human rights violations, and appeals campaigns waged by private groups and nongovernmental organizations. The centrality of private initiatives in the human rights campaign is clearly demonstrated by the fact that in the United Nations more meaningful initiatives have come from the Sub-Commission on Prevention of Discrimination and Protection of Minorities, which consists of experts appointed in their personal capacity and not as representatives of member states. The subcommission is not, of course, without counterpressures of the state's-right orientation within it. The main frustration of its initiatives, however, comes from its parent body, the Commission on Human Rights, which consists of state representatives. Not surprisingly, as Kuper notes, the commision is sometimes described as "the graveyard of human rights." What this means in terms of change needed to ensure greater respect for human life at the United Nations, with its typically dilatory tactics to protect governments practicing death, is the institutional enhancement of individual initiatives. Kuper endorses, in particular, the proposed five-year appointment of a "high commissioner for human rights" whose duties would be to pay "particular attention to urgent situations appearing to involve threats to life" and to sound an international alert.

Despite its title, *The Prevention of Genocide* is a topically broader book that contains such chapters as "The Right to Self-Determination," with a full case study of the secession of Bangladesh; "Implementation of the Anti-Slavery Conventions"; "Political Mass Murder"; and even an epilogue, "The Nuclear

Arms Race and Genocide." While the book is somewhat disorganized and tends toward repetitive comments, it is both informative and elucidating on the state of human rights protection at the United Nations.

SUNG HO KIM

Ohio University
Athens

PERRIS, ARNOLD. *Music as Propaganda: Art to Persuade, Art to Control.* Pp. x, 247. Westport, CT: Greenwood Press, 1985. $29.00.

In *Music as Propaganda*, Arnold Perris surveys the history of music as a medium for articulating political values, challenging established social orders, and reinforcing religious beliefs and practices. His scope is ambitiously broad, with individual chapters on musical nationalism in nineteenth-century Europe, opera and symphonic music in the Soviet Union and the People's Republic of China, sacred music in the Hindu, Islamic, Judaic, and Christian traditions, social commentary in the Broadway musical, and protest songs of the 1960s. Perris invites the reader to "relisten" and "to respond to the music as its first audience did," outlining the political context of compositions as diverse as Beethoven's *Fidelio* and Mozart's *Marriage of Figaro*, as Wagner's *Ring of the Nibelungs* cycle and Shostakovich's *Lady Macbeth of Mtsensk District,* as Malvina Reynolds's *Little Boxes* and the Who's *Tommy.*

Though he has written with style and spirit, Perris fails to overcome the obvious risks in extending his reach so far and wide. The work is uneven, neither systematic nor comprehensive. Too often, Perris settles for simple plot summaries of librettos, or catalogs of suggestive song titles, to make a point when the material begs for more careful analysis. At his best, in chapters on Beethoven and nationalist composers such as Smetana, Dvořak, and Sibelius, Perris offers a lucid historical overview of their music and interesting anecdotes on the politics of early

public performances of their compositions. At his worst, in the chapter on protest music in the 1960s, he neglects significant contrasts among popular singers and songwriters, glossing over the dramatic changes that took place as the music evolved from the acoustic performances of the coffeehouse to the amplified spectacles of the arena.

The book also suffers from a weak conceptualization of propaganda. Borrowing a simple dictionary definition, Perris includes virtually any music with a social or political message. When he considers the institutional controls and ideological goals in music making in Nazi Germany, the Soviet Union, and China, use of the term seems appropriate. But when he applies the term to liturgical compositions and popular song, regardless of whether or not its makers have been participants in organized movements for social or political change, its use seems too inclusive. As a result, the thematic continuity of the work is undermined, and the utility of such broad comparisons remains uncertain.

The lack of sophisticated analysis seems likely to disappoint much of the potential readership of this book. Communications historians, for example, or cultural anthropologists interested in religious ritual and music will find nothing new here and will regret that Perris neglected the important insights of their respective disciplines. Social or political historians will find his text thin and poorly developed. Finally, for most readers, the lesson that music in all genres reflects the social and political concerns of its age will have been learned long ago.

KEVIN GOSNER

University of Arizona
Tucson

QUANDT, WILLIAM B. *Camp David: Peacemaking and Politics.* Pp. xvi, 426. Washington, DC: Brookings Institution, 1986. $32.95. Paperbound, $12.95.

The Camp David accords, signed by Egyptian President Anwar el-Sadat and Israeli Prime Minister Menachem Begin on 17

September 1978, were a major event in modern Middle Eastern history and the most notable foreign policy achievement of the Carter administration. Quandt's account of the negotiations is a major scholarly achievement in its own right.

Quandt is one of those rare people who can combine meticulous scholarship with an insider's view of the policy process at work—he served on the National Security Council staff from 1977 to mid-1979 with special responsibility for the Middle East and participated in the Camp David negotiations—and do justice to both domains. He argues that the accords were a major achievement, but also notes the flaws of the protagonists and their limited room for maneuvers, particularly in the case of Carter and Sadat. Carter was sincere in his desire for a general settlement, but could not distinguish between questions better left to private persuasion and those requiring the application of pressure in public.

Quandt finds Sadat a generalist, impatient with the details of negotiation, gambling on a direct approach to Begin in Jerusalem and seeking essentially to exert pressure on Carter as a mediator to press Begin. Quandt mentions "an aura of collusion between Washington and Cairo." Sadat sought to remove Israeli forces from the Sinai. His concern for the broader issues of the West Bank, the Palestinian question, the Palestine Liberation Organization, and Syria was somewhat rhetorical. He did not want to be isolated in the Arab world in dealing with Israel, but often regarded the other Arab leaders with contempt.

But Begin seems to win Quandt's grudging respect as the most able and determined of the negotiators in gaining the maximum—and giving up the minimum—for his country. History and religion buttressed his insistence on maintaining control and sovereignty over the West Bank—so-called Judea and Samaria. Secretary of State Vance observed that the more one pushed Begin, the more intransigent he became. Secretary of Defense Brown quipped that "we have him just where he wants us."

Begin was helped by Carter's plight in this endeavor. The American president had hoped that the Egyptian-Israeli talks in Geneva would be expanded to deal with West Bank and Palestinian issues. The talks would be an "'umbrella' to pull in Jordan, the Palestinians, and perhaps even the Syrians." But the umbrella could not be raised until the Syrians and Palestinians were satisfied. If they perceived Geneva as merely a "fig leaf" for another separate Egyptian-Israeli agreement—"Sinai III"—they had little reason to go along. "Yet if they were allowed to veto Egyptian moves—no progress could be made in negotiations."

In assessing gains Quandt argues that Egypt recovered territory and Israel could concentrate all of its resources against Syrian threats. But by following Begin into "legalistic formulations," Carter and Sadat "lost sight" of the Palestinians and Jordanians. The Camp David accords "avoided any reference to eventual Israeli withdrawal from the West Bank, self determination, or a freeze on settlements. Indeed, the details make it seem as if everything had been worked out before the Palestinians and Jordan were invited to join the negotiations." Quandt would have preferred a vaguer, more open-ended formula.

Camp David, in his view, could be seen as either a model or an obstacle. As a model, Camp David could mean that Israel, with the Egyptian threat removed, would be more willing to make territorial concessions and peace with other Arab states. They, in turn, would be more willing to make peace with Israel. Others disagreed. Camp David would serve as an obstacle. Without the Egyptian threat Israel would have no reason to make further territorial concessions. Without such concessions, other Arab leaders would have no incentive to make peace with Israel.

I agree with Quandt that the Egyptian-Israeli treaty deals with the easiest issue in the Middle East conundrum. The rest will be very difficult—if not impossible—to settle. But the ambiguous lessons of the Camp David accords will be some elements that will be of great value to future negotiations while others will be "irrelevant or in need of revision."

ROGER HAMBURG
Indiana University
South Bend

AFRICA, ASIA AND LATIN AMERICA

HART, ALAN. *Arafat: Terrorist or Peacemaker?* Pp. 501. London: Sidgwick & Jackson, 1985. $19.95.

British journalist Alan Hart's evaluation of Yasser Arafat has two main purposes: (1) to give the PLO chairman a "fair hearing"; and (2) "to promote a more informed and more honest debate about the way to peace in the Middle East." He fails because of a total lack of objectivity, leaving only an apologia for Arafat that is crystallized in the opening claim: "Within the limits of what is politically possible on each side, no leader, Arab or Jew, has done more than Arafat to prepare the ground for a comprehensive settlement of the Arab-Israeli conflict." No honest dialogue about peace can start on the premise that "public opinion has been conditioned to accept Zionist propaganda as historical truth." The whole book that follows is full of assertion and bias, relying on but one principal source—the leadership of the PLO.

Hart attempts a three-dimensional portrait of Arafat: as individual; as leader of the PLO; and as rival to Arab governments. In the first dimension, we are introduced to virtue: Arafat the ascetic, the sensitive, the saint, the martyr, the wit. Even negative qualities, such as Arafat's notorious temper, are dismissed or transformed into positive traits. Violence is condoned or attributed to others. The role of personality and leadership is one of the more neglected areas of international relations; yet, particularly in the Middle East, uncritical accounts of individuals and automatic conclusions about the

influence of childhood and adolescence on later policymaking hardly substitute for careful psychohistory.

The sociological treatment is more promising. The best part of the book addresses Al Fatah's genesis and the personal relationships among the top leadership. Al Fatah and the PLO in general appear more lifelike than their chairman, for Hart discusses both conflict and cooperation regarding the purposes and methods of Palestinian nationalism.

Political rivalry is central also to Hart's description of Arafat's relations with key Arab countries, such as Egypt, Jordan, and Syria, and their leaders. He details Arafat's historical mistrust of the Arab world's commitment to the political and humanitarian resolution of the Palestinian question, adding insight into the Middle Eastern conundrum.

Hart's plea for peace in the Middle East is laudable. The path to peace will be trodden only if the roadblocks of mutual ignorance, fear, and misinformation are removed. Hart's myopia, however, leads us into a cul-de-sac.

LILY GARDNER FELDMAN
Tufts University
Medford
Massachusetts

LASATER, MARTIN L. *The Taiwan Issue in Sino-American Strategic Relations.* Pp. xi, 283. Boulder, CO: Westview Press, 1985. Paperbound, $18.00.

STOLPER, THOMAS E. *China, Taiwan and the Offshore Islands.* Pp. xiii, 170. Armonk, NY: M. E. Sharpe, 1985. $30.00.

These two books deal with Taiwan as an issue between the United States and the People's Republic of China. Although similar in general focus, the books are very much different in their approach and in the conclusions their authors reach. *China, Taiwan and the Offshore Islands* is essentially a history of the offshore-islands crises, though some implications are drawn that relate to current United States-China relations. *The Taiwan*

Issue in Sino-American Strategic Relations concerns the strategic role Taiwan plays at the present time in Washington-Peking-Moscow relations.

Stolper's main theme is that the fighting over the offshore islands from the Chinese perspective was a matter of jockeying for advantage and publicity and an effort—by Peking—to influence the U.S. decision to sign a defense pact with Nationalist China. In other words, Mao did not really want to liberate the offshore islands.

Stolper's analysis is best on the first offshore-islands crisis, in 1954 and 1955, though he argues convincingly that nothing really changed in 1958 in terms of China's goals and American policy. On the other hand, this book is short on analysis that tells us where we are going from here.

Lasater's central thesis is that Taiwan was an issue that did not impede a warming of Sino-American relations because the rapprochement was built primarily on strategic concerns, namely the growing Soviet military threat. Subsequently, however, each nation became disappointed with the other and realism set in regarding the value of the so-called China connection to the United States and China's plan to promote a united front against Soviet hegemonism, a plan that failed. Taiwan then emerged as a "problem." Lasater deals with this deftly though he avoids the issues of sovereignty.

Peking was also motivated to complain about Taiwan, says Lasater, because (1) Chinese leaders wanted to put Washington on the defensive and make U.S. policymakers feel guilty over Taiwan in order to extract economic concessions from the United States, which they did successfully; (2) China saw the United States as a soft negotiator, unlike the Soviet Union; (3) increases in U.S. global strength made it less necessary for Peking to help cope with the Soviet threat; and (4) opposition to pro-American policies by the Party and government bureaucracies and the military weakened Deng's leadership.

Both books are well researched and well written. Stolper and Lasater have demonstrated a talent for looking beyond the simple and obvious and have presented analysis that any scholar will consider top rate. The two also complement one another, though there is a considerable time gap: Stolper focuses almost exclusively on the 1954-55 period and Lasater begins in 1969 and focuses primarily on the events of the 1980s. If one is reading both books, Stolper should be read before Lasater. If one has time for only one of the pair and is interested in the Taiwan problem—if the Taiwan problem is really that—and all of its intricacies and how it relates to international politics, then Lasater's book is the book to read.

JOHN F. COOPER

Rhodes College
Memphis
Tennessee

PALMER, NORMAN D. *The United States and India: Dimensions of Influence.* Pp. xiv, 302. New York: Praeger, 1984. Paperbound, $14.95.

CHAUDHRI, MOHAMMAD AHSEN, ed. *Pakistan and Regional Security.* Pp. 146. Karachi: Distributed by Royal Book Company [1982?]. No price.

When John Kenneth Galbraith was ambassador to India—and I was one of his distant underlings—he once remarked that he could influence India to do anything that India had already made up its mind to do. Norman Palmer bears out the essence of this observation when he carefully documents the little influence the United States has had on India and the equally small amount India has had on the United States. Palmer's work is an extensive review of American-Indian relations, especially since 1971, a period in which relations between the two largest democracies have been cold to lukewarm. He notes also that the era before 1971 was similarly characterized and in doing so brings back memories of such Indian antagonists as Krishna Menon, as well as of the unwavering views of John Foster Dulles on nonalignment. He does not, however, ignore, in chapter 8, the important point that individual relationships have often been close and rewarding and that key individuals, such as Chester Bowles and Vijayalakshmi Pandit, have contributed positively to Indo-American understanding.

Palmer's discussion of the security relationship, in chapter 6, is a valuable study of the place given by the United States to the relative importance of India and of Pakistan in South Asian regional terms. This and the preceding chapter on economic assistance, however, strike me to a considerable degree as another example of American apologetics; the problem, it seems to be argued, is misunderstanding by Americans of the importance of India, and the errors are very largely on the American side. Palmer also provides, in chapter 7, an excellent review of the nuclear issue, centering on the Tarapur supply question. It is the best I have seen. Palmer corrects an earlier error, on page 84, by stating in this chapter that the Tarapur supply agreement was that and not a treaty.

No one—and no library—with interests in South Asia will want to be without this excellent work, even if all the conclusions may not be accepted by all readers.

The six papers in the Chaudhri volume each contribute to our understanding of Pakistani points of view on international issues. They are, not unexpectedly, written with a strong Pakistani bias. Chaudhri provides an overview of Pakistani foreign policy that is uncritical and finds India as the villain. Latif Ahmed Sherwani's review of Sino-Pakistani relations seems to me not to be up to his usual high standards. Pervaiz Iqbal Cheema provides an interesting discussion of Pakistan's nuclear option, accusing the West of alarmism, but seeming to conclude that Pakistan might do well to avoid weapons building. Mujtaba Razvi and Shafqat Ali Shah look at developments in Southwest Asia as they relate to Pakistan and the latter finds flaws in the Carter policy, especially on the Palestine question. Talat Ayesha Wizarat comments on Pakistan's energy future and seems to see a nuclear future as the necessary one. It is an interesting collection of essays, by now quite out of date, that will be helpful to students of the region.

CRAIG BAXTER
Juniata College
Huntingdon
Pennsylvania

EUROPE

BENNIGSEN, ALEXANDRE and S. ENDERS WIMBUSH. *Mystics and Commissars: Sufism in the Soviet Union.* Pp. viii, 195. Berkeley: University of California Press, 1985. No price.

This brief work largely repeats the kind of information published in Bennigsen's recent works "Official Islam and Sufi Brotherhoods in the Soviet Union Today" (in *Islam and Power*, edited by A. S. Cudsi and A. E. Hillal Dessouki) and *The Islamic Threat to the Soviet State* (with Marie Broxup). It represents a significant advance over the previous works, however, in that it concentrates particularly on the Sufi aspect of Islam in the Soviet Union. It begins with a concise history of Sufism in czarist and Soviet Russia, carefully noting that not all Sufis are politicized, nor are all politicized Muslims Sufis. It is Bennigsen and Wimbush's thesis, however, that the specific nature and organization of Sufi orders account to a large extent for the phenomenal survival and proliferation of Islam in the Soviet Union. As they point out, Soviet polls indicate that some 80 percent of the Muslim population of the Soviet Union claims religious affiliation, as compared to only 15 percent in previously Christian areas.

In chapters entitled "Structure of the Sufi Brotherhoods," "Sufi Adepts: Numbers, Recruitment, Women," "The Organization of the Sufi Brotherhoods," and "The Inner Life of the Sufi Brotherhoods," the work profiles four Sufi brotherhoods as they have evolved within the Soviet Union and emphasizes two unique aspects of their politicization. First, the Soviet Union has witnessed a recent wave of popular Islamic fundamentalism, just as has been experienced throughout the rest of the Islamic world. In the Soviet Union, however, this trend has been generally harmonious with Sufi activity, whereas in the rest of the Islamic world the fundamentalist trend has been for the most part anti-Sufi. Perhaps even more interesting, the politicization of Soviet-dominated Sufism is not necessarily coterminus with the current cries of *jihad* ("holy war" against the infidels). Rather, it seems to have permeated the very nature of the orders themselves. This is perhaps best exemplified by Bennigsen and Wimbush's observation that often members of the most mystical and traditionally other-worldly orders, such as the Yasawiya, appear to be the most deeply politicized.

Also included is an illuminating discussion of the relationship of Sufism to what is known as official Islam—that represented by the four Spiritual Boards of Soviet Islam—stressing the overwhelming popular rejection of the latter in favor of the former. Among the most interesting speculations concerns the relationship of the Soviet Sufis with their confreres across the borders, especially in Iran and Afghanistan. Drawing primarily on official Soviet condemnations of what the Soviet press calls criminal foreign influence, Bennigsen and Wimbush consider it highly likely that at least unofficial links have been made with Afghan *mojahidin* groups.

Bennigsen and Wimbush may tend to exaggerate the role of Sufism when they extrapolate beyond Soviet borders. They quote a Soviet expert to the effect that the current "renaissance of Islam" throughout the world can only take place under the banner of Sufism. But as they themselves caution, their analyses are preliminary. They nevertheless represent a valuable contribution to a long-neglected area and will, it is hoped, stimulate further investigation.

TAMARA SONN

Temple University
Philadelphia
Pennsylvania

BRADLEY, JOSEPH. *Muzhik and Muscovite: Urbanization in Late Imperial Russia.* Pp. xvi, 422. Berkeley: University of California Press, 1985. $37.50.

RALEIGH, DONALD J. *Revolution on the Volga: 1917 in Saratov.* Pp. 373. Ithaca, NY: Cornell University Press, 1986. $32.50.

Moscow around 1900 was a rapidly growing, sprawling city of over 1 million people. But with all its emerging modernization, Moscow—unlike St. Petersburg—retained the quality of a big village.

Immigrant muzhiks—peasants from the country—made up the bulk of this swelling population. The urban problems that this influx created were many: slums, poor transportation, vagrancy and unemployment, infectious disease, and drunkenness, to name the most important. Bradley, professor at the University of Tulsa, addresses himself principally to "the areas of poor relief and housing reform" to illustrate "the struggle of the educated elite, and in particular the professionals," in Moscow "against the poverty and ignorance of the common people." Such campaigns of improvement were carried on through official channels as well as by charitable societies. The discussions of the Imperial Foundling Home and its activities and of the Moscow Workhouse are informative. By and large, Bradley succeeds in his delineation of welfare activities in Moscow.

Raleigh, professor at the University of Hawaii, centers his study upon the revolutionary disturbances of 1917 in the Volga town of Saratov—the town of the famous nineteenth-century Russian radical, Nicholas Chernyshevski. Raleigh's work not only furnishes a detailed narrative of what happened; it also attempts to correct an imbalance of what is alleged to be overconcentration of scholars and students upon Petrograd and Moscow for the revolutions of 1917. As Raleigh well realizes, however, how representative is Saratov of the revolutions in "the Russian heartland"?

These two books are linked by an interest in local history, broadly construed. Each is the product of extensive research in Russian sources. Each also includes useful illustrations to supplement the text.

Raleigh tells us that he was never able to visit Saratov because it was a "closed city." Even so, it is to his credit that he makes Saratov come alive. A vivid sense of provincial oppressiveness about this town never quite fades. By contrast, there is something dead about the Moscow of Bradley's study— and this despite his firsthand knowledge of Moscow and his use of accounts by contemporaries. Incidentally, the name of the famous Baedeker of the tourist guides is spelled wrong on page 60 and in the index.

It remains to be said that both monographs make a contribution to their respective subjects.

DAVID HECHT

Pace University
New York City

LITTLEJOHN, GARY. *A Sociology of the Soviet Union.* Pp. viii, 286. New York: St. Martin's Press, 1984. $25.00.

This review begins with a negative note about the style of the book. It must do so precisely because the style gets in the way of easy—and in some instances, of any—comprehension. This deficiency is probably due to the fact that the book is an adaptation of a dissertation and as such it has all the faults of the poorest example of such a genre. Its generally turgid language is illustrated by a 110-word sentence on page 259 that defies a single reading. On this point the readers will have to take my word given the lack of space here to reproduce this and other lengthy sentences.

A more serious shortcoming of this study is the impression it conveys of an unfocused effort. Littlejohn begins with a statement that he intends to provide a sociological overview of the Soviet Union. Initially this is done without any qualification, thereby implying that the totality of Soviet society—

including all key groups, namely, the Party elite, the government bureaucracy, the military, the KGB, and the scientific and technical community—will be analyzed, as would be appropriate to such an overview. Yet this is not the case: the last three groups are not examined, even superficially. This omission cannot be a matter of space, since many pages are devoted to minute and abstract, if not extraneous, analysis of ideological postulations. These pages could have been better devoted to these important groups and to the more relevant *nomenklatura* structure underlying the class system in the Soviet Union. Instead, *nomenklatura* is mentioned in passing and essentially tossed off in one footnote. Indeed, even though *nomenklatura* is the heart of the class system in the Soviet Union, it does not even rate a citation in the book's index.

At the same time, the lack of focus is reinforced by a somewhat contradictory later admission that it is beyond the capability of one person to provide an all-embracing view of the vast and complex Soviet society.

Readers, then, are left puzzled about whether they will be enlightened by an objective analysis of Soviet society or be persuaded to accept Littlejohn's views on the main aim of his study: to determine whether social classes exist in the USSR. It is determined that such classes do not exist, and that the Soviet leadership has accomplished this by rough equalization of incomes. The latter conclusion is strange since anyone with the slightest familiarity with the Soviet salary and wage reality knows of the sizable compensation disparity between the top layers in the Party, military, KGB, arts and literature, and science and industry versus the *prostoi narod* ("common people").

But any pay comparison within the USSR, or with the United States, does not take into account the even more important perquisites of the Soviet elite such as access to special stores, *dachas,* chauffeured cars, travel abroad, and separate lounges at rail stations and airports. These and other material and intangible forms of privilege have long separated "the vanguard of the proletariat" from the proletariat in the USSR.

In this connection, it is also strange that the basis for such inequality—the *nomenklatura* system—is barely mentioned in passing, when in reality it forms the essence of economic, social, and political inequality in the USSR.

To reach his main conclusions, Littlejohn goes through a lot of minute and abstract discussion of ideology and theory, including Marx's and Weber's views of class structure and the relation of producers to the means of production. He also gives a historical review of the more practical social and economic aspects of the Soviet system such as the welfare system and consumption, including housing, health, and social security. He ends his study with an analysis of the Soviet class structure, including the relationships of women, *kolkhozniki,* and *intelligentsia* to and within the Soviet system. All of these analyses are done to reach his somewhat obfuscated main finding: "The conclusion that the relations of production within the state sector do not give rise to class relations within it does not mean that there are no class relations in the Soviet Union." Here Littlejohn seemingly reflects the effect of delving into Soviet matters, since his language resembles Soviet pronouncements with their double and even triple negatives.

Thus it is unclear how Littlejohn's findings add to our understanding of the Soviet system. For example, does it matter whether classes existed or exist in the USSR except as a philosophical proposition for intellectual exercise? The answer would seem to be that it is irrelevant in the face of Soviet history and present reality, which shows the vanguard ruling in the name of the proletariat without ever giving it a chance to determine its own fate and to act on its own desires.

No free elections were ever held after the disbanding of the Constituent Assembly, either in the USSR or in any other Communist state for that matter; this is the clearest confirmation of the lesson learned by the Soviets; never take a chance on genuinely free elections. And hence, the vanguard—embodying the Communist Party elite and associated key groups cited earlier—has ruled the USSR ever since 1917, perpetuated by *nomenklatura.*

Not only does Littlejohn add little to our understanding, but he actually makes errors in judgment. He asserts that "conditions on collective farms are steadily improving." It would be interesting to have this documented in the face of contrary evidence, reflected even by the Soviet leaders themselves. Gorbachev has said that private plots should be allowed to flourish to give Soviet farmers additional income incentive, despite the long-standing effort of Party zealots to abolish such plots. Presumably Gorbachev would not call for toleration of ideologically embarrassing private plots if the approved *kolkhozy* were meeting their own needs, on top of the Soviet state's harvest delivery requirements. Then, too, the few foreigners allowed to visit the few collective farms can confirm how inadequate most farms are in collectively required equipment and supplies, not to speak of personal and household items; the latter are traditionally and notoriously in short supply as evidenced by bare shelves in rural stores. Since most of the *kolkhozy* are off-limits and only the best few are shown to foreigners, we can imagine how far worse off are those farms not shown to foreign visitors.

To end on a positive note, Littlejohn deserves credit for amassing interesting data and drawing appropriate conclusions about some societal aspects of the Soviet system examined in individual chapters, even if he falls short of providing the overview promised by the title.

JOHN R. THOMAS

U.S. Department of State
Washington, D.C.

REID, DONALD. *The Miners of Decazeville: A Genealogy of Deindustrialization.* Pp. vi, 333. Cambridge, MA: Harvard University Press, 1985. $25.00.

Donald Reid's study of the southwestern coal-mining community of Decazeville from the late eighteenth to the mid-twentieth century traces the progress from industrialization to deindustrialization and the consequences for Decazeville's miners. Drawing on a rich collection of local and national primary sources, the book makes a significant contribution to contemporary French labor history.

Reid divides his study into three chronological sections. The first, the prelude to the large-scale industrialization of the central discussion, describes the period up to the 1820s. The second section covers the period from the July Monarchy through the late-nineteenth-century long depression. This period witnessed the initial growth and subsequent swings of prosperity and decline in the commune of Decazeville that had been established in the early 1830s on the site of the new coal mines and ironworks.

By the 1840s, the Houillères et Fonderies had become France's fourth largest industrial firm. However, the company town of Decazeville, dependent on heavy metallurgy and coal mining, suffered from the general mid-century depression, technological changes rendering its low-grade iron ore less industrially useful, and the Second Empire's free-trade policy undercutting its iron market. By 1860, coal had replaced iron as the primary industry of the Aubin basin, a change hinting at the town's eventual deindustrialization. The company's collapse in the late 1860s and the attendant unrest among the miners paved the way for new management by the Nouvelle Société with links to Le Creusot and industry outside the southwest. The 1870s witnessed both renewed prosperity and expanded links between the town and the national arena; company director Deseilligny, both mayor of Decazeville and its representative in the Chamber of Deputies, used his position to secure contracts for the town. In seeking to create a community loyal to the company, the company acted as an agent of modernization by constructing houses and a hospital and by introducing improvements like gas lighting. Paradoxically, it thereby fostered a labor solidarity subsequently directed against management. Decazeville's prosperity proved

short-lived; its isolated location made effective competition difficult with the northern industrial regions. The economic adversity of the century's fourth quarter pitted labor against management, triggering several strikes, most significantly in 1886 when a company supervisor was murdered, troops were summoned, and workers stayed off the job for over three months. To Reid, the social conflict was significant in developing workers' class and national consciousness, in transforming them into Frenchmen. In that respect, it paralleled the effects of universal, compulsory education and military service. Again, economic decline triggered a change in management with the transfer of ownership in 1892 to the large coal, iron, and steel conglomerate, Comambault.

The third period, which opened with the boom of a second industrial revolution from the mid-1890s to World War I, was characterized by renewed prosperity and labor shortage. Use of immigrant workers, initially from Spain and after the war from Eastern Europe, compensated for local labor scarcity, but altered the character of the industrial work force. Prosperity did not eliminate social discontent as the unions utilized the general strike weapon to pressure parliament into passing social legislation. The cycles of prosperity and depression continued with the expansion of the war period followed by depression in the early 1920s, a brief revival at the end of the decade, and more prolonged depression through the 1930s and World War II. The nationalization of the mines in 1946, the culmination of the process of increased state intervention, centralized the administration, but did not resolve the basic problem of an outmoded industry. Development of alternative energy sources like oil, gas, and hydroelectric power and creation of the European Coal and Steel Community in 1951, which exposed expensive French coal and steel to the competition of cheaper German goods, dealt the death blow. The miners, increasingly isolated from their technocratic society, succumbed to pessimism as their strikes and protests failed to halt the closure of unproductive mines in the early 1960s.

Reid's book is an excellent case study of the process by which a prosperous nineteenth-century town tied to the early stages of the industrial revolution experienced the cycles of prosperity and depression until the collapse of its industrial base in the mid-twentieth century. It provides interesting insights into the course of economic development and its effects on the labor force.

MARJORIE M. FARRAR
Chestnut Hill
Massachusetts

TURNER, HENRY ASHBY, Jr. *German Big Business and the Rise of Hitler.* Pp. 504. New York: Oxford University Press, 1985. $25.00.

Henry Turner introduces his highly publicized *German Big Business and the Rise of Hitler* as a work of debunking—an expose of lies, an explosion of myths, a clearing up of misconceptions—and one could discuss it as such were it not that no reputable non-Socialist-bloc scholar specializing in this subject any longer accepts the theory he attacks: that the leaders of finance and industry engineered Hitler's takeover of the *Reich.* The prosecution in the Trials of Nuremberg Industrialists first made this charge, Marxists have reiterated it endlessly, and until 1970 historians had seldom challenged it. It was then, however, that Turner himself began to chip away at the existing orthodoxy. In a succession of tightly written articles and provocative scholarly exchanges he demonstrated beyond serious doubt that German big business was neither pro-Weimar nor pro-Hitler but divided; that historians had exaggerated the importance of the aid given Hitler by individual industrialists such as Fritz Thyssen; that the Nazi Party had its own sources of campaign funding for the critical elections between 1930 and 1932; and that no major business figure was involved in the machinations of January 1933 resulting

in the formation of the Hitler-Papen cabinet. These are also the main conclusions of *German Big Business and the Rise of Hitler,* but in it Turner is, among historians at least, preaching to the converted.

German Big Business and the Rise of Hitler is more than a supplement to Turner's previous work, for it presents a new thesis about its response to the National Socialist phenomenon. Far from having pursued the goal of a Hitler dictatorship with single-minded intensity, he shows that Germany's leading industrialists and financiers were at the mercy of economic events, divided in political outlook, and all but immobilized in actual practice. Turner builds his case confidently: document by document, episode by episode, crisis by crisis, wherever possible allowing his material to speak for itself, even following it faithfully when it appears for a time to be pointing to conclusions different from his own. Although a more thorough analysis of the business problems faced by producers and bankers during the depression would have strengthened Turner's case, his results are impressive. He shows that the Nazis had no economic policy worthy of the name, sent out only scrambled signals to big business, and failed in an effort to put out feelers because of the incompetence, corruption, and opportunism of their agents. Turner also demonstrates that big business was unable to arrive at agreement over recovery policy, could not decide as to which of the several contending political horses to back, feared Nazi labor demagogy and anti-Semitism, made no more than half-hearted attempts to influence Nazi policy prior to 1933, and was never aware of the momentousness of an eventual Nazi takeover. Turner freely admits that members of the German big-business community may have been politically short sighted, even stupid, but he puts to rest for all time the reproach that they conspired to bring Hitler to power.

In writing *German Big Business and the Rise of Hitler* Turner decided to resolve a specific historical controversy rather than exhaust his subject. It is hard to quibble with the choice of one who has produced such an impeccable work of scholarship. Yet, while Turner never says anything he cannot document, he fails to address a couple of important questions. Did not certain business decisions—as opposed to political decisions made by businessmen—contribute to the collapse of the Weimar system? And why was it that Germany's producers adapted so readily to the Third Reich and served Hitler so faithfully? Was there not some underlying compatibility of aims in the background of the relationship between the National Socialists and big business during the years from 1930 to 1933? Although the search for answers to these questions may involve more theorizing, or speculating, than Turner finds congenial, it is to be hoped that such activity will be preliminary to further studies faithful to his fastidious empiricism.

JOHN GILLINGHAM
University of Missouri
St. Louis

UNITED STATES

GRAFTON, CARL and ANNE PERMALOFF. *Big Mules and Branchheads: James E. Folsom and Political Power in Alabama.* Pp. xiv, 307. Athens: University of Georgia Press, 1985. $27.50.

James E. Folsom was born in 1908 on a farm near Elba, in southeast Alabama. As a young boy, he accompanied his father, a deputy sheriff and tax collector, on his rounds throughout rural Coffee County. Folsom also fondly recalled boyhood trips to the county courthouse and politicos who visited his home. The young Folsom worshiped his Populist uncle, who thrilled him with tales of embattled Alabama farmers of the 1890s, faraway political conventions, and ancestors who opposed the Civil War. These early influences were crucial in shaping Folsom's grass-roots political philosophy, which emerged during his two terms as governor of Alabama during the years 1947-51 and 1955-59.

Big Jim Folsom as governor was an anachronism in Alabama politics—his populistic ideas about the people versus the interests seemed more akin to the 1890s than the 1940s and 1950s. Unlike many of his political contemporaries, he avoided race baiting and aggressively championed the cause of Alabama's black underclass. His campaign speeches, official statements, and press interviews reveal that he also favored greater participatory democracy for other forgotten citizens—poor whites and women. Despite his failure to deal effectively with hostile lawmakers, Folsom consistently fought for reapportionment of the legislature, abolition of the poll tax and other voting barriers, and the placement of women on juries. He also supported increases in state welfare allotments, old-age pensions, and teachers' salaries. On occasion, however, his keen interest in highway expansion—especially in rural areas—took precedence over other legislative proposals.

Grafton and Permaloff conclude that Folsom's basic naiveté, administrative ineptitude, and alcoholism prevented his achieving greatness as governor; yet their final assessment of his influence is quite positive: "Although Folsom's measurable impact was minimal, he represented something important in Alabama politics and history that cannot be quantified." In short, he mobilized ordinary citizens and successfully challenged the hegemony of the Big Mules of the Black Belt and Birmingham, thereby significantly altering the traditional pattern of Alabama politics.

There is much about this book that is praiseworthy, particularly Grafton and Permaloff's prodigious research effort and their concerted quest for objectivity in dealing with Folsom. Also, they have captured the minute, colorful details of Alabama politics during the period after World War II. Descriptions of Folsom's various campaigns are especially well done.

Like Grafton and Permaloff's protagonist, however, this book has a number of flaws. After devoting nine years to this project, Grafton and Permaloff understandably were eager to share their rich source material with the reader. Some judicious excising of lengthy quotations and historical background material, however, would have strengthened this book immeasurably. In providing so much superfluous data, Folsom, the central figure, is allowed to drift out of focus. Moreover, in the book's treatment of corruption in state government under Folsom, one is left with the impression that he was only indirectly responsible for illegal acts since in most cases his aides were the guilty parties. Nevertheless, Folsom selected these men and helped create their working environment. The theme of business as usual in politics also permeates this analysis. For example, at one point, it is asserted that Folsom's "use of legal and illegal means to influence the legislature" simply followed "a pattern set by other Alabama and southern governors." Although Grafton and Permaloff obviously wrestled over whether or not to indict Folsom for such acts, they failed to reach a very decisive conclusion. Finally, there is a serious problem with the use of confidential interviews in this work. The late T. Harry Williams employed such sources to perfection in his masterful biography of Huey Long. Unfortunately, Grafton and Permaloff have relied too heavily on unattributed interviews. Journalists and scholars will encounter great difficulty in assessing the evidence in this book because of footnotes that read: "many interviews with legislators in these areas, 1973-80," "countless people in Marshall County, Apr. 1974," and "newspaper reporter's notes, Montgomery."

These deficiencies detract from many of the positive aspects of this work. For interested readers there is an alternative volume—George E. Sims's *Little Man's Big Friend: James E. Folsom in Alabama Politics, 1946-1958* (University: University of Alabama Press, 1985). Both of these books contain a wealth of information—substantive and trivial—and will be welcomed by veteran Folsom watchers and students of Alabama politics.

DAVID E. ALSOBROOK

Carter Presidential Library
Atlanta
Georgia

LANE, ROGER. *Roots of Violence in Black Philadelphia, 1860-1900.* Pp. 213. Cambridge, MA: Harvard University Press, 1986. $25.00.

Roger Lane has written a first-rate book. His examination of black Philadelphia over the latter decades of the nineteenth century is done with care for detail and it offers a breadth of insight that is scholarship at its best. All of this is done in plain English, easily accessible to the general reader. The argument Lane constructs is simple in its essentials, but intricately woven from the fabric of historical evidence. To those who would talk glibly of such problems as disorganization in the black family, welfare dependency, or unemployment among black teenagers as if these problems emerged from some misguided problem of the 1960s, Lane offers a powerful antidote. Through his carefully wrought Philadelphia story he traces the unique and corrosive impact of the urban experience on black America.

A short review cannot do justice to this profoundly important book. In examining the processes through which Philadelphia blacks were squeezed out of various lines of work as well as out of sundry forms of legitimate business enterprise, Lane is fully persuasive in showing how an increasingly tenuous economic position inevitably gave rise to a subculture of crime and violence, which has stereotyped and handicapped even the most peaceable and law-abiding members of the black middle class. *Roots of Violence in Black Philadelphia* is an honest and courageous book. Readers will find that Roger Lane genuinely understands why civil rights legislation alone is not enough to free us from a past in which blacks were confined to the margins of the nation's post-agricultural economy.

CLARENCE N. STONE

University of Maryland
College Park

McDONALD, FORREST. *Novus Ordo Seclorum: The Intellectual Origins of the*

Constitution. Pp. xiii, 359. Lawrence: University Press of Kansas, 1985. $25.00.

The appearance of this book on the intellectual origins of the Constitution could not come at a better time. As we approach the bicentennial of the Constitution, McDonald has given us a superb treatment of the basic ideas and experiences that influenced the Framers in 1787.

These men had a very large body of political theory at their disposal as they searched for a form of government that would protect life, liberty, and property. Often they have been acclaimed as practical, hardheaded men who had a disdain for theory, but McDonald says that theories permeated their thinking more than they cared to admit and perhaps more than they knew. Between 1776 and 1787 a number of public men took pains to study the writings of the theorists of republicanism. Notable, of course, were Locke, Montesquieu, and Hume. McDonald says, "American republican ideologues could recite the central points of Montesquieu's doctrine [of separation of powers] as if it had been a catechism."

In regard to basic concepts of political economy, the attitudes of the Framers depended upon two considerations: beliefs as to what was possible and perceptions as to what was desirable. Of enormous importance was the impact of Adam Smith's "An Inquiry into the Nature and Causes of the Wealth of Nations." Most of the public men in America had some acquaintance with Smith's work.

Contributing, too, to the ideas of the Framers were the lessons derived from experience during the years from 1776 to 1787. The diverse experiences of the several states—financial and otherwise—were never far from their thinking. Noteworthy was Madison's concern over the tendency of factions to put their interests ahead of those of the public. Shays's Rebellion shocked many into reconsidering their ideas about republican forms of government and the means of safeguarding liberty and property. As the delegates grappled with their enormous problems, there was a general realization of the need to strengthen and reorganize the central authority. In the last analysis, the Framers relied heavily on common sense, collective wisdom, and their willingness to compromise.

McDonald insists that political theories and ideologies were of limited practical use to the Framers. The theories, he says, helped shape their perspectives, but experience provided the surer guide. Ultimately, the authors of the Constitution did indeed create "a new order of the ages." As McDonald says, "The constitutional reallocation of powers created a new form of government, unprecedented under the sun."

RAYMOND H. GUSTESON
Ohio University
Athens

McGERR, MICHAEL E. *The Decline of Popular Politics: The American North, 1865-1928.* Pp. ix, 307. New York: Oxford University Press, 1986. $24.95.

The setting is a familiar one: a late nineteenth-century American political campaign, and the party faithful parade, singing songs and carrying torches. Some of the paraders are not yet old enough to vote, but they itch for the day they can. Michael McGerr personalizes this slice of Americana, describing the activities of one Michael Campbell, an Irish-American factory worker who in 1880 boosted local and national Democratic candidates in New Haven, Connecticut. The spectacular style of campaigning built party loyalty and turned out the voters successfully—more than 75 percent of them voted in presidential elections between 1876 and 1900. McGerr concludes that the flamboyant style of parades and rallies provided entertainment and prompted men to vote.

What reversed this urge to vote? What caused "the decline of popular politics"?

McGerr effectively argues that much of the decline came from a change in political style. As early as Samuel J. Tilden's campaign in 1876, upper-class liberal reformers set out to replace popular politics with subdued campaigns based on educating voters rather than exciting them. Dismayed that party wheelhorses manipulated the immigrants, the illiterate, and the propertyless, the liberals developed a style of politics that quieted partisanship, permitted ticket splitting, and emphasized intellectual debates in a flood of pamphlets and brochures. Thus the liberals' educated style of politics refocused the attention from party loyalty to the candidates themselves and the complicated issues of the day. This new "deliberative and educational canvass" proved to be stultifying to thousands of Northern voters, who found politics increasingly boring and less personally involving. Voter participation dwindled. Next, the liberals mixed the educational style with the power of advertising, further undercutting party loyalty and making the mass of voters—especially if they were illiterate or poor—more spectators than participants. McGerr's excellent chapter on "advertised politics" analyzes the increasing use of various types of advertising by the major parties from the 1890s though the 1920s. Clever campaign managers such as Republican George B. Cortelyou, leading Theodore Roosevelt's election drive in 1904, demonstrated how potent advertising could be. By 1916 advertising battles were so intense that Democrat George Creel had fleeting thoughts of hiring film director D. W. Griffith as a consultant to the Woodrow Wilson campaign. The use of advertising continued the trend toward political passivity and reduced voter turnout, supporting McGerr's conclusion that "the decline of popular politics in the North is also the origin of modern American politics."

Making wonderful use of a wealth of manuscript collections from many archives, McGerr sprinkles his narrative with many delightful quotations that provide insights into American political life. Furthermore, he shows excellent command of the many quantitative studies of recent years. McGerr's well-written book is highly recommended to both political scientists and historians.

JOSEPH G. DAWSON III
Texas A&M University
College Station

SOCIOLOGY

GOLBY, J. M. and A. W. PURDUE. *The Civilisation of the Crowd: Popular Culture in England, 1750-1900.* Pp. 224. New York: Schocken Books, 1985. $20.00.

In this wide-ranging survey, John Golby and William Purdue, staff tutors at the Open University, trace the development of English popular culture from the beginnings of the industrial revolution through the great social and economic transformations of the nineteenth century. Theirs is not a work of original research; it seeks, rather, to synthesize the voluminous literature that has appeared on this subject in the last several years and to develop an interpretation based on what they see as the most persuasive of the recent contributions.

Golby and Purdue reject, or at least criticize, several related notions that seem to them to have dominated some of the most influential scholarship in this field: that early modern Europe, including England, can be seen—following Peter Burke—as a peasant society with an essentially communal traditional culture, which the elites gradually abandoned and which eventually yielded to such forces of modernization as individualism and the market economy; that in England the old culture finally collapsed at the end of the eighteenth century under the impact of industrialization and urbanization; that the destruction of the old culture, as Robert Malcolmson has argued, left a gap that was slow to be filled; that what filled it was a commercialized mass culture, which the new working class absorbed as passive and alienated consumers and which lacked the spirit and vitality of the traditional culture it replaced; and that attempts to sustain a more authentic popular culture were snuffed out by the bourgeoisie, which directly repressed the old practices and, more insidiously, supplanted them with the new commercialized leisure activities, reinforcing what in Gramscian terms would be called its ideological hegemony. Popular recreations, in this view, were "arenas of class conflict and the frontiers of social control."

Golby and Purdue, in contrast, argue that eighteenth-century English society was already markedly commercialized and individualistic in ways that set it apart from all societies on the Continent; here they perhaps accept too uncritically the now-discredited thesis of Alan Macfarlane. In popular culture, they suggest, the transition from a rural preindustrial society to an urban industrial society was characterized by continuity and adaptation, rather than by gaps and "vacuums," with the growing middle classes mediating between the lower orders and the elite. They hold, too, that the essentially urban mass culture that emerged in the latter nineteenth century was to a large extent "created by the people themselves" and was in many respects superior to the popular culture of an earlier era—"more varied, more generous and more rewarding." In all of this, the would-be reformers of popular culture, whether Evangelicals, radicals, or socialists, had only a slight influence, the apparent assimilation of middle-class values in mass culture—such as a decline in violence and cruelty—reflecting less the penetration of the bourgeoisie than a common search for domesticity and respectability, which the working classes increasingly found within their grasp as they came to enjoy a shorter work week and a higher standard of living. As Golby and Purdue see it, the class-conflict model has severe limits; in their use of leisure, they suggest, the working and middle classes converged as the century wore on, and their shared pastimes should be treated with respect rather than condescension. How sympathetically readers receive this interpretation will depend in part on their affinity for academic Marxism; Golby and Purdue write that their own view "will no doubt be called populist"—as indeed it is.

Along the way, Golby and Purdue offer numerous descriptions of popular recreations, customs, and the like, ranging from the old alehouses, fairs, and Punch and Judy shows to working-class choirs and bands, music halls, railway outings and seaside holidays, organized sports, the mass-circulation press, and the Victorian Christmas.

Much of this material is fascinating; not all of it is closely tied to the book's theoretical points, some of which wind up dangling as unproved assertions. In fairness, however, it should be emphasized that this work is not intended as a closely argued and thickly documented demonstration for specialists, but rather as an introduction for students, for historians and social scientists in neighboring fields, and presumably also for the curious general reader, since Golby and Purdue seem bent on bridging the gap between academic scholarship and the larger culture. As such it largely succeeds, although the book's casual organization and occasionally discursive and repetitious writing may discourage the less determined among its large potential readership.

MATTHEW RAMSEY

Vanderbilt University
Nashville
Tennessee

ROBINSON, DAVID. *The Unitarians and the Universalists.* Pp. xiii, 368. Westport, CT: Greenwood Press, 1985. $35.00.

This is the first volume in an ambitious series of denominational histories to be published by Greenwood Press. Denominational history has lately been out of fashion, both because it isolates particular groups from the context of American religious history and because so often in the past it served denominational chauvinism. But after a generation of bountiful harvests in understanding American religious trends generally while denominational history has lain fallow, it is time for new, more critical, and more contextual denominational histories.

The Unitarians and the Universalists, by David Robinson, director of American Studies at Oregon State, represents this new denominational history, eschewing apologetics—although he occasionally speaks of persons "maturing" or "growing" into Unitarianism; might not one also mature into right-wing Fundamentalism?—and relating his subject to the main currents of American religious life. His emphasis is on the history of ideas, an appropriate emphasis for such a cerebral denomination as the Unitarians.

The early history of the two denominations is treated freshly, in line with newer studies of the two movements. John Murray's universalism is recognized as a kind of biblicist hyper-Calvinism that extended predestination to all, while W. E. Channing is portrayed as primarily interested not in anti-Trinitarian polemic but in moral and personal development. Robinson skillfully chronicles the impact of transcendentalism, liberal theology, and the social gospel upon the two denominations. In the twentieth century they are shown wrestling not only with the problem of unity with each other, but also with humanism on their left and the neo-orthodox critique of liberalism on their right. Appended to the volume is a very thorough bibliographical essay and a 133-page biographical dictionary of Unitarian and Universalist worthies that does a fine job of assessing the central significance of those described.

If there is any general shortcoming it is that Robinson has gone to the opposite extreme from denominational histories that triumphantly record institutional growth by ignoring institutional history almost entirely. Internecine arguments about institutionalization are recounted, and there is some analysis of Unitarian and Universalist Association membership in the mid-twentieth century, but there is little assessment of the social role and significance of these denominations and their members. Perhaps a summarizing conclusion—the narrative ends abruptly—might have been helpful in this regard and also in analyzing the long-range trends that Robinson mentions, such as the shifts away from theism, Boston dominance, and birthright membership.

DEWEY D. WALLACE, Jr.

George Washington University
Washington, D.C.

WHALLEY, PETER. *The Social Production of Technical Work*. Pp. xiv, 237. Albany: State University of New York Press, 1986. $29.50.

In studying the work lives of engineers in two British factories, Peter Whalley tests several theories that posit a growing crisis of legitimacy in the capitalist firm. These theories predict, albeit for very different reasons, conflict between the values and/or role of technical knowledge workers and the organizational purposes and structure of capitalist firms. Whalley compares the training, autonomy, career prospects, supervisory functions, and attitudes toward professional and union organizations of engineers in a relatively new, high-tech equipment manufacturing firm to those of engineers in an old-line, metal products manufacturer. In his concluding chapter, he also compares British engineers to French and American engineers.

The study reveals substantial national differences in the work lives of engineers as well as important differences based on the nature of the firm. British engineers differ from their French and American counterparts in that their work exhibits a much wider range of skill levels, including what in the other countries is technicians' work. British engineers are much less likely to have advanced, specialized degrees, and they are less likely to function in a supervisory capacity or move into management. British engineers also are more disposed to unionize than are engineers in the other countries. There are differences, though less marked, along these same lines when the British high-tech firm is compared with the British industrial firm.

Lest this analysis be taken as support for the notion of a new class of British workers, in the process of being deskilled or proletarianized, whose interests are antagonistic to the interests of capital, Whalley suggests that British engineers in both firms studied, along with their French and American counterparts, share the role of trusted worker. Employers, rather than attempting to control engineers by deskilling and reallocating their work, either allow them autonomy from organizational and market concerns so that they may pursue creative and satisfying technical projects or direct their attention to the opportunities for advancement that management positions offer. In other words, formal and informal controls make the engineers' expertise subservient to the needs of the firm. The controls, however, emphasize the long term—that is, the career of the engineer—and are thereby less salient than the controls over less skilled workers.

LAWRENCE E. ROTHSTEIN
University of Rhode Island
Kingston

WRIGHT, KEVIN N. *The Great American Crime Myth.* Pp. x, 227. Westport, CT: Greenwood Press, 1985. $29.95.

That discrepancies abound between the realities of crime and public images of it is not a new idea to criminologists, but Kevin N. Wright has given it a useful new twist. Written for the educated general reader, this book examines 11 myths—seen as creations chiefly of news media, politicians, and justice agencies—that together undergird a general myth that American society is engulfed in an unprecedented flood of violent and predatory crime, but that the adoption of stern law enforcement policies can stanch it.

The first five myths, constituting part 1, relate to beliefs about the amount and trends of crime and the risks of victimization. To debunk these myths, Wright examines several distortions and misuses of criminal statistics. I can only cite some examples here: (1) media sensationalization of crimes of violence obscures the fact that most crime is against property, not persons; (2) workers in the vineyards of justice find it useful to cultivate this myth—the Federal Bureau of Investigation's alarming crime-clock graphs are shown by Wright to be overblown and misleading; (3) while cold comfort to victims, the chances of being attacked by a rapist or robber are statistically too low to justify our pervasive fear of these kinds of offenses—our neighborhoods, even deprived ones, are much less dangerous than we suppose.

Six more myths, composing parts 2 and 3, center upon the beliefs, encouraged especially by law-enforcement interests, that our confidence in the deterrent effect of swift and sure justice, weakened by two decades of misplaced concern for the rights of offenders over those of victims, should be renewed and that enforcement branches of government can, if backed by increased budgets and sterner laws, stem the rising tide of crime. Wright argues, as have others, that enforcement agencies tend invariably to seek aggrandizement by exaggerating both the magnitude of the crime problem and their capacity for dealing effectively with it if given the tools. Alleged weakening of justice by exclusionary rules is a myth given particular scrutiny by Wright. He thinks that popular feeling against these arises from the false assumption that large numbers of guilty persons elude justice thereby, but available evidence shows that only a tiny proportion of offenders are freed on grounds of improperly gathered evidence.

Our crime problem, Wright concludes, comes not from law-enforcement weaknesses but from certain forces embedded in American culture. Until these forces abate we shall continue to have a rate of crime considerably higher than other industrialized countries. We can live with it, thinks Wright, but we should demythologize it.

R. W. ENGLAND, Jr.
University of Rhode Island
Kingston

ECONOMICS

ABT, VICKI, JAMES F. SMITH, and EUGENE MARTIN CHRISTIANSEN. *The Business of Risk: Commercial Gambling in Mainstream America.* Pp. xiv, 286. Lawrence: University Press of Kansas, 1985. $29.95. Paperbound, $14.95.

The Business of Risk is a timely and enlightening study of a major and rapidly expanding institution in American society: legal commercial gambling. Over the past two decades the selective legalization of gambling has proceeded apace, with 21 states now operating lotteries and 36 states permitting pari-mutuel betting. In 1983, according to Abt, Smith, and Christiansen's careful estimates, some 66 million Americans collectively wagered $134 billion on various forms of legal gambling, producing commercial revenues to operators—whether private businesses or state governments—of nearly $12 billion and direct tax revenues to government of $3.4 billion.

The impressive growth and dimensions of this activity suggest that legal gambling has become a large-scale and mainstream social institution, and it is in this light that Vicki Abt and her coauthors analyze commercial gambling. They dispel common misconceptions about gambling, for example, that all gambling is compulsive and harmful behavior, that gambling is dominated by organized crime; describe the characteristics and operations of diverse gambling games and the varied motives and behaviors of gamblers; and chart the historical development of commercial gambling. But the central purpose of the book is to analyze the nature of commercial gambling as a conventional institution and its economic, cultural, and political significance and consequences for American society.

The figures previously cited indicate that gambling is today a big business, dominated by large corporate and public enterprises, with "hundreds of thousands of jobs and billions of dollars of invested equity." It is also a largely legitimate business, with organized crime controlling only about 17 percent of the gambling market, as measured by gross revenues, by the calculations of Abt and her colleagues. *The Business of Risk* is very informative about the economics of the gambling industry and about the unique role of government in it; in very few other industries is there a comparable degree of public ownership! Unfortunately, however, the book does not directly analyze the relative size or weight of the gambling industry within the larger leisure industry, service sector, or national economy, so that the macroeconomic significance of commercial gambling is left unclear.

Commercial gambling is not only a big business but also an increasingly important leisure activity and cultural institution. According to Abt and her coauthors, the rise of commercial gambling both reflects and shapes larger trends in the evolution of American culture, especially the shift from a productive to a consumptive ethic and the pervasive commercialization of leisure and culture. They mount a sharp and cogent critique of the commercialization of gambling—which in their view perverts the potential cultural significance of gambling as creative and pleasurable play—and of the new gambling ideology being disseminated by corporate and governmental interests to justify their agressive promotion of gambling. I wish that Abt, Smith, and Christiansen had more fully developed their hints that state lotteries and other gambling games function to legitimate class inequality by the promise, illusory for all but a few, of great wealth at a bargain price.

Perhaps the most important contribution of *The Business of Risk* is its political analysis. As is shown in this book, the decisive—though not the only—force in the expansion of legal gambling has been the revenue requirements of government. State and local jurisdictions increasingly rely upon commercial and tax revenues from gambling for a small but politically significant share of their funds. State lotteries are swiftly becoming a normal method of public finance, though their presumed character as sources of voluntary taxes is surely compromised by their relentless promotion and though they may well be regressive in the incidence of their tax burden. Abt and her coauthors raise and intelligently discuss a series of important but widely ignored issues about the direct, growing, and interested relationship of government to commercial gambling. Above all, they question whether a public policy on gambling dictated largely by the "revenue imperative" of government, in conjunction with the pecuniary needs of private interests, is consistent with the public interest.

The Business of Risk is a scholarly work based on extensive research and considerable reflection. It contains an appendix and glossary for aid on technical matters. I hope this book gains a wide audience, because it makes a vital contribution to the understanding of an increasingly significant public issue.

ANDREW C. BATTISTA

East Tennessee State University
Johnson City

ILGEN, THOMAS L. *Autonomy and Interdependence: U.S.-Western European Monetary and Trade Relations 1959-1984.* Pp. x, 166. Totowa, NJ: Rowman & Allanheld, 1985. $34.95.

U.S. economic performance, both at home and abroad, has been relatively dismal since the early 1970s. The near-full employment of the 1960s gave way to sluggish growth, declining productivity, high unemployment, and double-digit inflation in the 1970s. The comfortable trade surpluses of the 1950s and 1960s have now turned into disturbing deficits. This is both because oil prices and, therefore, oil imports dramatically increased in the 1970s and because American industrial competitiveness lagged. The once-mighty American dollar, suffering under several speculative attacks, limped through the 1970s and early 1980s.

The reasons for the U.S. economy's rather dismal record over much of the last decade or so are now well understood by economists and policymakers alike. Chief among the reasons are, of course, the oil crisis of 1973 and the round of oil-price hikes in 1979. But oil was not the only culprit. Other events, such as agricultural shortfalls and shifts in money demand, have also been blamed for U.S. economic woes. Most—though not all—of the culprits, however, were worldwide

events leading to global, not just American, stagflation. Why did the United States adjust so poorly, relative to Europe, to these worldwide events? What accounts for America's relatively poor performance in the last decade or so and even now?

According to Ilgen, the current American difficulties in the world economy are largely the result of the success, not the failure, of U.S. postwar foreign policy objectives. At least in the economic sphere, American postwar foreign policy has had two main goals. First, the United States has successfully created a network of interdependence among the Western allies. Such interdependence has been fostered largely through the trade-liberalization efforts of the General Agreement on Tariffs and Trade. Second, while fostering interdependence among the allies, the United States has insisted on complete autonomy for itself. Whenever its autonomy seemed seriously threatened, Ilgen argues, Washington would simply change the rules of the game.

According to Ilgen, the oil crisis and other worldwide events in the 1970s quite forcefully demonstrated the incompatibility of the twin U.S. goals of increasing the interdependence among the allies while protecting its own freedom of action. The inherent logic of the liberal order fostered by U.S. foreign policy was to weave together the fortunes of the advanced industrial nations through trade, foreign investment, and capital flows. Like it or not, Washington found itself drawn into the web of interdependence. As a result, even Americans are now aware of the fact that we live in one economic world where Washington is not the only center of power and policy. How closely the world's economies—including the U.S. economy—are now linked together is underscored by the fact that U.S. exports as a percentage of gross national product doubled over the period covered by this book. Moreover, each day throughout the world, several hundred billion dollars in financial assets flow among nations.

But old habits die hard. The American habit of autonomy made it more difficult to deal with the consequences of the United States' interdependence with the European allies. Ironically, according to Ilgen, Europe's postwar weakness led to American policies making Europe better able to cope with current worldwide economic problems.

The Reagan years, Ilgen argues, have been a retreat to the insistence on autonomy in the making of domestic economic policy. These years have demonstrated "the will to put the domestic economy through the wringer to rid it of inflation and begin the process of restoring industrial competitiveness." But Washington has recently designed its domestic policies with little regard for their consequences in an interdependent global economy. For example, the recent U.S. policy of high interest rates, while damping inflation and strengthening the dollar, had serious consequences for many nations. Of course, with its faith in free-market solutions, the present administration is unlikely to pay much attention to policy coordination among the allies.

This slim and readable volume surveys and synthesizes much of postwar international monetary and trade relations beginning in the late 1950s, when currency convertibility had been restored and Europe's recovery from the war was largely complete. This survey is used to support Ilgen's novel, but persuasive, argument that Washington's postwar policy of encouraging interdependence among the allies while maintaining domestic economic autonomy left the United States relatively ill prepared to deal with the consequences of worldwide economic events in the 1970s and beyond. Clearly, Ilgen's analysis calls for greater coordination in the future management of global interdependence. But, because political realities both here and abroad demand that primary attention be focused at home, intergovernmental efforts at policy coordination are likely to have a very uneven record in the foreseeable future.

JON HARKNESS

Queen's University
Kingston
Canada

ROSEN, GEORGE. *Western Economists in Eastern Societies: Agents for Change in South Asia, 1950-1970.* Pp. xxii, 270. Baltimore, MD: Johns Hopkins University Press, 1985. $30.00.

This is a careful, well-researched, and well-documented account of the Ford Foundation's activities in sending out Western economists under its own auspices or through the Massachusetts Institute of Technology, Harvard, Yale, and Williams College "to assist in economic training or the development of research institutions or to provide assistance to policy makers" as advisers or researchers in the two decades that were critical in the history of two of the world's largest new nations, India and Pakistan, and in the emergence and development of the discipline of economic development. The account "is largely chronological, centering on specific institutions and programs . . . with a greater treatment of the personalities of the economists involved than normally occurs in an economics book." Excluded from the study are the large number of economists, along with social scientists interested in development—Western as well as from the Soviet-type economies—who went to these countries during this period to pursue their own research or academic interest or to serve as advisers in one capacity or another. By keeping his focus on the manageable narrower subset of economists, Rosen has achieved coherence and tightness, but at the cost of some of the intellectual excitement that went with the interaction between the broader Western, Indian, and Pakistani economists, social scientists, administrators, and politicians.

Rosen sets out to answer five sets of general questions: (1) the impact of the American view of the world in 1950 on the American economic advisory and training programs in South Asia; (2) the effects of these programs on economic policymaking and on the economic profession in India and Pakistan; (3) the impact of this experience on the field of economic development; (4) the meaning of this experience for the notion that economics is a positive science; and (5) lessons for institution building or advising for other less developed countries.

Rosen chooses to discuss the third set only briefly because "Ian Little's books deals with this issue at some length." I would have liked him to discuss that issue at greater length, simply because it may be the most interesting issue to academics. He deals with the other four competently and responsibly. Despite his own involvement in these programs for four years, he tells the story with admirable fairness and objectivity. His style, in its sensitivity, also exemplifies what many in the host countries have looked for in the personalities of their guest scholars or advisers.

Two American academic institutions, The India Project of the Massachusetts Institute of Technology's Center for International Studies and the Harvard Advisory Group in Pakistan, which were involved for the longest time in sending economists to the subcontinent, come in for a lengthy discussion. In an otherwise excellent discussion of why Western economists went to India and Pakistan, Rosen fails to mention that for some it may simply have been the economics of a job out there just as others who opted not to go abroad may have seen the short-term rewards of work abroad as an impediment to upward mobility in careers in the home market, in which domestic issues have traditionally been more important than international issues—more so in the continental United States than perhaps in the United Kingdom. "In the period after 1972," Rosen tells us, "I have not worked on problems of overseas development, nor have I worked in these two countries." One wonders how many other economists who worked overseas would say the same. It is in this context that one feels that a greater discussion of the impact of overseas experience on the field of economic development would have been helpful.

In an otherwise clear and concise narrative there are a few—very few—fuzzy spots.

Indian ideas on economic policy were largely independent of foreign thinking on development. Indian leaders and planners were interested in foreign experience in the economic area and in the ideas of economists that could be applied to India. This interest was especially great because the First Plan was an apparent success . . . [in] those days India was the Mecca of planners and economists from all over the world (p. 58).

If the First Plan was their own baby, and it was a success, why indeed did the Indians look overseas, especially to overseas economists, for ideas? More important, I found the use of the term "myth" "in the sense that Fussell uses it" very unclear, especially because Fussell's use is never described in this book.

The book is rewarding reading for those interested in the history of U.S. relations with India and Pakistan—and Bangladesh— or for those interested in working in less developed countries as advisers, teachers, researchers, or planners. For development economists the book has special appeal as a story of the discipline's formative years when the theories and ideas of economists and other thinkers from all over were competing in an unprecedented setting in which a half billion people were trying to work their way out of age-old poverty in a democratic polity.

SHANTI S. TANGRI
Rutgers University
New Brunswick
New Jersey

OTHER BOOKS

American Foreign Policy: Current Documents, 1983. Pp. lxiv, 1477. Washington, DC: Department of State, 1985. $27.00.

ANANYEV, P. et al. *Economies of the Countries of Latin America.* Translated by Glenis Ann Kozlov. Pp. 406. Moscow: Progress, 1985. Distributed by Imported Publications, Chicago. $7.95.

BARKER, JEFFREY H. *Individualism and Community: The State in Marx and Early Anarchism.* Pp. xiii, 235. Westport, CT: Greenwood Press, 1986. $35.00.

BARNETT, A. DOAK and RALPH N. CLOUGH, eds. *Modernizing China: Post-Mao Reform and Development.* Pp. xii, 136. Boulder, CO: Westview Press, 1986. $23.85. Paperbound, $12.85.

BAUER, E. E. *China Takes Off: Technology Transfer and Modernization.* Pp. xvi, 227. Seattle: University of Washington Press, 1986. $20.00.

BAUMOL, WILLIAM J. *Superfairness: Applications and Theory.* Pp. xi, 266. Cambridge, MA: MIT Press, 1986. $20.00.

BENDAHMANE, DIANE B. and JOHN W. McDONALD, Jr., eds. *Perspectives on Negotiation: Four Case Studies and Interpretations.* Pp. xi, 315. Washington, DC: Center for the Study of Foreign Affairs, Foreign Service Institute, 1986. Paperbound, $7.50.

BLASI, VINCENT, ed. *The Burger Court: The Counter-Revolution That Wasn't.* Pp. xxii, 326. New Haven, CT: Yale University Press, 1986. Paperbound, $12.95.

BLAU, PETER M. *Exchange and Power in Social Life.* Pp. xxxv, 352. New Brunswick, NJ: Transaction Books, 1986. Paperbound, $14.95.

Blocking the Spread of Nuclear Weapons: American and European Perspectives. Pp. x, 153. New York: Council on Foreign Relations, 1986. Paperbound, $6.95.

BOLSHAKOV, VLADIMIR. *This Whole Human Rights Business.* Pp. 327. Moscow: Progress, 1985. Distributed by Imported Publications, Chicago. Paperbound, $2.95.

BRAILLARD, PHILLIPPE and MOHAMMAD-REZA DJALILI. *The Third World and International Relations.* Pp. xii, 301. Boulder, CO: Lynne Rienner, 1986. $38.50.

BRIGGS, DOROTHY CORKILLE. *Celebrate Yourself: Enhancing Your Own Self-Esteem.* Pp. 226. New York: Doubleday, 1986. Paperbound, $7.95.

BROWN, LESTER R. et al. *State of the World, 1986.* Pp. xvii, 263. Washington, DC: Worldwatch Institute, 1986. Paperbound, $9.95.

BROWNING, RUFUS P., DALE ROGERS MARSHALL, and DAVID H. TABB. *Protest Is Not Enough: The Struggle of Blacks and Hispanics for Equality in Urban Politics.* Pp. xvi, 317. Berkeley: University of California Press, 1986. Paperbound, $10.95.

BUTLER, DAVID and GARETH BUTLER. *British Political Facts, 1900-1985.* 6th ed. Pp. xix, 536. New York: St. Martin's Press, 1986. $45.00.

BYERS, R. B. *The Denuclearisation of the Oceans.* Pp. xiv, 270. New York: St. Martin's Press, 1986. $29.95.

CAMPBELL, TOM et al., eds. *Human Rights: From Rhetoric to Reality.* Pp. vii, 262. New York: Basil Blackwell, 1986. $45.00. Paperbound, $19.95.

CARINO, THERESA CHONG. *China and the Overseas in Southeast Asia.* Pp. vii, 116. Quezon City, Philippines: New Day, 1985. Distributed by Cellar Book Shop, Detroit, MI. Paperbound, $7.25.

COUNCIL ON FOREIGN RELATIONS. *Blocking the Spread of Nuclear Weapons: American and European Perspectives.* Pp. x, 153. New York: Council on Foreign Relations, 1986. Paperbound, no price.

DAOUDI, M. S. and M. S. DAJANI. *Economic Diplomacy: Embargo Leverage* and World Politics. Pp. xiii, 258. Boulder, CO: Westview Press, 1985. $30.00.

DASHEFSKY, ARNOLD, ed. *Contemporary Jewry.* Vol. 7. Pp. xii, 207. New Brunswick, NJ: Transaction Books, 1986. $19.95.

DAVIDOV, ROBERT., ed. *The Palestine Question: Documents Adopted by the United Nations and Other International Organizations and Conferences.* Translated by Glenis Koslov. Pp. 248. Moscow: Progress, 1985. Distributed by Imported Publications, Chicago. Paperbound, $4.95.

DAVIS, HOWARD and RICHARD SCASE. *Western Capitalism and State Socialism: An Introduction.* Pp. vi, 202. New York: Basil Blackwell, 1985. $24.95. Paperbound, $9.95.

DE VRIES, MARGARET GARRITSEN. *The IMF in a Changing World, 1945-85.* Pp. x, 226. Washington, DC: International Monetary Fund, 1986. Paperbound, no price.

DIAMOND, EDWIN and STEPHEN BATES. *The Spot: The Rise of Political Advertising on Television.* Pp. xiv, 416. Cambridge, MA: MIT Press, 1986. Paperbound, $15.00.

Directory of Organizations Providing Business and Economic Education Information. Pp. vii, 232. San Francisco, CA: Foundation for Teaching Economics. Paperbound, $5.00.

ETZIONI-HALEVY, EVA. *Bureaucracy and Democracy: A Political Dilemma.* Pp. xi, 266. New York: Methuen, 1983. Paperbound, $9.95.

EULAU, HEINZ. *Politics, Self, and Society: A Theme and Variations.* Pp. viii, 567. Cambridge, MA: Harvard University Press, 1986. $39.95.

FISKE, DONALD W. and SHWEDER, RICHARD A., eds. *Metatheory in Social Science.* Pp. x, 390. Chicago: University of Chicago Press, 1986. $35.00. Paperbound, $16.95.

FOELL, EARL W. and RICHARD A. NENNEMAN, eds. *How Peace Came to*

the World. Pp. xii, 257. Cambridge, MA: MIT Press, 1986. $13.95.

FURTAK, ROBERT. *The Political Systems of the Socialist States: An Introduction to Marxist-Leninist Regimes.* Pp. xi, 308. New York: St. Martin's Press, 1986. $32.50.

GELFAND, LAWRENCE E. and ROBERT J. NEYMEYER, eds. *Changing Patterns in American Federal-State Relations during the 1950's.* Pp. 82. Iowa City, Iowa: Center for the Study of the Recent History of the United States, 1985. Paperbound, $9.95.

GLENNON, JOHN P., EDWARD C. KEEFER, and DAVID W. MABON, eds. *Foreign Relations of the United States, 1958-1960.* Vol 1. Pp. xxvi, 774. Washington, DC: Government Printing Office, 1986. No price.

GOODSELL, CHARLES T. *The Case for Bureaucracy: A Public Administration Polemic.* 2nd ed. Pp. xi, 212. Chatham, NJ: Chatham House, 1986. Paperbound, $11.95.

GOODWIN, CRAUFURD D. and MICHAEL NACHT. *Decline and Renewal: Causes and Cures of Decay among Foreign-Trained Intellectuals and Professionals in the Third World.* Pp. x, 75. New York: Institute of International Education, 1986. Paperbound, no price.

GRAEBNER, NORMAN A., ed. *The National Security: Its Theory and Practice, 1945-1960.* Pp. xii, 316. New York: Oxford University Press, 1986. Paperbound, $8.95.

GRIFFIN, KEITH, ed. *Institutional Reform and Economic Development in the Chinese Countryside.* Pp. x, 336. Armonk, NY: M. E. Sharpe, 1985. $37.50. Paperbound, $18.95.

GRINSPOON, LESTER, ed. *The Long Darkness: Psychological and Moral Perspectives on Nuclear Winter.* Pp. 213. New Haven, CT: Yale University Press, 1986. $25.00. Paperbound, $7.95.

HAFER, R. W., ed. *The Monetary versus Fiscal Policy Debate: Lessons from Two*

Decades. Pp. vii, 171. Totowa, NJ: Rowman & Allanheld, 1986. $38.50.

HAMRIN, CAROL LEE and TIMOTHY CHEEK, eds. *China's Establishment Intellectuals.* Pp. xix, 266. Armonk, NY: M.E. Sharpe, 1986. $35.00. Paperbound, $14.95.

HANLEY, SUSAN B. and ARTHUR WOLF, eds. *Family and Population in East Asian History.* Pp. xx, 360. Palo Alto, CA: Stanford University Press, 1985. No price.

JANITSCHEK, HANS. *Mario Soares: Portrait of a Hero.* Pp. xii, 116. New York: St. Martin's Press, 1985. No price.

JENNINGS, JAMES and MEL KING, eds. *From Access to Power: Black Politics in Boston.* Pp. vii, 196. Cambridge, MA: Schenkman Books, 1986. $18.95. Paperbound, $11.25.

JURIS, HERVEY, MARK THOMPSON, and WILBUR DANIELS, eds. *Industrial Relations in a Decade of Economic Change.* Pp. vi, 407. Madison, WI: Industrial Relations Research Association, 1986. Paperbound, $15.00.

KELLY, ROBERT J., ed. *Organized Crime: A Global Perspective.* Pp. 300. Totowa, NJ: Rowman & Allanheld, 1986. $29.50.

KEOHANE, ROBERT O. *After Hegemony: Cooperation and Discord in the World Political Economy.* Pp. ix, 290. Princeton, NJ: Princeton University Press, 1984. $30.00. Paperbound, $8.95.

KIHL, YOUNG WHAN and LAWRENCE E. GRINTNER, eds. *Asian-Pacific Security: Emerging Challenges and Responses.* Pp. xiv, 282. Boulder, CO: Lynne Rienner, 1986. $25.00.

KIM, H. EDWARD, ed. *In Pursuit of Commitments: President Chun Doo Hwan's Visit to the United States.* Pp. 96. Seoul: Chong Wa Dae Press Corps, 1985. No price.

KINDLEBERGER, CHARLES P. *The World in Depression, 1929-1939.* Pp. xxiii, 355. Berkeley: University of California Press, 1986. $38.50. Paperbound, $10.95.

KOSUKHIN, NIKOLAI. *Revolutionary Democracy in Africa.* Translated by Glenis Kozlov. Pp. 167. Moscow: Progress, 1985. Distributed by Imported Publications, Chicago. Paperbound, $3.95.

KUHN, RAYMOND, ed. *Broadcasting and Politics in Western Europe.* Pp. viii, 174. Totowa, NJ: Frank Cass, 1986. $29.50.

LARIONOV, V. et al. *World War II: Decisive Battles of the Soviet Army.* Translated by William Biley. Pp. 527. Moscow: Progress, 1984. Distributed by Imported Publications, Chicago. $10.95.

LENGYEL, PETER. *International Social Science: The UNESCO Experience.* Pp. xii, 133. New Brunswick, NJ: Transaction Books, 1986. $29.95. Paperbound, $9.95.

LINK, WERNER, *The East-West Conflict: The Organisation of International Relations in the 20th Century.* Pp. x, 198. New York: St. Martin's Press, 1986. $27.50.

LORENCE-KOT, BOGNA. *Child-Rearing and Reform: A Study of the Nobility in Eighteenth-Century Poland.* Pp. ix, 170. Westport, CT: Greenwood Press, 1985. $29.95.

LUCASH, FRANK S., ed. *Justice and Equality Here and Now.* Pp. 172. Ithaca, NY: Cornell University Press, 1986. $22.50. Paperbound, $7.50.

LUTZKER, MARILYN and ELEANOR FERRALL. *Criminal Justice Research in Libraries: Strategies and Resources.* Pp. xvi, 167. Westport, CT: Greenwood Press, 1986. $37.50.

MAALOUF, AMIN. *The Crusades through Arab Eyes.* Translated by Jon Rothschild. Pp. xvi, 293. New York: Schocken Books, 1985. $16.95.

MALTSEV, GENNADY. *An Illusion of Equal Rights.* Translated by Frances Longman. Pp. 299. Moscow: Progress, 1985. Distributed by Imported Publications, Chicago. Paperbound, $2.95.

McLEAN, SCILLA, ed. *How Nuclear Weapons Decisions are Made.* Pp. xv, 264. New York: St. Martin's Press, 1986. $29.95.

MILNE, R. S. and DIANE K. MAUZY. *Malaysia: Tradition, Modernity, and Islam.* Pp. xix, 199. Boulder, CO: Westview Press, 1986. $28.00.

MORRISON, STEVEN and CLIFFORD WINSTON. *The Economic Effects of Airline Deregulation.* Pp. xi, 84. Washington, DC: Brookings Institution, 1986. Paperbound, $7.95.

MOWER, GLENN A. *International Cooperation for Social Justice: Global and Regional Protection of Economic/Social Rights.* Pp. x, 267. Westport, CT: Greenwood Press, 1985. $35.00.

MUNSUN, CHRIS. *The White House Sucks.* Pp. 518. Los Angeles: Dare-Co, 1986. Paperbound, $8.95.

NICKERSON, RAYMOND S. *Using Computers: Human Factors in Information Systems.* Pp. xiv, 434. Cambridge, MA: MIT Press, 1986. $22.50.

PARET, PETER, ed. *Makers of Modern Strategy: From Machiavelli to the Nuclear Age.* Pp. vii, 942. Princeton, NJ: Princeton University Press, 1986. $45.00. Paperbound, $12.95.

PARK, MICHAEL ALAN. *Anthropology: An Introduction.* Pp. xv, 398. New York: Harper & Row, 1986. Paperbound, no price.

PENNOCK, J. ROLAND and JOHN W. CHAPMAN, eds. *Justification: NOMOS XXVIII.* Pp. xv, 368. New York: New York University Press, 1986. Distributed by Columbia University Press, New York. $42.50.

PIERRE, ANDREW J., ed. *The Conventional Defense of Europe: New Technologies and New Strategies.* Pp. xii, 185. New York: Council on Foreign Relations, 1986. Paperbound, $6.95.

PLOCK, ERNEST D. *The Basic Treaty and the Evolution of East-West Relations.* Pp. xiii, 272. Boulder, CO: Westview Press, 1986. Paperbound, $26.00.

POPENOE, DAVID. *Sociology.* 6th ed. Pp. xv, 624. Englewood Cliffs, NJ: Prentice-Hall, 1986. No price.

PORTER, J. M. and RICHARD VERNON, eds. *Unity, Plurality, and Politics: Essays in Honor of F. M. Barnard.* Pp. 194. New York: St. Martin's Press, 1986. $27.50.

QUESTER, GEORGE H. *Deterrence before Hiroshima.* Pp. xxix, 193 New Brunswick, NJ: Transaction Books, 1986. $24.95.

RAMET, PEDRO. *Nationalism and Federalism in Yugoslavia, 1963-1983.* Pp. xviii, 299. Bloomington: Indiana University Press, 1985. $27.50.

REJWAN, NISSIM. *The Jews of Iraq: 300 Years of History and Culture.* Pp. ix, 274. Boulder, CO: Westview Press, 1986. $30.00.

RESNICK, STEPHEN and RICHARD WOLFF. *Rethinking Marxism: Struggles in Marxist Theory.* Pp. xxxiv, 428. Brooklyn, NY: Automedia, 1986. $27.95. Paperbound, $12.95.

ROCCATAGLIATA, GIUSEPPE. *A History of Ancient Psychiatry.* Pp. viii, 206. Westport, CT: Greenwood Press, 1986. $45.00.

ROSET, I. *The Psychology of Phantasy.* Translated by Sergei Savchenko and Alexander Parnakh. Pp. 247. Moscow: Progress, 1985. Distributed by Imported Publications, Chicago. $7.95.

RYAN, ALAN. *Property and Political Theory.* Pp. viii, 198. New York: Basil Blackwell, 1986. Paperbound, $12.95.

RYMYANTSEV, A. M. *A Dictionary of Scientific Communism.* Pp. 288. Moscow: Progress, 1985. Distributed by Imported Publications, Chicago. $7.95.

SCHAEFER, MORRIS. *Designing and Implementing Procedures for Health and Human Services.* Pp. 155. Beverly Hills, CA: Sage, 1985. Paperbound, no price.

SCHOOL, J. W., J. J. VAN DER LINDEN, and K. S. YAP, eds. *Between Basti Dwellers and Bureaucrats: Lessons on Squatter Settlement Upgrading in Karachi.* Pp. xiii, 305. New York: Pergamon Press, 1983. $35.00. Paperbound, $17.00.

SCHOTT, KERRY. *Policy, Power, and Order: The Persistence of Economic Problems in Capitalist States.* Pp. ix, 206. New Haven, CT: Yale University Press, 1984. $20.00.

SCHRAM, STUART R., ed. *The Scope of State Power in China.* Pp. xxxiv, 381. New York: St. Martin's Press, 1986. $35.00.

SHULMAN, MARSHALL D. *East-West Tensions in the Third World.* Pp. 243. New York: W.W. Norton, 1986. $16.95. Paperbound, $6.95.

SOMJEE, A. H. *Political Society in Developing Countries.* Pp. xii, 202. New York: St. Martin's Press, 1984. $27.50.

SOROKIN, ALEXEI. *The People's Army.* Translated by William Biley. Pp. 247. Moscow: Progress, 1985. Distributed by Imported Publications, Chicago. Paperbound, $4.95.

STANCIU, ION G. H. and PAUL CERNOV-ODEANU. *Distant Lands: The Genesis and Evolution of Romanian-American Relations.* Pp. vii, 293. Boulder, CO: East European Monographs, 1985. Distributed by Columbia University Press, New York. $38.00.

SULEIMAN, EZRA N., ed. *Parliaments and Parliamentarians in Democratic Politics.* Pp. 255. New York: Holmes and Meier, 1986. $37.50. Paperbound, $19.95.

SUVOROV, VICTOR. *Inside the Aquarium: The Making of a Top Soviet Spy.* Pp. 249. New York: Macmillan, 1986. $17.95.

THIBAUT, JOHN W. and HAROLD H. KELLY. *The Social Psychology of Groups.* Pp. xxvi, 313. New Brunswick, NJ: Transaction Books, 1986. Paperbound, $14.95.

Trotsky's Notebooks, 1933-1935: Writings on Lenin, Dialectics, and Evolutionism. Translated and annotated by Philip Pomper. Pp. viii, 166. New York: Columbia University Press, 1986. $25.00.

TULCHIN, JOSEPH, ed. *Habitat, Health, and Development: A New Way of Looking at the Third World.* Pp. xvi, 182. Boulder, CO: Lynne Rienner, 1986. No price.

VERMES, GABOR. *Istvan Tisza: The Liberal Vision and Conservative Statecraft of a Magyar Nationalist.* Pp. xii, 627. East European Monographs, 1986. Distributed by Columbia University Press, New York. $50.00.

VROMAN, WAYNE. *The Funding Crisis in State Unemployment Insurance.* Pp. xi, 199. Kalamazoo, MI: W.E. Upjohn Institute for Employment Research, 1986. $16.95. Paperbound, $11.95.

WEEKS, JOHN. *Limits to Capitalist Development: The Industrialization of Peru, 1950-1980.* Pp. xii, 254. Boulder, CO: Westview Press, 1985. $20.00.

WILLIAMS, SIMON and RUTH KAREN. *Agribusiness and the Small-Scale Farmer: A Dynamic Partnership for Development.* Pp. xv, 319. Boulder, CO: Westview Press, 1985. $27.50.

WRIGHT, MOORHEAD, ed. *Rights and Obligations in North-South Relations: Ethical Dimensions of Global Problems.* Pp. x., 196. New York: St. Martin's Press, 1986. $27.50.

ZNANIECKI, FLORIAN. *The Social Role of the Man of Knowledge.* Pp. xxiii, 212. New Brunswick, NJ: Transaction Books, 1986. Paperbound, $19.95.

INDEX

Chicago

THE DYNAMICS OF DETERRENCE
FRANK C. ZAGARE

"This book provides a fundamental and extremely promising contribution to the deterrence issue. It is a theoretical breakthrough in the conflict/cooperation, war/peace problem area and opens a door for further sophisticated and relevant work. It is certain to make an important contribution to its field."—Robert North, Stanford University

Cloth $22.00   208 pages

THE PHILOSOPHY AND POLITICS OF FREEDOM
RICHARD E. FLATHMAN

"This book should reshape a great deal of the contemporary debate about liberty and [will] have considerable and deserved impact on one of the most important and long-standing issues in political philosophy."—James Fishkin, author of *Beyond Subjective Morality*

Paper $16.95   376 pages
Library cloth edition $42.50

Now in paper

STALIN STRIDES

GENDER JUSTICE
DAVID L. KIRP, MARK G. YUDOF, *and* MARLENE STRONG FRANKS

"*Gender Justice* has the rarity of being a book about public policy that is literate, jargon-free and even entertaining. The authors make a fascinating case for a gender policy centered on personal liberty."
—*New York Times Book Review*

$9.95   256 pages

POLITICAL PHILOSOPHY AND TIME
Plato and the Origins of Political Vision
JOHN G. GUNNELL

"Gunnell has made a substantial contribution to the history of political ideas. He has shown that a reading of some of the major texts in political theory can be...a substantial contribution to political science."—George Kateb, *American Political Science Review*

$13.95 (est.)   334 pages

THE EAGLE AND THE SMALL BIRDS
Crisis in the Soviet Empire: From Yalta to Solidarity
MICHAEL CHARLTON

"This excellent volume provides insight and illumination to anyone interested in the nature of the Soviet System and empire and in relations between the Soviet Union and the United States."—Robert Byrnes, *Political Science Quarterly*

$8.95   192 pages

The University of **CHICAGO** Press
5801 South Ellis Avenue, Chicago, IL 60637

NEW from Sage

INTERETHNIC COMMUNICATION
Current Research
edited by YOUNG YUN KIM, *Governors State University*

**Published in cooperation with the
Speech Communication Association Commission on
International and Intercultural Communication**

Problems in interethnic relations seem particularly acute in today's world. To the extent that societies regard harmonious interethnic relations as a significant social issue, systematic research is needed to help understand the ways individuals and groups with different ethnic backgrounds interact with, and relate to, each other. We need to strive to find ways of promoting effective communication and cooperative relationships across ethnic boundaries.

This volume is an attempt to bring together some of the current inquiries consistent with this theme, and to facilitate the further development of our scientific understanding of the dynamics of interethnic relations. The guiding principle in preparation of this volume was to present studies which bear direct relevance to interethnic contact and interaction of individuals. Thus, the communication-related concepts such as perception, attitude, language, verbal behavior, and interpersonal relationship development take the central place in the studies presented in this volume.

**International and Intercultural Communication Annual, Volume X
1986 / 320 pages (tent.) / $29.95 (c) / $14.95 (p)**

SAGE PUBLICATIONS, INC.
2111 West Hillcrest Drive,
Newbury Park, California 91320

SAGE PUBLICATIONS, INC.
275 South Beverly Drive,
Beverly Hills, California 90212

SAGE PUBLICATIONS LTD
28 Banner Street,
London EC1Y 8QE, England

SAGE PUBLICATIONS INDIA PVT LTD
M-32 Market, Greater Kailash I,
New Delhi 110 048 India

new from sage!

WOMEN IN EDUCATIONAL ADMINISTRATION

by CHAROL SHAKESHAFT, *Hofstra University*

The traditional literature in school administration has largely ignored women. Although there have always been women in school administration, we know very little of their histories, their issues, and their management strategies. **Women in Educational Administration** fills this gap.

This book presents the history of women in administration and the status of women in the field today. Specifically, it illustrates women's place in school administration, making clear that women's history in school is different from men's and that the "typical" woman school administrator varies in important respects from her male counterpart. Barriers that have kept women out of school administration are also presented, and proven strategies for overcoming them are discussed.

An examination of the working world of women administrators shows how women's day-to-day experiences create a female culture that differs from the world males occupy in schools. Current theory in educational administration is analyzed, demonstrating how it fails to take into account the experiences of women and speculating upon ways that such distortions damage both women and school life in general. Suggestions for building theory and practice that include female experiences are discussed.

To aid in this reconceptualization of the theory of the field, an attempt has been made in this book to bring together as much as possible of what we know about women in educational administration. Three kinds of data have been drawn upon. The first is a synthesis of research literature on women in administration using the synthesis techniques of listing of factors, taking a vote, averaging statistics, and meta-analysis. The second source of data comes from survey, interview, and observational studies conducted by the author over the past seven years. The third source of evidence is the author's experience in directing a program for women in administration from 1980 to the present. The result is a book that challenges traditional theory and practice in educational administration as inappropriate for women administrators.

CONTENTS: Acknowledgments / Introduction // **I. Where are the Women Managers?** 1. Women School Administrators: Too Few for Too Long / 2. Profiles and Career Paths of Women in Administration // **II. Getting Women into Administration** // 3. Barriers to Women's Advancement into School Administration / 4. Demolishing the Barriers // **III. Female Culture and Educational Administration** // 5. Androcentric Bias in Educational Administration Theory and Research / 6. Differences Between the Ways Women and Men Manage Schools / 7. The Female World of School Administration / Bibliography

1986 (December) / 300 pages (tent.) / $25.00 (c)

SAGE PUBLICATIONS, INC.
2111 West Hillcrest Drive
Newbury Park, California 91320

SAGE PUBLICATIONS, INC.
275 South Beverly Drive
Beverly Hills, California 90212

SAGE PUBLICATIONS LTD
28 Banner Street
London EC1Y 8QE, England

SAGE PUBLICATIONS INDIA PVT LTD
M-32 Market, Greater Kailash I
New Delhi 110 048 India

new from sage

EDUCATION AND RURAL DEVELOPMENT
by SUDHA V. RAO
Foreword by T. Scarlett Epstein

This pioneering book explores, through a detailed case study, the relationship between education and the development process in rural areas. The author scrutinizes a widespread assumption: that the provision of educational opportunities promotes upward mobility, reduces disparities between class groups, and accelerates the process of socioeconomic development.

Rao set out to examine this common belief by studying a village in Southern India. She found that there was a considerable demand for education, as it is considered the passport to urban employment. However, the poorer inhabitants were unable to make use of the educational facilities due to high rates in opportunity costs. In addition, the minority of individuals who managed to secure urban employment came from families of higher social standing. All this has left a growing residue of educated but unemployed youth. What has developed? A group of frustrated and angry individuals who, by joining forces, may trigger radical changes.

Interdisciplinary in its approach, full of insights into the dynamics of economic development, and firmly rooted in current political and economic realities, **Education and Rural Development** will appeal to a wide range of scholars and policymakers, especially those involved in both education and rural development.

1986 / 334 pages / $25.00 (c)

SAGE PUBLICATIONS, INC.
2111 West Hillcrest Drive
Newbury Park, California 91320

SAGE PUBLICATIONS, INC.
275 South Beverly Drive
Beverly Hills, California 90212

SAGE PUBLICATIONS LTD
28 Banner Street
London EC1Y 8QE, England

SAGE PUBLICATIONS INDIA PVT LTD
M-32 Market, Greater Kailash I
New Delhi 110 048 India

Of Related Interest

EDUCATIONAL PUBLIC RELATIONS

by PHILIP T. WEST
Department of Educational Administration,
Texas A&M University

"The collective effort of any group or person to win the esteem of people, by its conduct to deserve that esteem, and by its communications to maintain it" is how the National School Public Relations Association defines good educational public relations. West believes that educators can no longer ignore the importance of public relations. School administrators who have not kept up with the principles and practices of effective PR are, he insists, at a "distinct disadvantage."

Educational Public Relations stresses both principles and practices. It offers an array of strategies that facilitate the initiation, implementation, and evaluation of public relations programs in school districts. How to determine public attitudes and expectations through surveys, how to increase community support for schools, how to establish a close working relationship with the media, and many other pragmatic matters are discussed. Case studies and vignettes bring abstract explanations of theory and research to life. Chapters on the history and future of educational public relations give the book a broad perspective.

Educational Public Relations is an ideal text for graduate courses in educational administration as well as a useful guide for the in-service training of educational professionals.

1985 / 288 pages / $25.00 (c)

SAGE Publications
The Publishers of Professional Social Science
Newbury Park ● Beverly Hills ● London ● New Delhi